Hemingway Didn't Say That

Hemingway Didn't Say That

The Truth Behind Familiar Quotations

Garson O'Toole

The Internet's Foremost Quote Investigator

Published by Little A, New York
www.apub.com

Amazon, the Amazon logo, and Little A are trademarks of Amazon.com, Inc., or its affiliates.

ISBN-13: 9781503933415 (hardcover)
ISBN-10: 1503933415 (hardcover)
ISBN-13: 9781503933408 (paperback)
ISBN-10: 1503933407 (paperback)

Cover design by Rex Bonomelli

Printed in the United States of America

First edition

In memory of my brother, Stephen

"In the future, everyone will be famous for fifteen minutes."

—Andy Warhol

"Eighty percent of success is showing up."

—Woody Allen

CONTENTS

INTRODUCTION

THE DETECTIVE, THE DATABASE, AND THE MECHANISMS OF ERROR

How did I begin investigating the dubious origins of familiar quotations? I will tell you: In the 1990s I developed an enthusiasm for electronic books. I felt they had enormous potential to advance access to the world's knowledge cheaply and efficiently. Massive digital libraries, every book in the public domain, shared worldwide at low cost on the Internet—the thought excited in me a desire to learn more about the potential applications of such technology.

Meanwhile, a pioneer in electronic publishing named Brad Templeton had assembled a groundbreaking CD-ROM, *Hugo and Nebula Anthology 1993*, a digital collection of five novels and numerous short stories, at the time the first e-book of contemporary writing. The works were all nominees for the Hugo and Nebula Awards, the top literary prizes for science fiction. The CD-ROM cost about as much as a hardcover book these days, $29.95. The forward-thinking fans of science fiction were ideal customers for this innovative collection, and as one of them, I couldn't resist. I purchased the CD-ROM as the harbinger of the future. But Templeton's project was many years too early and, sadly, never caught on.

In the early 2000s I read and commented on articles at a website devoted to e-reading called TeleRead. At the prompting of the founder, David Rothman, I began to contribute articles. Rothman envisioned a "well-stocked national digital library." He had been propounding the idea for over a decade in op-ed pieces published in periodicals such as *Computerworld*, and I was glad to find someone who shared the same viewpoint about the magnificent potential of electronic reading.

It would soon turn out that a central part of this idea was already being pursued by a former graduate student of Stanford University. Larry Page, the cocreator of Google, shared this dream of constructing a searchable digital library, one that might contain all the books of the world. In time he found himself in a position to do something about it. Google engineers developed efficient machines using multiple cameras and sensors to create scans of page after page of one volume after another, and in 2002 the machines were put to work. Beginning at his undergraduate alma mater at the University of Michigan, Page would pursue the stacks of the major research libraries in the United States and the United Kingdom. The Google Books database now contains more than thirty million searchable books.

The fantasy became reality very quickly. Despite complex questions of copyright that threatened, for a time, to shut the database down, the futurist library had been built. I wondered even then how one could prove to others the power and value of such an expansive library. The whole of linguistic history at one's fingertips: What is one to do? Searching for words, phrases, and statements would reveal a trove of connections and citations. But what could one learn?

To test the utility of the search procedure, I decided to explore the history of a hex that only sounds like a blessing:

May you live in interesting times.

The saying fit the project. Robert F. Kennedy had once labeled the statement a "Chinese curse" when he employed it during a commencement speech given at the University of Capetown, South Africa, in 1966. Indeed, others have called it "ancient." (More recently, Hillary Clinton included the saying in her memoir *Living History*.)

When I sought in 2007 to answer the question of where the saying had come from, I discovered that many people had already explored its history. *Wikipedia* volunteers had created an entry on the topic with an initial citation in 1950, and this entry functioned as my benchmark. If I could determine that the statement had appeared before 1950, then I would write an article for TeleRead illustrating the effectiveness and potency of performing research with Google Books.

It only took a few strokes of the keyboard for me to immediately locate within the Google Books database a 1930 citation for a short story in a magazine called *Astounding Science Fiction*. Had it really taken only my single search to best *Wikipedia*? No. This was my rocky introduction to the complexity and difficulty of searching within large textual databases like Google Books. While cross-checking the date of the issue in question, I determined that the story I had found, "U-Turn" by Duncan H. Munro, had in fact been published in 1950. I was befuddled. Why was Google Books supplying incorrect dates? The tight restrictions on what Google Books was able to display due to copyright laws hampered the resolution to this mystery. The issue containing the match was still under copyright, so Google Books would only display what is referred to as "snippets" of text: images containing only a few lines.

Eventually, I discovered that *Astounding Science Fiction* had *begun publishing* in 1930, so the database had erroneously assigned the year 1930 to many of the issues of the magazine while ignoring the individual publication dates. (This class of error was prevalent in Google Books back in 2007. Thankfully, the situation has improved over time.)

After discarding other matches that were improperly dated, I found a match in a 1944 book titled *The American Character* by Denis William Brogan. Now I was exposed to another type of error. Google Books stated that the match was located on page 169, but, bizarrely, the book was only 168 pages long according to the metadata. I visited a nearby library to examine a reprint edition published in 1956, but I was aggravated to find that the statement was entirely absent. I traveled to a more distant library to examine the original 1944 edition, and there it was on page 169, which was unnumbered—the quotation I sought:

It is, I have been told, one of the most formidable of Chinese imprecations to wish that your enemy lived "in interesting times." We live in very interesting times; times not to be made better by any simple formula.

Combining my research results, I proudly published an article on TeleRead titled "Is a Famous 'Ancient Chinese Curse' Really an Invention from 1950? An Investigation Using Google Book Search."

I had learned four important lessons:

1. The Google Books database is an enormously powerful and valuable tool for researchers.
2. Dates (and other items of metadata) provided by Google Books are sometimes inaccurate.
3. When a book is reprinted it may be revised, and a revision may shift the date of publication. Precise details about editions must be collected.
4. A book in the Google Books database that is only visible in snippets must be examined directly in hard copy to verify the quotation and to allow the construction of a complete and accurate citation.

Idealistically, I thought that by posting the 1944 citation I had advanced the shared enterprise of gathering public knowledge. The overall experience was very satisfying, and the successful pursuit of this task provides part of the explanation for my transition to becoming the Quote Investigator, or **QI**. Further impetus was supplied by an event I never expected.

Fred R. Shapiro is the editor of *The Yale Book of Quotations*, which is regarded as the most important modern reference source for familiar quotations. He pioneered the use of large-scale textual databases containing books, magazines, journals, pamphlets, and newspapers to perform research on the origin of quotations. Somehow he had learned about my blog article, read it, and, upon finishing the piece, left a comment.

The Yale Book of Quotations had an entry about the curse, he noted, and the earliest citation was dated 1939, five years before my contribution to humanity. I reacted with simple embarrassment. I had assumed that one of the many people who had worked on the *Wikipedia* entry for "May you live in interesting times" must have examined references such as *Bartlett's Familiar Quotations*, the *Oxford Dictionary of Quotations*, and *The Yale Book of Quotations*. But—in fact—no one had conducted that basic check.

I purchased a copy of the *The Yale Book of Quotations* and began purposefully scanning its entries. The notion of using the Google Books database to trace quotations and sayings was still worthwhile to me, but now my preparation would include consulting the best physical reference books. I titled a follow-up article on TeleRead "Google Book Search: A Powerful Tool for Investigating Phrase Origins." I presented new citations for adages such as "You cannot make an omelet without breaking eggs" and jokes such as "The operation was successful, but the patient died"—citations that were older than what I found in my physical reference. I was a neophyte just trying to make some progress.

A search in Google Books yields a fascinating earlier citation of the "omelet" quote in the 1856 *Journal of Adventures with the British Army*, Volume II, by George Cavendish Taylor. The military man, Taylor, discusses different battlefield strategies and then says the following regarding one rather bloody plan:

> Our loss would of course have been greater, but our success would have been more complete; and, as Pelissier observed, "one cannot make omelettes without breaking eggs."

The *Encyclopaedia Britannica* says that Pelissier was a "French general who distinguished himself in the conquest of Algeria and was the last French commander in chief in the Crimean War."

For the quip about a successful operation, I found a close variant in a book titled *Manual of Operative Surgery* published in 1887:

If a complicating injury be discovered, which of itself imperils
the life of the patient, all idea of an immediate operation must be
deferred. These thoughtful attentions will lessen the pungency of
the oft-repeated satirical expression, "The operation was successful,
but the patient succumbed."

So I was learning how to trace a quotation backward. I slowly broadened
my research by using newspaper databases such as GenealogyBank and
NewspaperARCHIVE.com; these electronic resources were originally created
to help genealogists and historians, but they have proven invaluable for exploring
quotations. To enhance my expertise, I subscribed to mailing lists for linguistics
researchers and research librarians; I began to use the interlibrary loan system to
obtain books from distant collections; and I cajoled friends, family members,
and colleagues to access the shelves and databases of major research libraries
around the United States.

The activity became a vigorous hobby.

Finally, in 2010, I started the Quote Investigator website and began to work
seriously for several hours a day on my research.

Using an Internet search engine to learn more about these sayings can be
both a revelatory and exasperating experience. Search engines contain link after
link to websites with faulty information, repetitive text, and incomplete data.
Moving beyond this mélange of misinformation is nearly impossible for the
average web user. It's no wonder, then, that such mistakes are perpetuated and
duplicated to the extreme.

Many truth-seekers have struggled with the cacophony of conflicting information online; too often, accurate data is overwhelmed by inaccurate data. One
wonderful aspect of operating my website is the opportunity it provides to aid
others in communicating the truth. This is a book that collects many of my
investigations, but it is also a book that is meant to reveal how these misattributions happen, what I call the "mechanisms of error."

Here is a short summary of each mechanism. (Note that often the history
of a quotation involves multiple mechanisms. For the sake of illustrating each
category of error, I have made certain judgment calls.)

SYNTHESIS (AND STREAMLINING)

Human memory naturally shortens and simplifies statements. Qualifiers are often omitted, and the vocabulary may change. A concise remark is more easily remembered than a rambling one, and a profound thought is more likely to be repeated than something mundane. Quotations are exposed to an evolutionary process that results in distortion and inaccuracy. The terms "synthesis" and "streamlining" refer to the evolution of the quotation.

VENTRILOQUY

An observer examines the writings, interviews, and speeches of a prominent person and develops a novel statement encapsulating an idea expressed by that person. The observer's crisp or elegant statement is not actually present in the writings or remarks of the well-known individual. In fact, it might even be misrepresentative. Nevertheless, the saying is so vivid and memorable that others eventually reassign the words directly to the luminary.

PROVERBIAL WISDOM

Accurate ascriptions are often lost or garbled when a quotation is retransmitted. A popular quotation with an unknown ascription may be elevated to the status of a proverb or an adage. When the origin of a statement is uncertain, the age of the statement also becomes uncertain.

TEXTUAL PROXIMITY

When a well-known name appears in a book or article, sometimes a nearby quotation (created by a different person) is scooped up and reassigned to the well-known name. This also occurs when the picture of a famous person is near a quotation. The probability that this mechanism might occur is heightened by two factors: (1) the quotation was actually crafted by a person who is less well known or by an anonymous person, and (2) the quotation fits the public personality of the well-known person. A fascinating version of this mechanism occurs when a list of quotations is published in a book or magazine. These lists often alternate between presenting names and quotations, and the reader must determine if a quotation was composed by the name given above or the name below; this is an error-prone process. If the list is alphabetized, then curious misattributions occur between names that are close together in the alphabet.

REAL-WORLD PROXIMITY

The ascription of a quotation shifts from one person to another because the two persons are close to one another in a network of connections in real-life space. Here are two examples: Jim Morrison and Ray Manzarek were founding members of the controversial rock band The Doors. This connection facilitated the improper reassignment of a statement spoken by Manzarek to the more charismatic Morrison. In a second case, the Wall Street trader Henry S. Haskins became acquainted with the libertarian Albert Jay Nock while they were in New York. Years later, when Haskins published an anonymous book, Nock provided the introduction, and this linkage led some observers to incorrectly reassign passages in the book from Haskins to Nock.

SIMILAR NAMES

An ascription can jump from one person to another person who shares a similar name. This mechanism is distinct from alphabetic ambiguity because the mistake is not caused by the misreading of a list of quotations. A gas station attendant with the nickname Socrates has the same name as the famous philosopher Socrates. Harrington Emerson might be confused for Ralph Waldo Emerson; the songwriter Poe could be mistaken for the horror master Edgar Allan Poe.

CONCOCTIONS

It is difficult to prove that a misquotation or misattribution was forged deliberately. The majority of quotation errors in this book emerged via multifarious accidents. Most of the time, the culprit is only inattentiveness or ineptitude. Yes, writers sometimes do concoct fanciful quotations as colorful asides. For example, a spurious Albert Einstein saying occurs in the movie *Powder,* and a fake Christopher Columbus saying occurs in *The Hunt for Red October.* Neither of these famous figures appears in those films. Also, incorrect quotations and attributions occur in the humorous anecdotes, heart-tugging tales, and imaginative incidents presented by comedians, raconteurs, and columnists. Now, in the Internet age, pranksters build memes with dubious quotations.

HISTORICAL FICTION

When a real-life character is dramatized in a film, play, or book, the author fabricates scenes with dialogues or inner monologues. Some readers incorrectly assume that the new quotations are genuine. This error occurs even when an author admits to using creative license. More controversially, a book characterized as nonfiction may contain invented or altered quotations.

CAPTURE

The largest section in this book is dedicated to a simple type of misattribution. A famous person employs a preexisting quotation that was originally crafted by a less famous or anonymous individual. The quotation is then reassigned to the prominent individual. In essence, the remark is reused and captured. This shift in attribution can occur even when the well-known person strives mightily to prevent it by carefully giving proper credit.

HOST

Mark Twain, Albert Einstein, Marilyn Monroe, Winston Churchill, Dorothy Parker, and Yogi Berra are quotation superstars. Personas of this type are so vibrant and attractive that they become hosts for quotations they never uttered. A remark formulated by a lesser-known figure is attached to a famous host. The relationship is symbiotic and often enhances the popularity of both the host and the quotation. Each host attracts specific types of quotations that conform to his or her character or accomplishments. For example, Twain receives credit for numerous witticisms that he never employed, and the list of malapropisms incorrectly ascribed to Berra is lengthy. Interestingly, over a long period, a popular expression can shift ascriptions multiple times as the fame of individuals expands and contracts.

You may be shocked by how fragile information is, and I fear it is only getting worse. Each transmission of a quote can sometimes seem to produce cracks in the truth. When familiar quotations and attributions have been retransmitted over the decades, the text has often changed and the linkages have shifted. But the modern age of large-scale databases provides an unprecedented chance to study these alterations and to correct misinformation.

The goal of expunging errors is only one of the attractions, however. Another wonderful aspect of the work involved in fact-checking attributions of popular sayings is the opportunity to show other inclined, casual researchers how to set the record right.

The textual databases of today are the largest in humankind's history and they continue to grow. At the same time, misinformation can be propagated around the world in milliseconds. Keeping track of who said what is one of the central tasks of properly recording history. The current generation of researchers has the tools to correct errors of attribution from the past and present, but will they respond to the challenge?

I
GROUP ERROR

SYNTHESIS * VENTRILOQUY * PROVERBIAL WISDOM

1. "Good artists copy; great artists steal."
2. "Behind every great fortune there is a crime."
3. "No one can make you feel inferior without your consent."
4. "The arc of the moral universe is long, but it bends toward justice."
5. "The only thing necessary for the triumph of evil is that good men do nothing."
6. "Genius is 1% inspiration and 99% perspiration."
7. "The question isn't who is going to let me, it's who is going to stop me."
8. "Don't bend; don't water it down; don't try to make it logical; don't edit your own soul according to the fashion."
9. "In the struggle for survival, the fittest win out at the expense of their rivals."
10. "Life is a journey, not a destination."
11. "640K [of computer memory] ought to be enough for anyone."
12. "Be kind; everyone you meet is fighting a hard battle."
13. "The purpose of life is to discover your gift. The meaning of life is to give your gift away."
14. "We do not inherit the Earth from our ancestors; we borrow it from our children."
15. "If you love someone, set them free. If they come back they're yours."

16. "Give a man a fish, and you feed him for a day. Teach a man to fish, and you feed him for a lifetime."
17. "Choose a job you love and you will never have to work a day in your life."
18. "A bird doesn't sing because it has an answer, it sings because it has a song."

SYNTHESIS

1. "Good artists copy; great artists steal."

—Pablo Picasso

In 1988 the *Sydney Morning Herald* in Australia printed an article that discussed lawsuits in the computer industry and the development of the Macintosh computer system. The article contained a controversial remark by Steve Jobs, the iconic entrepreneur and cofounder of Apple.[1]

> Steve Jobs said that while it was being developed he kept in mind a quote from Pablo Picasso, "Good artists copy. Great artists steal."

Jobs repeated the quip in front of the camera for a multipart PBS television program called *Triumph of the Nerds: The Rise of Accidental Empires*. (The interview was later released in its entirety as a full-length film called *The Lost Interview*.)[2]

Credit: Magnolia Pictures/PBS. "Good artists copy; great artists steal": Steve Jobs misattributing a phrase to Pablo Picasso in The Last Interview.

It comes down to trying to expose yourself to the best things that humans have done and then try to bring those things into what you're doing. I mean, Picasso had a saying. He said, "Good artists copy; great artists steal." And [my colleagues and I] have always been shameless about stealing great ideas. And I think part of what made the Macintosh great was that the people working on it were musicians, poets, artists, zoologists, and historians, who also happened to be the best computer scientists in the world.

A film critic at the *Philadelphia Inquirer* repeated Jobs in 1996, the same year that the PBS show debuted, but she changed the saying either through error or impulse.[3]

All of which goes to prove Pablo Picasso's statement that "bad artists copy, great artists steal."

But was Jobs right? Had Picasso ever said such a thing?

QI has located an intriguing precursor that appeared in an article titled "Imitators and Plagiarists" published in the *Gentleman's Magazine* in 1892. The author, W. H. Davenport Adams, wrote that "to imitate" was commendable, but "to steal" was unworthy. Adams extolled the works of the famed poet Alfred, Lord Tennyson, and he presented several examples in which Tennyson constructed his verses using the efforts of his artistic antecedents as a resource.[4]

> Of Tennyson's assimilative method, when he adopts an image or a suggestion from a predecessor, and works it up into his own glittering fabric, I shall give a few instances, offering as the result and summing up of the preceding inquiries a modest canon: "That great poets imitate and improve, whereas small ones steal and spoil."

Note that Adams seems to think that it is wrong for poets to steal, but Jobs is not only accepting of the artist who copied or stole—he seems to have cited Picasso as a way to say that the outright thieving turns a good artist into a great one. Adams concluded his essay on Tennyson with additional praise for the poet and a condemnation of plagiarists. Oddly, as **QI** will exhibit, the word "plagiarizes" was incorporated in later variants of the expression.

In 1920 the major poet T. S. Eliot published *The Sacred Wood: Essays on Poetry and Criticism*, where he presented his own version of the maxim. Eliot, ironically or not, interchanged the terminology used by *Gentleman's Magazine*— "to imitate" was shoddy, and "to steal" was praiseworthy. This change is closer to the modern incarnation of the expression employed by Jobs.[5]

> One of the surest of tests is the way in which a poet borrows. Immature poets imitate; mature poets steal; bad poets deface what they take, and good poets make it into something better, or at least something different. The good poet welds his theft into a whole of feeling which is unique, utterly different from that from which it was torn; the bad poet throws it into something which has no cohesion. A good poet will usually borrow from authors remote in time, or alien in language, or diverse in interest.

In 1949 a book review columnist in the *Atlantic Monthly* employed an instance of the maxim that replaced the word "steal" with "plagiarizes." The reviewer assigned the expression to Eliot, and this version has been circulating for decades.[6]

> T. S. Eliot once wrote that the immature poet imitates and the mature poet plagiarizes. Goethe to Eckermann, before Eliot, said: "If you see a great master, you will always find that he used what was good in his predecessors, and that it was this which made him great."

The book *Time of Apprenticeship: The Fiction of Young James Joyce* by Marvin Magalaner, published a decade later, contained another variant of the expression. Strangely, Magalaner seems to associate the quote with T. S. Eliot without making the connection that Eliot is perhaps the quote's author (so far as Magalaner might know). The word "poets" was replaced by "artists," and "borrow" was used instead of "imitate."[7]

> Obviously, any author is influenced by what he has read; even forty years ago T. S. Eliot knew that he was perpetuating a cliché in saying so, but in the case of such eclectic writers as Pound and Eliot and Joyce, this axiom is supremely true. They are concerned not merely with the general ideas and techniques of their predecessors, but with their very lines and words, which they reconstruct in a new mosaic of verbal power. To paraphrase a contemporary critic, "Immature artists borrow; mature artists steal"; and Joyce was a mature artist.

Three years later, in 1962, *Esquire* magazine printed a humorous piece titled "The Student Prince: Or How to Seize Power Through an Undergraduate" by Robert Benton and Gloria Steinem. Several quotations were presented by Benton and Steinem, and **QI** believes that the authors thought the quotes were genuine. Here are three of the sayings that appeared in a section of the piece called "Six Quotes to Get You Through Any Senior Exam. Use Them Wisely":[8]

> Indian summer is like a woman, ripe, hotly passionate but fickle.
> —Grace Metalious

Immature artists imitate. Mature artists steal. —Lionel Trilling

I think my favorite weapon is a twenty-dollar bill.
—Raymond Chandler

The statement credited to Grace Metalious did appear as the beginning line of her blockbuster novel *Peyton Place* in 1956, though the punctuation and capitalization were different. Raymond Chandler did write the words above in a comical letter in 1951. **QI** does not know whether the prominent literary critic Lionel Trilling made the statement above, but its appearance in *Esquire* catalyzed its wide dissemination with the attached ascription.

By the 1960s and 1970s, the quote attributed to Eliot could be heard in the same circles as the quote by Trilling and several new iconic voices (which may explain what could have led to Steve Jobs's confusion). In 1967 the Los Angeles–based music critic and lecturer Peter Yates published the book *Twentieth Century Music: Its Evolution from the End of the Harmonic Era into the Present Era of Sound*. In the work Yates claimed that he heard the prominent composer Igor Stravinsky employ an instance of the saying. Stravinsky's version did not reference "poets" or "artists"; it was tailored to "composers."[9]

> Igor Stravinsky said to me of his *Three Songs by William Shakespeare*, in which he epitomized his discovery of Webern's music: "A good composer does not imitate; he steals."

A 1974 book, concerning stage design of all things, included an instance of the saying credited to the Nobel Prize–winning author William Faulkner.[10]

> There is probably more truth than we care to admit in William Faulkner's observation that, "immature artists copy, great artists steal." Knowing what and when to steal is very much a part of the designer's self-education.

In 1975 Brendan Gill, a longtime writer at the *New Yorker* magazine, printed a version of the expression in his memoir. He credited the words to T. S. Eliot, but he incorrectly used the word "plagiarizes"; thus, he echoed the mistake in the *Atlantic Monthly* in 1949.[11]

> In senior year, I won a prize for writing a long narrative poem in what everyone must have seen was a pastiche of Frost. (I had not yet read Eliot's dictum: "The immature poet imitates, the mature poet plagiarizes." Nevertheless, I was obeying it.)

The popular 1977 collection *Peter's Quotations: Ideas for Our Time* by Laurence J. Peter, which happens to be the source of a great many misattributed quotations, it turns out, included the saying and attributed the words to T. S. Eliot. However, like Gill, Peter wrongly used the version printed in the *Atlantic Monthly*.[12]

The last instance of the saying known to **QI** before PBS taped the Steve Jobs interview in 1995 is found in a 1986 instructional text about preparing computerized documents called *LaTeX: A Document Preparation System*. The work credits Stravinsky with a further evolved version of the quotation. By the second edition the footnote was deleted:[13]

> "Lesser artists borrow; great artists steal."
>
> —Igor Stravinsky

Notes:

1. "Computers Keep the Courts Active," *Sydney Morning Herald*, April 11, 1988, 20, https://goo.gl/zxSf74.

2. "The Television Program Transcripts: Part III," companion website for 1996 PBS television program *Triumph of the Nerds*, accessed March 6, 2013, http://www.pbs.org/nerds/part3.html.

3. Carrie Rickey, "Arnold's Mission: Keeping Vanessa Williams Alive," *Philadelphia Inquirer*, June 21, 1996, 3.

4. W. H. Davenport Adams, "Imitators and Plagiarists, In Two Parts—Part II," *Gentleman's Magazine*, June 1892, 627–28, https://goo.gl/WqSo1N.

5. T. S. Eliot, *The Sacred Wood: Essays on Poetry and Criticism* (London: Methuen, 1920), 114. Accessed in Internet Archive, https://archive.org/stream/sacredwoodessays00eliorich#page /114/mode/2up.

6. Harvey Breit, "Reader's Choice," *Atlantic Monthly*, October 1949, 76–78.

7. Marvin Magalaner, *Time of Apprenticeship: The Fiction of Young James Joyce* (New York: Abelard-Schuman, 1959), 34.

8. Robert Benton and Gloria Steinem, "The Student Prince: Or How to Seize Power Through an Undergraduate," *Esquire*, September 1962, 85.

9. Peter Yates, *Twentieth Century Music: Its Evolution from the End of the Harmonic Era into the Present Era of Sound* (New York: Pantheon, 1967), 41.

10. Darwin Reid Payne, *Design for the Stage: First Steps* (Carbondale: Southern Illinois University Press, 1974), 236.

11. Brendan Gill, *Here at The New Yorker* (New York: Random House, 1975), 53.

12. Laurence J. Peter, *Peter's Quotations: Ideas for Our Time* (New York: William Morrow, 1977), 385.

13. Leslie Lamport, *LaTeX: A Document Preparation System* (Reading, MA: Addison-Wesley, 1986), 7, footnote 2.

2. "Behind every great fortune there is a crime."

—Honoré de Balzac

The popular 1969 novel *The Godfather* by Mario Puzo recounts the violent tale of a Mafia family, and bears this spurious epigraph:[1]

Behind every great fortune there is a crime.

—Balzac

QI believes that this adage was inspired by a sentence that was written by Honoré de Balzac, but the expression has been simplified in an evolutionary process. Here is the original in French from a serialization of *Le Père Goriot* published in *Revue de Paris* in 1834:[2]

Le secret des grandes fortunes sans cause apparente est un crime oublié, parce qu'il a été proprement fait.

Balzac published a series of interlinked novels called *Comédie Humaine* or *The Human Comedy*, and *Le Père Goriot* was part of this series. Eventually, all were translated into English. Here is a rendering of the statement above published in 1896:[3]

The secret of a great success for which you are at a loss to account is a crime that has never been found out, because it was properly executed.

Here is another translation into English that was published in 1900:[4]

The secret of a great fortune made without apparent cause is soon forgotten, if the crime is committed in a respectable way.

Note that Balzac did not pronounce a general rule that larceny was at the root of all large fortunes. However, the simplified statement that is popular in modern times is arguably more provocative and consequently more memorable.

The simplification process is illustrated by an instance of the saying printed in a newspaper in 1912, within an account of a dinner held in London. The article's author was Pierre Mille, who is described as "a literary man of Paris." The following words were credited to an unidentified "French writer." **QI** hypothesizes that they were inspired by a schematic memory of Balzac's words.[5]

> One evening at the Carlton Hotel, where he had invited me to dinner, the conversation fell on certain money kings of America, those great modern powers that one cannot help dreaming about. One of the guests recalled the words of a French writer. "At the base of every great fortune there is a great crime." I could not help saying how false this statement was. At the base of great American fortunes to-day there is boldness, the genius of concentrating economic fortunes, a vigorous mentality in calculating and combining, but never a trace of crime.

The above account was first printed in the French periodical *La Petit Journal*, according to the newspaper report. So this concise maxim was disseminated in two languages.

In 1915 a Chicago business publication reported remarks made by a Washington, DC–based government functionary who pronounced a concise dictum.[6]

> What kind of a creature is this Frank P. Walsh that the United States has let loose on an unoffending American people? Mr. Walsh is chairman of the federal commission on industrial relations. He is quoted as saying in an address in this city this week that "every great fortune is a fundamental wrong"; that "every man with a fortune must at some time have crossed the line of ethics and of criminal law"; that "the government ought to get back the land which has been taken by fraud."

In 1922 a Kentucky newspaper printed a short story by the playwright and novelist Samuel Merwin. An instance of the aphorism was spoken by a figure in the story.[7]

> In every instance, Rob. The facts support us. Every great fortune—every one—is founded on evil, usually on crime. In the building of every one there were moments—crises, you understand—when only a criminal act of some nature could save the thing.
>
> The purchase of a legislature or a judge, robbing a vault of records or evidence, even violence against an individual.

A 1925 collection of essays by British politician James Henry Yoxall included a simplified version of the adage that Yoxall tentatively ascribed to Balzac.[8]

> Somebody said—I think it was Balzac—that at the root of every great fortune there was a crime, which is not true, let us hope; but at the root of every honourable success there has been capacity of some kind, depend on it—strength, splendid health, or assiduity, courage, enterprise, wisdom . . .

The 1956 work *The Power Elite* by American sociologist C. Wright Mills credited Balzac with an instance of the maxim.[9]

> Two general explanations for the fact of the very rich—now and in the past—are widely available. The first, of muckraker origin, was best stated by Gustavus Myers, whose work is a gigantic gloss in pedantic detail upon Balzac's assertion that behind every great fortune there lies a crime.

In 1958 the writer Daniel Bell reviewed the work of Mills in the pages of the *American Journal of Sociology*. Bell presented a slightly altered version of the maxim that Mills ascribed to Balzac.[10]

It is interesting that Mills quotes with approval Balzac's dictum, "Behind every fortune is a crime," and sees it as a judgment which applies equally today.

As mentioned at the beginning of this section, the 1969 bestseller *The Godfather* by Mario Puzo contained an epigraph credited to Balzac. The novel was a popular sensation that was made into an acclaimed film.

In 1976 the financial columnist Jane Bryant Quinn employed a version of the saying with an anonymous attribution.[11]

It has been said that every great fortune is founded on a great crime, a maxim that Miller's book documents down through the Harding administration.

In conclusion, Balzac did write a statement linking large fortunes to crime, but it was a nuanced remark about a subset of great fortunes. Over the years his expression has been dramatically simplified, and no single person can be credited with the construction of the modern concise and forceful version.

Notes:

Thanks to Fred R. Shapiro for the analysis of this quotation given in the *The Yale Book of Quotations*, which included the important 1956 citation.[12]

1. Mario Puzo, *The Godfather* (New York: G. P. Putnam's Sons, 1969), 9 (epigraph). Verified in hard copy.
2. Honoré de Balzac, "Le Père Goriot," *Revue de Paris* 12 (1834): 258. Accessed in Google Books, https://goo.gl/EcNnGU.
3. "Old Goriot (Le Père Goriot)" in Honoré de Balzac, *Comédie Humaine*, ed. George Saintsbury, trans. Ellen Marriage (London: J. M. Dent, 1896), 124. Accessed in Google Books, https://goo.gl/5ytwfX.
4. Honoré de Balzac, *La Comédie Humaine of Honoré de Balzac*, trans. Katharine Prescott Wormeley, standard Wormeley ed. (Boston: Hardy, Prat, 1900), 142. Accessed in Google Books, https://goo.gl/S5ZUes.

5. "Conan Doyle's Yarn," *News and Courier* (Charleston, SC), May 18, 1912, 8. Accessed in GenealogyBank.

6. Walsh's Philosophy, *Economist*, March 13, 1915, 449. Accessed in Google Books, https://goo.gl/4PMemq.

7. Samuel Merwin, "The Gold One," *Lexington Herald* (Lexington, KY), April 16, 1922, 9. Accessed in GenealogyBank.

8. James Henry Yoxall, *Live and Learn* (London: Hodder and Stoughton, 1925), 111. Accessed in the digital collection of the Bodleian Library, Oxford University, http://goo.gl/RG3csQ.

9. C. Wright Mills, *The Power Elite* (New York: Oxford University Press, 1956), 95. Verified in hard copy.

10. Daniel Bell, "The Power Elite–Reconsidered," *American Journal of Sociology* 64, no. 3 (November 1958): 238–39. Accessed in JSTOR.

11. Jane Bryant Quinn, "Staying Ahead: Fathers of Country Also Good Hustlers," *Seattle Daily Times*, September 22, 1976, A19. Accessed in GenealogyBank.

12. Fred R. Shapiro, *The Yale Book of Quotations* (New Haven: Yale University Press, 2006), 42. Verified in hard copy.

3. "No one can make you feel inferior without your consent."

—Eleanor Roosevelt

The above saying has been attributed to Eleanor Roosevelt for more than seventy-five years. **QI** believes the streamlined version of an enigmatic statement made by the First Lady originated in the pages of *Reader's Digest* in September 1940, when the magazine was coming into its heyday. At its peak, the publication was almost as popular as the Bible and distributed globally, in multiple editions, and in Braille:[1]

No one can make you feel inferior without your consent.

—Eleanor Roosevelt

However, the magazine gives no supporting reference, and the quote stands alone at the bottom of a page with an unrelated article's text above it. Quotation experts such as Rosalie Maggio and Ralph Keyes have explored the origin of this saying. Surprisingly, a thorough examination of the books the First Lady authored, along with her other archives, has failed to reveal any instances of the quote in her writings.[2]

QI has located some intriguing evidence as to the words actually expressed by Roosevelt, and **QI** now believes that the creation of this maxim can be traced back to comments about an awkward event in 1935. The secretary of labor in the Franklin D. Roosevelt administration was invited to give a speech at University of California, Berkeley, on the school's charter day. The customary host of the event was unhappy because she felt that the chosen speaker should not have been a political figure. Thus she refused to serve as the host, and several newspaper commentators viewed her action as a rebuff and an insult.

Eleanor Roosevelt was asked at a White House press conference whether the labor secretary had been snubbed, and her response was widely disseminated in newspapers. Here is an excerpt from an Associated Press article:[3]

> "A snub," defined the first lady, "is the effort of a person who feels superior to make someone else feel inferior. To do so, he has to find someone who can be made to feel inferior."

Roosevelt may have performed this reformulation herself, but currently there is no evidence to support that possibility. More likely, an unknown someone between 1935 and 1940 synthesized a compact and stylish aphorism based on the commentary made by Roosevelt, and that statement was published in the September 1940 *Reader's Digest*. **QI** notes that this 1935 statement by Roosevelt contains the key elements of the quotation that was assigned to her by 1940, perhaps knowingly, by a skilled, not entirely honest editor. The precise wording given for Roosevelt's statement varied slightly in competing press outlets almost as soon as the sentiment appeared in *Reader's Digest*. Here is an example that a syndicated newspaper column called So They Say! printed the following week:[4]

> I think it is the effort of a person who feels superior to make someone else feel inferior. First, though, you have to find someone who can be made to feel inferior.

The next month, October 1940, the saying appeared as the first line of an editorial in an Iowa newspaper. The words were placed between quotation marks, but no attribution was given.[5]

> "No one can make you feel inferior without your consent."

> That is a good thing to remember. If you feel uncertain of yourself, it is a good pointer to remember. If you feel uncertain of yourself, it is easy to make you feel inferior by making a slighting remark. But if you feel confident you can laugh it off.

At the end of October 1940, the maxim appeared as a freestanding item in an Alaska newspaper, credited to Roosevelt:[6]

> Eleanor Roosevelt, First Lady: "No one can make you feel inferior without your consent."

The next summer the aphorism appeared in an Alabama newspaper column titled Sermon-o-grams, which was dedicated to the topics of "Home, Church, Religion, Character."[7]

In February 1944 the saying appeared in Walter Winchell's widely read syndicated column, where it was again credited to Roosevelt.[8] A year later, Winchell, who had a flair for creating colloquial vocabulary, repeated it:[9]

> Mrs. F.D.R. can turn out punchlines with the best of 'em. Frixample [*sic*]: "No one can make you feel inferior without your consent."

The Yale Book of Quotations contains a compelling precursor to the quote listed as a cross-indexed term. More than one hundred years before the citations above, in 1838, the American clergyman William Ellery Channing said the following:[10]

> No power in society, no hardship in your condition can depress you, keep you down, in knowledge, power, virtue, influence, but by your own consent.

Notes:

1. [Freestanding quotation], *Reader's Digest*, September 1940, 84. Verified in hard copy.
2. Ralph Keyes, *The Quote Verifier: Who Said What, Where, and When* (New York: St. Martin's, 2006), 97–98. Verified in hard copy.
3. "Heart Balm Suit Ban Given Support by Mrs. Roosevelt," *News and Courier* (Charleston, SC), March 26, 1935, 7. Accessed in GenealogyBank.
4. So They Say!, *Owosso Argus-Press* (Owosso, MI), April 2, 1935, 4. Accessed in Google News Archive, https://goo.gl/6pD4x1. Column is located beneath linked article.

5. Ardell Proctor, "The Little Newsance: Editorial," *Lake Park News* (Lake Park, IA), October 10, 1940, 7. Accessed in NewspaperARCHIVE.com.

6. [Freestanding quotation], *Fairbanks Daily News-Miner* (Fairbanks, AK), October 30, 1940, 2. Accessed in NewspaperARCHIVE.com.

7. "Sermon-o-grams," *Huntingdon Daily News* (Huntingdon, PA), June 6, 1941, 11. Accessed in NewspaperARCHIVE.com.

8. Walter Winchell, "Notes of an Innocent Bystander," in New York, *Augusta Chronicle* (Augusta, GA), February 29, 1944, 4. Accessed in GenealogyBank.

9. Walter Winchell, "Lint from a Blue Serge Suit," *St. Petersburg Times* (St. Petersburg, FL), February 25, 1945, 24. Accessed in Google News Archive, https://goo.gl/vbfprn.

10. Fred R. Shapiro, *The Yale Book of Quotations* (New Haven: Yale University Press, 2006), 143. Verified in hard copy; William Ellery Channing, *Self-Culture: An Address Introductory to the Franklin Lectures, Delivered at Boston, September* (Boston: Dutton and Wentworth, 1838), 80. Accessed in Google Books, https://goo.gl/JwvgAf.

4. "The arc of the moral universe is long, but it bends toward justice."

—Martin Luther King Jr.

Sometimes things aren't exactly as they seem. **QI** has encountered many cases that show what can happen when an iconic figure plucks a figure of speech from daily rotation, perhaps one that has been circulating as a general anonymous saying. In 2009 *Time* magazine published an article by President Barack Obama crediting Martin Luther King Jr. with a powerful image of history.[1]

> [W]hile you can't necessarily bend history to your will, you can do your part to see that, in the words of Dr. King, it "bends toward justice." So I hope that you will stand up and do what you can to serve your community, shape our history and enrich both your own life and the lives of others across this country.

In 2010 the quote appeared in the pages of *Time* again, and the words were credited to King.[2]

> Martin Luther King Jr. once said, "Let us realize the arc of the moral universe is long, but it bends toward justice."

Theodore Parker was a Unitarian minister and prominent American Transcendentalist born in 1810 who called for the abolition of slavery. In 1853 Parker published *Ten Sermons of Religion*. The third sermon, titled "Of Justice and the Conscience" included figurative language about "the arc of the moral universe":[3]

> Look at the facts of the world. You see a continual and progressive triumph of the right. I do not pretend to understand the moral universe, the arc is a long one, my eye reaches but little ways. I

cannot calculate the curve and complete the figure by the experience of sight; I can divine it by conscience. But from what I see I am sure it bends towards justice.

Things refuse to be mismanaged long. Jefferson trembled when he thought of slavery and remembered that God is just. Ere long all America will tremble.

The words of Parker's sermon above foreshadowed the US Civil War fought in the 1860s. The passage was reprinted in later collections of Parker's works. A similar statement using the same metaphor was printed in a book called *Morals and Dogma of the Ancient and Accepted Scottish Rite of Freemasonry* with a copyright date of 1871 and publication date of 1905. The author was not identified:[4]

We cannot understand the moral Universe. The arc is a long one, and our eyes reach but a little way; we cannot calculate the curve and complete the figure by the experience of sight; but we can divine it by conscience, and we surely know that it bends toward justice. Justice will not fail, though wickedness appears strong, and has on its side the armies and thrones of power, the riches and the glory of the world, and though poor men crouch down in despair. Justice will not fail and perish out from the world of men, nor will what is really wrong and contrary to God's real law of justice continually endure.

In 1918 a concise instance of the expression similar to the modern version was printed in the book *Readings from Great Authors* in a section listing statements attributed to Theodore Parker:[5]

The arc of the moral universe is long, but it bends toward justice.

In 1932 a columnist for the *Cleveland Plain Dealer* in Ohio reported on an adage that he had seen posted at a church. This saying nearly matched the 1918 expression, but the word "moral" was omitted.[6]

A Euclid Avenue church which displays weekly epigrams on its bulletin board, has this current offering: "The arc of the universe is long, but it bends toward justice." I don't know where the quotation is from—it sounds like Emerson—but I have tried in vain for three days now to puzzle out a meaning for it. It sounds so good that it really ought to mean something. Perhaps it is a vague and poetic way of claiming that nature is eventually just.

A newspaper reader recognized that the statement was based on the words of Theodore Parker and notified the columnist. Fourteen days after the original article was published, the columnist reprinted the relevant excerpt from Parker's sermon as published in 1853 and then praised his words.[7]

In 1934 Reverend Seth Brooks, pastor of the First Parish Church of Malden, Massachusetts, used a version of the phrase in a sermon, as reported in the *Lowell Sun* newspaper. No attribution was given.[8]

We must believe that the arc of the universe is long, but that it bends toward justice, toward one Divine end towards which creation moves onward and onward, forever.

A 1940 New Year's message by Rabbi Jacob Kohn in Los Angeles did not include the attribution.[9]

"Our faith is kept alive by the knowledge, founded on long experience, that the arc of history is long and bends toward justice," Rabbi Jacob Kohn told his audience at Temple Sinai. "We have seen so many ancient tyrannies pass from earth since Egypt and Rome held dominion that our eyes are directed not to the tragic present, but to the beyond, wherein the arc of history will be found bending toward justice, victory and freedom."

In 1958 the *Gospel Messenger* printed an article by Martin Luther King Jr. that employed the saying. King placed it between quotation marks to signal that it was a preexisting aphorism.[10]

Evil may so shape events that Caesar will occupy a palace and Christ a cross, but that same Christ arose and split history into A.D. and B.C., so that even the life of Caesar must be dated by his name. Yes, "the arc of the moral universe is long, but it bends toward justice." There is something in the universe which justifies William Cullen Bryant in saying, "Truth crushed to earth will rise again."

Six years later King delivered the baccalaureate sermon at the commencement exercises for Wesleyan University in Middletown, Connecticut, and he included the saying:[11]

"The arc of the moral universe is long," Dr. King said in closing, "but it bends toward justice."

In conclusion, **QI** believes that Theodore Parker should be credited with formulating this metaphor about historical progress, which was published in a collection of his sermons in 1853. By 1918 a concise version of the saying was being credited to Parker. In 1958 Martin Luther King Jr. included the expression in an article, but he placed the words in quotation marks to indicate that the adage was already in circulation. King apparently found the phrase attractive and included it in several of his speeches.

Notes:

In memoriam: Thanks to my brother Stephen, who asked about this saying. Special thanks to David Weinberger, who pointed out that *Ten Sermons of Religion* was published in 1853.

1.   Barack Obama, "A New Era of Service Across America," *Time*, March 19, 2009, http://content.time.com/time/magazine/article/0,9171,1886571,00.html.
2.   Shohreh Aghdashloo, "Heroes: Mir-Hossein Mousavi," *Time*, April 29, 2010, http://content.time.com/time/specials/packages/article /0,28804,1984685_1984949_1985221,00.html.
3.   Theodore Parker, *Ten Sermons of Religion* (Boston: Crosby, Nichols, 1853), 66, 84–85, https://goo.gl/7wtO9m.

4. *Morals and Dogma of the Ancient and Accepted Scottish Rite of Freemasonry* (Charleston: The Council, 1871), 828, 838, https://goo.gl/b8ZFbs.

5. John Haynes Holmes et al., *Readings from Great Authors Arranged for Responsive, or Other Use in Churches, Schools, Forums, Homes, Etc.* (New York: Dodd, Mead, 1918), 17–18. Accessed in Internet Archive, https://archive.org/details/readingsfromgre01goldgoog.

6. Ted Robinson, Philosopher of Folly's, *Cleveland Plain Dealer* (Cleveland, OH), October 14, 1932, 10. Accessed in GenealogyBank.

7. Ted Robinson, Philosopher of Folly's, *Cleveland Plain Dealer* (Cleveland, OH), October 28, 1932, 8. Accessed in GenealogyBank.

8. "Real Happiness Found Only in Making Others Happy, Says Malden Pastor in Lecture Here," *Lowell Sun* (Lowell, MA), March 13, 1934, 10, 12. Accessed in NewspaperARCHIVE.com.

9. "Jews Usher in New Year: Services Conducted at Scores of Synagogues and Temples in City," *Los Angeles Times* (Los Angeles, CA), October 3, 1940, 14. Accessed in ProQuest.

10. Martin Luther King Jr., "Out of the Long Night," *Gospel Messenger*, February 8, 1958, 14. Accessed in Internet Archive, https://archive.org/details/gospelmessengerv107mors.

11. John Craig, "Wesleyan Baccalaureate Is Delivered by Dr. King," *Hartford Courant* (Hartford, CT), June 8, 1964, 4. Accessed in ProQuest.

5. "The only thing necessary for the triumph of evil is that good men do nothing."

—Edmund Burke

The wonderful resource *The Quote Verifier* by Ralph Keyes discusses the mixed-up quotations that President John F. Kennedy sometimes declaimed in his speeches. Keyes says that the quote above has not been successfully traced, though Kennedy attributed it to Edmund Burke. He went on to note the following:[1]

> [The quote] . . . was judged the most popular quotation of modern times (in a poll conducted by editors of *The Oxford Dictionary of Quotations*). Even though it is clear by now that Burke is unlikely to have made this observation, no one has ever been able to determine who did.

The most recent popular utterance of the phrase is found in the 2015 TV series *The Man in the High Castle,* which reimagines a Philip K. Dick story about a Nazi occupation of the United States. A character expresses the saying to explain his bravery. (**QI** has not found the phrase in Dick's titular novel.) Amazon Studios produced the show and used the phrase without attribution in their marketing posters and billboards.

Credit: Jason Morgan / dailybillboardblog.com

The search for the origin of this famous quotation has led to controversy. One disagreement involves the important reference book *Bartlett's Familiar Quotations* and the well-known word maven William Safire.

In 1968 the quotation appeared in the fourteenth edition of *Bartlett's Familiar Quotations*. The words were attributed to Burke and a 1795 letter was specified as support:[2]

> The only thing necessary for the triumph of evil is for good men
> to do nothing.
>
> —Letter to William Smith dated January 9, 1795

In 1980 *New York Times* language columnist William Safire wrote about the quote and challenged the attribution. He did so based on information from a persistent correspondent (not **QI**) who stated that the letter cited by Bartlett's did not contain the quote:[3]

The trouble is that it may be a phony. When I used the "triumph of evil" quotation recently to condemn complacency, a man named Hamilton A. Long of Philadelphia wrote to ask where and when Burke had said it . . .

Then the quotation sleuth sprung his trap. "It's not in that letter," Mr. Long replied triumphantly. "Nor any other source quoted in the quotations books I've found. They are false sources."

In the fifteenth edition of *Bartlett's Familiar Quotations*, released in 1980, the editor noted that the quotation had not been located in Burke's writings, and the reference work had been updated to reflect that fact. In 1981 Safire again discussed the quote.[4] In the sixteenth edition of *Bartlett's*, however, the quote is again listed under Burke, though a footnote indicates that vigorous searches have failed to find the words in Burke's oeuvre.

QI has solved the case. Edmund Burke and John Stuart Mill both produced apothegms that are loosely similar to the quotation under investigation; yet they are unmistakably distinct. By a process of synthesis and streamlining, the idea put forth by Burke was repeated by Mill and hewn further over time into a catchy aphorism.

In 1770 the Irish statesman and philosopher Burke wrote about the need for good men to associate to oppose the cabals of bad men. The second sentence in the excerpt below is listed in multiple quotation references and shares some points of similarity to the saying under investigation, but it is clearly dissimilar.[5]

No man, who is not inflamed by vain-glory into enthusiasm, can flatter himself that his single, unsupported, desultory, unsystematic endeavours are of power to defeat the subtle designs and united Cabals of ambitious citizens. When bad men combine, the good must associate; else they will fall, one by one, an unpitied sacrifice in a contemptible struggle.

In 1867 the British philosopher and political theorist Mill delivered an inaugural address at the University of St. Andrews. The second sentence in the excerpt below expresses part of the idea of the quotation under investigation.[6]

Let not any one pacify his conscience by the delusion that he can do no harm if he takes no part, and forms no opinion. Bad men need nothing more to compass their ends, than that good men should look on and do nothing.

In 1895 a medical bulletin printed a comment that was similar to Mill's adage. The wording of the second half matched closely, though no attribution was given.[7]

He should not be lulled to repose by the delusion that he does no harm who takes no part in public affairs. He should know that bad men need no better opportunity than when good men look on and do nothing. He should stand to his principles even if leaders go wrong.

Burke's quote continued in use in the early 1900s. In 1910 a pithy form of the saying appeared in the *Chicago Daily Tribune*:[8]

Burke said, "When bad men combine, good men must organize."

In October 1916 the *San Jose Mercury Herald* reported on a speech by Charles F. Aked in favor of prohibition. Aked used an expression similar to the quotation under investigation, though he uncoupled it from a source by offering the disclaimer "it has been said . . ." to signal that he was not claiming originality. Thus the saying was probably in circulation before 1916, but this mention is the earliest citation known to **QI**. Here is a longer excerpt.[9]

"The people in the liquor traffic," said the speaker, "simply want us to do nothing. That's all the devil wants of the son of God—to be let alone. That is all that the criminal wants of the law—to be let alone. The sin of doing nothing is the deadliest of all the seven sins. It has been said that for evil men to accomplish their purpose it is only necessary that good men should do nothing."

QI believes that Aked was a prominent preacher and lecturer who moved from England to the United States. A piece in the June 1920 issue of *100%: The Efficiency Magazine* attributed the expression above directly to Aked, providing further dissemination for the words. The article attributed the saying to the preacher twice—once in the subheading and once in the body. The following passage refers to a "constructive publication" that is never identified.[10]

> The slogan of a recently established constructive publication is "For evil men to accomplish their purpose, it is only necessary that good men do nothing," quoting the Rev. Charles F. Aked. While this is recognized as true of municipal politics, is it not also being evidenced as an actual condition in American industry?

The same month, a different version of the saying appeared anonymously in *Railway Carmen's Journal*. This variant used the term "bad men" and occurred in isolation at the beginning of an editorial section:[11]

> For bad men to accomplish their purposes it is only necessary that good men do nothing.

A July 1920 address to the Fourth International Congregational Council by British temperance crusader Sir R. Murray Hyslop contained a version of the now famous statement. In his speech at the church conference, Hyslop attributed the saying to Burke. This is the earliest example of this precise attribution known to **QI**.[12]

> Burke once said: "The only thing necessary for the triumph of evil is that good men should do nothing." Leave the Drink Trade alone and it will throttle all that is good in a nation's life. Let it alone, that is all that is required. Cowardice will suffice for its triumph. Courage will suffice for its overthrow.

In July 1920 a business digest periodical that lists articles published in other magazines included an entry for the aforementioned *100%: The Efficiency*

Magazine piece. The digest's listing reproduced the subheading, so the maxim appeared in this digest magazine and further propagated.[13]

> Are We Helping the Radicals? "For Evil Men to Accomplish Their Purpose, It Is [O]nly Necessary That Good Men Do Nothing." Perhaps the "Do Nothing" Attitude Is Responsible for Much of the Industrial Unrest. By Charles H. Norton, General Manager Collins Service. 100% June '20 p. 64. 1000 words.

In 1924 the *Surrey Mirror and County Post* of Surrey, England, reported on a meeting of an organization called the World Brotherhood Federation. A speaker named Robert A. Jameson employed an instance of the saying that he attributed to Burke:[14]

> As Edmund Burke had said, much more than 100 years ago: "The only thing necessary for the triumph of evil was that good men should do nothing."

In 1950 the saying appeared in the *Washington Post* and was attributed to Burke, as noted in *The Yale Book of Quotations*:[15]

> It is high time that the law-abiding citizens of Washington, and particularly those in organized groups dedicated to civic better-ment, became alert to this danger and demanded protection against organized gangdom.
>
> This situation is best summed up in the words of the British statesman, Edmund Burke, who many years ago said: "All that is necessary for the triumph of evil is that good men do nothing."

In 1955 a US congressman named O. C. Fisher wrote a short piece in the *Rotarian* where he used an instance of the saying and credited Burke.[16]

> He is a good man but he does nothing. His inaction is often the handmaid of evil. As the great Edmund Burke once said, for evil to succeed, it is only necessary for good men to do nothing.

Garson O'Toole

In 1961 President John F. Kennedy addressed the Canadian parliament and used a version of the quotation that he also credited to Burke.[17]

> At the conference table and in the minds of men, the free world's cause is strengthened because it is just. But it is strengthened even more by the dedicated efforts of free men and free nations. As the great parliamentarian Edmund Burke said, "The only thing necessary for the triumph of evil is for good men to do nothing."

It is possible that Aked created an adage with conscious or unconscious inspiration from Burke or Mill. Perhaps Hyslop heard the phrase and assigned it to Burke because he believed it sounded similar to Burke's style. Kennedy kept a notebook of quotations that he found worth recording. He may have heard a version attributed to Burke and noted it for future use. The record is too incomplete to make strong claims about who crafted the quote. But **QI** believes that the quotations from Burke and Mill are conceptually related to the quote under examination, though neither expression is close textually.

Notes:

1. Ralph Keyes, *The Quote Verifier: Who Said What, Where, and When* (New York: St. Martin's, 2006), 59, 109, 286. Verified in hard copy.
2. John Bartlett and Emily Morison Beck, eds., *Bartlett's Familiar Quotations*, 14th ed. (Boston: Little, Brown, 1968), 454. Verified in scans.
3. William Safire, "On Language: The Triumph of Evil," *New York Times Magazine*, March 9, 1980, SM2. Accessed in ProQuest.
4. William Safire, "On Language; Standing Corrected," *New York Times Magazine*, April 5, 1981, SM4. Accessed in ProQuest.
5. Edmund Burke, *Thoughts on the Cause of the Present Discontents*, 3rd ed. (London: J. Dodsley, 1770), 106. Accessed in Google Books, https://goo.gl/vkcgYG.
6. John Stuart Mill, "Inaugural Address, on a Course of Study," *Littell's Living Age* 4, no. 50 (March 16, 1867): 664. Accessed in Google Books, https://goo.gl/Zts8VL.
7. Mariott Brosius, "The Medical Profession and the State: Alumni Oration," *Medical Bulletin: A Monthly Journal of Medicine and Surgery* 17, no. 6 (June 1895): 203. Accessed in Google Books, https://goo.gl/RSNAJM.

8.   "Capen Pleads for Reforms," *Chicago Daily Tribune* (Chicago, IL), August 28, 1910, 4. Accessed in ProQuest.

9.   Charles F. Aked, "On Liquor Traffic," *San Jose Mercury Herald* (San Jose, CA), October 31, 1916, 1. Verified in newspaper scans from Archive of Americana. Thanks to Mike at Duke University of obtaining those scans. Also thanks to Ken Hirsch for pointing out this citation in a post by J. L. Bell at the website Boston 1775, http://boston1775.blogspot.com /2009/04/only-thing-necessary-for-triumph-of.html.

10. Charles H. Norton, "Are We Helping the Radicals?" *100%: The Efficiency Magazine*, June 1920, 64. Accessed in Google Books, https://goo.gl/mJFTeu.

11. "Editorial Notes," *Railway Carmen's Journal* 25, no. 1 (January 1920): 366. Accessed in HathiTrust, https://goo.gl/yebJmi.

12. Sir R. Murray Hyslop, J. P., "Some Present Features of the Temperance Crusade" (address, Fourth International Congregational Council, Boston, MA, June 29–July 6, 1920), 166. Accessed in Google Books, https://goo.gl/7knZd9. Barry Popik located this citation, which is noted on his webpage, "All That Is Necessary for the Triumph of Evil Is That Good Men Do Nothing," The Big Apple, November 7, 2009, http://www.barrypopik.com /index.php/new_york_city/entry/all_that_is_necessary_for_the_triumph_of_evil_is_that _good_men_do_nothing/.

13. "Labor," *Business Digest and Investment Weekly* 26, no. 5 (July 30, 1920): 75. Accessed in Google Books, https://goo.gl/vwW2VX.

14. "Redhill Brotherhood," *Surrey Mirror and County Post* (Surrey, UK), August 29, 1924, 5. Accessed in British Newspaper Archive.

15. Harry N. Stull, "District Affairs: Indifference Fosters Gangsterism," *Washington Post* (Washington, DC), January 22, 1950, B8. Accessed in ProQuest; Fred R. Shapiro, *The Yale Book of Quotations* (New Haven: Yale University Press, 2006), 143. Verified in hard copy.

16. O. C. Fisher, "Yes, He's a 'Party Hack,' Believes O. C. Fisher," *Rotarian*, November 1955, 9. Accessed in Google Books, https://goo.gl/ekPKRL.

17. "Address by President Kennedy to the Canadian Parliament [Extracts], May 17, 1961," *Documents on Disarmament 1961*, Publication 5 (Washington, DC: United States Arms Control and Disarmament Agency, 1962), 149. Accessed in HathiTrust, https://goo.gl /SdalYj.

6. "Genius is 1% inspiration and 99% perspiration."

—Thomas Edison

In 1892 a newspaper in Massachusetts reacted to a statement by a prominent lecturer named Kate Sanborn. The newspaper indicated that sayings about the composition of genius were already being disseminated:[1]

> Kate Sanborn is getting lots of credit for having said that "talent is perspiration." That idea has been expressed very often; in fact, much in the same terms. A common way of saying it is that "genius is perspiration more than inspiration."

In 1893 Sanborn delivered a lecture that was reported in a Riverside, California, newspaper. According to the article, Sanborn suggested in her talk that genius was composed of three ingredients, but she did not give a memorable fractional breakdown:[2]

> Her subject was "What is Genius?" She quoted copiously from ancient and modern writers, giving their definitions of the word genius, and wittily added that "genius is inspiration, talent and perspiration."

In April 1898 *Ladies' Home Journal* printed a remark about genius that it credited to Thomas Edison.[3] The main ingredient mentioned was "hard work," and the ratio was 98 to 2. Expert Ralph Keyes listed this citation in *The Quote Verifier* reference work:[4]

> Once, when asked to give his definition of genius, Mr. Edison replied: "Two per cent. is genius and ninety-eight per cent. is hard work." At another time, when the argument that genius was

inspiration was brought before him, he said: "Bah! Genius is not inspired. Inspiration is perspiration."

Also, in April 1898, the *Youth's Companion* printed similar remarks from Edison that presented a ratio of ninety-eight to two:[5]

"Ninety-eight per cent. of genius is hard work," says Thomas A. Edison, and he adds, "As for genius being inspired, inspiration is in most cases another word for perspiration." As the foremost example in the world of one type of genius, Mr. Edison is an authority on the subject, and his aphorism corroborates Johnson's often-quoted definition of genius, "the infinite capacity for taking pains."

In May 1898 the president of a shoe company delivered a speech to high school students, in which he incorporated an adage he ascribed to Edison. But the speaker did not list "hard work" as an ingredient. Instead, two constituents were given: inspiration and perspiration, and the ratio was two to ninety-eight:[6]

Even Mr. Edison is quoted as having said that genius may be divided into two parts, of which inspiration is 2 per cent and perspiration 98.

In June 1898 a Montana newspaper published a version of the aphorism and attributed it to a person who was writing about Edison instead of Edison himself:[7]

Speaking of the life and labors of Thomas A. Edison, a writer says that two per cent of his great discoveries and inventions can be credited to inspiration, while the other 98 per cent is due to perspiration.

At last, in 1901, the modern version of the saying with a ratio of 1 to 99 emerged in an Idaho newspaper, where it was credited to Edison:[8]

Genius is another name for hard work, honest work. "Genius," says Edison "is 1 per cent inspiration and 99 per cent perspiration." People who take pains never to do any more than they get paid for, never get paid for anything more than they do.

Multiple versions of Edison's maxim were in circulation at the same time. For example, in 1902 the magazine *Scientific American* presented the following instance with a ratio of two to ninety-eight:[9]

To those who believe that Edison's work is the product of an inspiration given by nature to but few, the story of the manner in which he achieves success will seem shockingly unromantic. In the genius who works by inspiration Edison has no great faith. "Genius is two per cent inspiration and ninety-eight per cent perspiration," is the incisive, epigrammatic answer he once gave to a man who thought that a genius worked only when the spirit moved him.

In 1904 the *Chicago Tribune* published a profile of Edison that included a version of the saying:[10]

[H]is fondness for epigrams led him away from the spirit of the true genius when he took occasion to say that "Genius is 2 percent inspiration and 98 percent perspiration."

The saying inspired variations. For example, in 1907 a store selling shirts published an advertisement with the following formulation for success:[11]

We carry the elements of success under our hats
1 per cent Luck.
2 per cent Inspiration.
97 per cent Perspiration.
Watch us perspire when we show you shirts, as we have so many to show you[.]

A 1910 biography, *Edison: His Life and Inventions*, also ascribed the most common modern version of the maxim to Edison:[12]

> The idea of attributing great successes to "genius" has always been repudiated by Edison as evidenced by his historic remark that "Genius is 1 per cent. inspiration and 99 per cent. perspiration." Again, in a conversation many years ago at the laboratory between Edison, Batchelor, and E.H. Johnson, the latter made allusion to Edison's genius as evidenced by some of his achievements, when Edison replied: "Stuff! I tell you genius is hard work, stick-to-it-iveness, and common sense."

In 1932 a man who worked in Edison's laboratory named Martin André Rosanoff published an article in *Harper's* magazine that quoted Edison taking credit for the modern saying:[13]

> You may have heard people repeat what I have said, "Genius is one per cent inspiration, ninety-nine per cent perspiration."

In conclusion, the basic idea that genius is composed of inspiration and perspiration was in circulation before Edison's adage was published. But Edison can be credited with presenting a clever fractional breakdown. Indeed, evidence suggests that he presented two different ratios: two to ninety-eight and one to ninety-nine.

Notes:

In memoriam: thanks to my brother Stephen, who asked about Edison quotations.

1. "Men, Women, and Affairs," *Springfield Republican* (Springfield, MA), December 4, 1892, 4. Accessed in GenealogyBank.
2. "Miss Sanborn's Lecture," *Riverside Daily Press* (Riverside, CA), April 21, 1893, 4. Accessed in GenealogyBank.

3. "The Anecdotal Side of Edison," *Ladies' Home Journal*, April 1898, 8. Accessed in ProQuest American Periodicals.

4. Ralph Keyes, *The Quote Verifier: Who Said What, Where, and When* (New York: St. Martin's, 2006), 77, 292. Verified in hard copy.

5. Current Topics, *Youth's Companion* 72, no. 16 (April 21, 1898): 194. Accessed in ProQuest American Periodicals.

6. "Peace Has Its Victories: An Interesting Address to High School Boys, Delivered by Mr. J. K. Orr," *Savannah Tribune* (Savannah, GA), May 21, 1898, 4. Accessed in GenealogyBank.

7. Brevities, *Helena Independent* (Helena, MT), June 19, 1898, 2. Accessed in GenealogyBank.

8. Doing One's Best, *Idaho Daily Statesman* (Boise, ID), May 6, 1901, 4. Accessed in GenealogyBank. Top researcher Barry Popik located this citation.

9. "Thomas Alva Edison," *Scientific American*, December 27, 1902, 463. Accessed in ProQuest American Periodicals.

10. Jonas Howard, "Thomas A. Edison as He Is Today," *Chicago Tribune*, November 6, 1904, E2. Accessed in ProQuest.

11. [Advertisement for shirts, Harry Weiss], *Repository* (Canton, OH), November 12, 1907, 2. Accessed in GenealogyBank.

12. Frank Lewis Dyer and Thomas Commerford Martin, *Edison: His Life and Inventions*, vol. 2 (New York: Harper, 1910), 607. Accessed in Google Books, https://goo.gl/R6zYtZ.

13. M. A. [Martin André] Rosanoff, "Edison in His Laboratory," *Harper's* 165 (September 1932): 406. Verified in microfilm.

7. "The question isn't who is going to let me, it's who is going to stop me."

—Ayn Rand

In 2013 the *Time* magazine website published an article about the fashion retailer Forever 21 selling an "Unstoppable Muscle Tee" with a controversial message.[1] Displayed on this garment was a quotation attributed to Ayn Rand, the influential author and combative capitalist philosopher:

> The question isn't who is going to let me, it's who is going to stop me.
>
> —Ayn Rand

The *Time* writer seemed to disapprove of the garment. A client of **QI**'s had a different reaction: "Are these really the words of Ayn Rand? I have searched for them and cannot find them in any of her novels or essays."

QI has been unable to find this precise quotation in the writings of Rand. However, **QI** hypothesizes that the sentence was derived from a dialogue in her bestselling 1943 novel *The Fountainhead*.

In the work, the main character, Howard Roark, attends a school called the Stanton Institute of Technology to learn about architecture. He refuses to follow the design precepts that he considers anachronistic and wrong-headed, and he is expelled from the school for insubordination.

Howard's modernistic designs of glass and concrete have shocked many of the teachers at the institute, and the school dean, when meeting for a final discussion before Roark is expelled, appears truly confused:[2]

> "Do you mean to tell me that you're thinking seriously of building that way, when and if you are an architect?"
>
> "Yes."

"My dear fellow, *who will let you?*"

"That's not the point. The point is, *who will stop me?*"

"Look here, this is serious. I am sorry that I haven't had a long, earnest talk with you much earlier . . . I know, I know, I know, don't interrupt me, you've seen a modernistic building or two, and it gave you ideas. But do you realize what a passing fancy that whole so-called modern movement is?"

QI conjectures that the third and fourth lines above were altered and combined to generate a single sentence, and this sentence was directly assigned to Rand. The process may have occurred via multiple intermediary steps.

The 2001 book *Welch: An American Icon* by Janet Lowe told the story of the business executive Jack Welch, who became chairman of General Electric corporation. The third chapter used a jumbled quotation attributed to Rand as an epigraph:[3]

★ *chapter three* ★

The Companies General Electric Dumped

I do everything for a reason—most of the time the reason is money.　　Suzy Parker, fashion model and actress[1]

The question is not "who is going to let me," it's "who is going to stop me?"　　Ayn Rand, *The Fountainhead*

Wiley/Welch: An American Icon

In 2003 the expression appeared in the book *Love It, Don't Leave It: 26 Ways to Get What You Want at Work*. The authors did not give an attribution and treated the remark critically:[4]

> The question isn't who is going to let me—it's who is going to stop me.
>> If that sounds like you, consider yielding occasionally because:
>> You can't always be right. Sometimes someone else has a better solution, updated information, or a fresh perspective.

In May 2013 the *Forbes* magazine website published an article titled "Top 100 Inspirational Quotes," and the statement under investigation was listed ninety-third:[5]

> The question isn't who is going to let me; it's who is going to stop me.
>
> —Ayn Rand

The critical story published on the *Time* website in 2013 apparently had repercussions. After it appeared, **QI** was unable to find the shirt emblazoned with the misquotation in the online store of Forever 21. In this case, the phrase "who is going to stop me" had been answered.

Notes:

Great thanks to astute *Wall Street Journal* reporter Jason Zweig, who pointed out the article on *Time*'s website and questioned the accuracy of the quotation on the shirt. The inquiry gave impetus to **QI** to formulate this question and initiate this exploration. Also, thanks to Skylar for her library help on multiple occasions.

1.   Courtney Subramanian, "Forever 21 Is Now Selling a Shirt with an Ayn Rand Quote on It," *Time*, October 10, 2013, http://newsfeed.time.com/2013/10/10/forever-21-cashes-in-on-ayn-rands-objectivist-philisophy/.

2. Ayn Rand, *The Fountainhead*, reprint of 1943 Bobbs-Merrill edition (New York: Penguin, 1971), 23. Verified in scans.

3. Janet Lowe, *Welch: An American Icon* (New York: John Wiley and Sons, 2001), 81. Verified in hard copy.

4. Beverly L. Kaye and Sharon Jordan-Evans, *Love It, Don't Leave It: 26 Ways to Get What You Want at Work* (San Francisco: Berrett-Koehler, 2003), 398, https://goo.gl/biAIXa.

5. Kevin Kruse, "Top 100 Inspirational Quotes," *Forbes*, May 28, 2013, http://www.forbes.com/sites/kevinkruse/2013/05/28/inspirational-quotes/3/.

VENTRILOQUY

8. "Don't bend; don't water it down; don't try to make it logical; don't edit your own soul according to the fashion."

—Franz Kafka

The comedian Russell Brand has written two bestselling autobiographies, *My Booky Wook: A Memoir of Sex, Drugs,* and *Stand-Up* (2007) and *Booky Wook 2: This Time It's Personal* (2010). The sequel bears a mistaken epigraph on its opening page:[1]

Part One

Don't bend; don't water it down; don't try to make it logical; don't edit your own soul according to the fashion. Rather, follow your most intense obsessions mercilessly.

Franz Kafka

Credit: Booky Wook 2/HarperCollins

Brand may have seen a user-generated post on the website Goodreads, which attributed the quotation to Franz Kafka, and which matches the one in *Booky Wook 2: This Time It's Personal*.[2] However, **QI** discovered that the quote wasn't written by Kafka at all, but by another famous author in the late twentieth century.

The exact string of words appears in the foreword to a 1995 collection of Kafka's works titled *The Metamorphosis, In the Penal Colony, and Other Stories*. The passage, written by the bestselling horror author Anne Rice, is part of a larger introductory summary for what Rice imagines as Kafka's imperatives to himself and thereby other writers. Rice was not actually quoting Kafka. She was conjuring him, you might say—but some readers apparently misunderstood her intentions.[3]

> Kafka became a model for me, a continuing inspiration. Not only did he exhibit an irrepressible originality—who else would think of things like this!—he seemed to say that only in one's most personal language can the crucial tales of a writer be told. Don't bend; don't water it down; don't try to make it logical; don't edit your own soul according to the fashion. Rather, follow your most intense obsessions mercilessly. Only if you do that can you hope to make the reader feel a particle of what you, the writer, have known and feel compelled to share.

QI believes that the philosophy of creativity outlined above is Rice's, not Kafka's. Rice is stating that she adopted a method that she gleaned from reading Kafka's stories. To her, Kafka is the author of the sentiment, if not the particular words.

QI shared these discoveries on the Quote Investigator website in 2013.

Two years later, **QI** received a startling and confusing message. Anne Rice herself had recently shared with her fans a 2013 post from an Anne Rice Facebook fan page that repeated the attribution to Kafka. **QI**'s correspondent helpfully included a link:

> "Don't bend; don't water it down; don't try to make it logical; don't edit your own soul according to the fashion. Rather, follow your

most intense obsessions mercilessly." Franz Kafka said this. Thanks to Granny Goodwitch for the quote. This is Kafka's birthday.[4]

QI notes that 3,485 users had "liked" something that Kafka didn't write.

QI sent a private message of inquiry to Rice, who explained that one of her fans had sent her the quotation with the ascription to Kafka. Rice hadn't recognized the words, but she found them attractive, so she shared the message with her Facebook followers. **QI** learned with gratification that the article on the Quote Investigator website had been more than enough proof to convince Rice that she was the actual author.

In June 2015 Rice corrected the misattribution via a message on her Facebook page.[5]

> I just found out something hilariously funny. Years ago, I wrote a brief introduction to a collection of Kafka's short stories, including the Metamorphosis, and something I said in the intro, about Kafka's influence on me has been recently quoted all over the internet as a quote from Kafka! This is truly very amusing. "Don't bend; don't water it down; don't try to make it logical; don't edit your own soul according to the fashion. Rather, follow your most intense obsessions mercilessly." Those are my words struggling to define the impression Kafka's example made on me! And it's being attributed worldwide to Kafka.

Notes:

Many thanks to Nathaniel Tan, whose inquiry gave impetus to **QI** to formulate this question and perform this exploration. Thanks also to the Project Wombat group. In addition, many thanks to Anne Rice for her response.

1. Russell Brand, *Booky Wook 2: This Time It's Personal* (London: HarperCollins, 2010), 1.
2. "Franz Kafka > Quotes > Quotable Quote," Goodreads, accessed November 8, 2013, https://www.goodreads.com/quotes/201816-don-t-bend-don-t-water-it-down-don-t-try-to-make.

3. Anne Rice, foreword to *The Metamorphosis, In the Penal Colony, and Other Stories*, by Franz Kafka (New York: Schocken, 1995), 1–3. Great thanks to the helpful librarian at the Beaufort County Library in Beaufort, South Carolina, who accessed the 1995 citation.

4. "Anne Rice Fan Page" post dated July 13, 2013, Facebook, accessed November 11, 2013, https://www.facebook.com/annericefanpage/posts/10151768484880452.

5. "Anne Rice Fan Page" post dated June 26, 2015, Facebook, accessed June 27, 2015, https://www.facebook.com/annericefanpage/posts/10153485424645452.

9. "In the struggle for survival, the fittest win out at the expense of their rivals."

—Charles Darwin

The scholars working on the authoritative Darwin Correspondence Project based at Cambridge University have constructed an important database of 7,500 letters written or received by Charles Darwin. On the basis of this hoard of personal writings, **QI** assumes, the board has placed the statement above into a set of "Six Things Darwin Never Said."[1] And yet, every now and then, a publication will claim the quote comes from Darwin's seminal work *The Origin of Species*. For example, the *MIT Technology Review* on July 15, 2014, led with the quote in a story called "Evolving Beyond Coupons and Mobile Apps."[2]

The earliest appearance of the statement found by **QI** is located within a history textbook titled *Civilization Past and Present* by T. Walter Wallbank, Alastair M. Taylor, and Nels M. Bailkey. Many editions of this work were published beginning in 1942. **QI** has inspected the 1962 edition.

A chapter titled "Einstein, Darwin, and Freud" presents a summary of the "Darwinian hypothesis" crafted by the textbook authors (as opposed to Darwin). Item three below precisely matches the expression that has been misattributed to Darwin in modern times.[3]

> There are five main points in the Darwinian hypothesis. First, all existing vegetable and animal species are descended from earlier and, generally speaking, more rudimentary forms. Second, the variation in species has come about because the environment and the use or disuse of organs have brought about changes in structure that are inherited.
>
> Third, in the struggle for survival, the fittest win out at the expense of their rivals because they succeed in adapting themselves best to their environment. Fourth, differentiation among the species is also brought about by sexual selection, which Darwin declared is

"the most powerful means of changing the races of man." Finally, some variations seem to arise spontaneously, a view of Darwin's which pointed toward the doctrine of mutation.

In 1971 *The Living Clocks* by Ritchie R. Ward included an instance of the quotation. The author did not credit Darwin; instead, a footnote indicated that the text was excerpted from an edition of *Civilization Past and Present*.[4]

An especially clear modern summary of the five main points that Darwin made in the two works is available to college students today: "First, all existing vegetable and animal species are descended from earlier and, generally speaking, more rudimentary forms. Second, the variation in species has come about because the environment and the use or disuse of organs have brought about changes in structure that are inherited. Third, in the struggle for survival, the fittest win out at the expense of their rivals because they succeed in adapting themselves best to their environment.

By 2006 the quotation had been reassigned to Darwin directly. This development was accordant with a mechanism known to **QI** for the generation of misattributions:

Step 1: The thoughts of a famous person are summarized or restated to yield a short passage in a book or newspaper.

Step 2: Some reader misinterprets the passage and ascribes the words directly to the famous person.

Step 3: The misattribution is widely propagated by unsuspecting individuals.

Here is an example of the erroneous ascription in the *Guardian* newspaper in 2006:[5]

In the struggle for survival, the fittest win out at the expense of their rivals because they succeed in adapting themselves best to their environment.

—Charles Darwin, *The Origin of Species*

Having seen the first part of the TV series *Extinct* (ITV1, Saturday), I think I get what Darwin was on about. But perhaps if he was around now, and just coming up with his theory, he may have worded it slightly differently—"In the struggle for survival, the cutest win out at the expense of the less cute because they appeal more to celebrities and, through them, to a live television audience."

In 2009 a book titled *Wisdom Well Said* included the following instance.[6]

Charles Darwin (1809–1882), the famous English naturalist who first formulated the concept of evolution, wrote in his history-making *Origin of the Species*: "In the struggle for survival, the fittest win out at the expense of their rivals because they succeed in adapting themselves best to their environment."

In conclusion, **QI** believes that one or more of the authors of the history textbook *Civilization Past and Present* constructed the quotation. The statement was part of a description and explication of Darwin's ideas. The words were not written by Darwin in *The Origin of Species* or anywhere else.

Notes:

Special thanks to Edward Carilli and Lauren Foster, whose inquiries about another quotation misattributed to Darwin led **QI** to the Darwin Correspondence Project website. At the website **QI** saw an inquiry that led him to formulate this question and perform this exploration.

1. "Six Things Darwin Never Said—And One He Did," Darwin Correspondence Project, accessed December 18, 2014, http://www.darwinproject.ac.uk/people/about-darwin /six-things-darwin-never-said-and-one-he-did.

2. Manju Bansal, "Evolving Beyond Coupons and Mobile Apps: Retail Technologies in the Sensor Economy," *MIT Technology Review,* July 15, 2014, accessed in Google News Archive.

3. T. Walter Wallbank, Alastair M. Taylor, and Nels M. Bailkey, *Civilization Past and Present,* single-volume ed. (Chicago: Scott, Foresman, 1962), 575, 578. Verified in photocopies.

4. Ritchie R. Ward, *The Living Clocks* (New York: Alfred A. Knopf, 1971), 74. Verified in hard copy.

5. Sam Wollaston, "Pop Stars, Buildings, Now Endangered Species . . . Is Nothing Safe from the Phone Vote Format?" The Weekend's TV, *Guardian* (London, UK), December 10, 2006. https://www.theguardian.com/media/2006/dec/11/broadcasting.tvandradio.

6. Charles Francis, ed., *Wisdom Well Said* (El Prado, NM: Levine Mesa, 2009), 7. Accessed in Google Books, https://goo.gl/48YXPq.

10. "Life is a journey, not a destination."

—Ralph Waldo Emerson

QI believes that an exact match for the expression above has not been found in the oeuvre of Ralph Waldo Emerson. Yet, Emerson did write a thematically related remark:[1]

> To finish the moment, to find the journey's end in every step of the road, to live the greatest number of good hours, is wisdom.

This sentence suggests a psychological vantage point in which the intermediate advances of the journey are representative of the completion of the journey. This is arguably a distinct statement from the statement that is listed in *The Dictionary of Modern Proverbs* without attachment to a specific person.[2]

Interesting precursors of the expression were in circulation in the nineteenth century. In 1854 *Sunday at Home: A Family Magazine for Sabbath Reading* printed a "Page for the Young" with the following advice.[3]

> You should learn in early youth that your life is a journey, not a rest. You are travelling to the promised land, from the cradle to the grave.

In 1855 another religious text used a variant phrase and provided an explanation.[4]

> All life is a journey, not a home; it is a road, not the country; and those transient enjoyments which you have in this life, lawful in their way,—those incidental and evanescent pleasures which you may sip,—are not home; they are little inns only upon the road-side of life, where you are refreshed for a moment, that you may take

again the pilgrim-staff and journey on, seeking what is still before you—the rest that remaineth for the people of God.

A decade later the passage above was reprinted in a collection entitled *A Cyclopaedia of Illustrations of Moral and Religious Truths*; however, it was labeled "Anon."[5]

The earliest strong match located by **QI** appeared in 1920 in a periodical called the *Christian Advocate*. The phrase was used by the theologian Lynn H. Hough during "The Sunday School Lesson" in the February 19, 1920, issue. Hough is discussing a letter from Saint Peter.[6]

He wanted his friends to realize that life is a journey and not a destination; that the heart must be set upon those matters of character which are eternal and not upon those matters of sensation which pass away.

In 1922 another variant of the saying was printed that emphasized an experiential theme instead of a religious one.[7]

But we stupid mortals, or most of us, are always in haste to reach somewhere else, forgetting that the zest is in the journey and not in the destination.

In 1926 the trope was applied to the domain of love, within a verse using eccentric capitalization.[8]

LOVE To SOME men Is NOT a DESTINATION. It is just A FLIGHT OF FANCY. A RUSHING EMOTION between BUSINESS and AMBITION that Keeps them FOREVER ON THE HOP.

In 1929 an essay by a high school student employed a version of the saying with the word "success." The words were enclosed in quotation marks, suggesting that the adage was already in circulation.[9]

You know, "success is not a destination, but a journey."

Yet another variant of the expression was in circulation by 1930.[10]

Prof J. C. Archer of Yale University will speak on "Religion a Journey and Not a Destination" at the monthly "church night" gathering at Memorial church tomorrow night.

In 1935 a story in the *Cleveland Plain Dealer* presented a variant.[11]

"Helen, somebody has said that happiness is a journey—not a destination. You have it as you go along. You've been very happy with two different people.

In 1936 the book *I Knew Them in Prison* by Mary B. Harris included another version of the adage.[12]

Reformation, like education, is a journey, not a destination.

In 1937 another instance of the maxim about education was printed in a California newspaper.[13]

Reporting on education, Mrs. S. G. Stooke said that education is a journey and not a destination, for we must keep developing.

In 1993 the rock band Aerosmith released the single "Amazing." The lyrics were written by Steven Tyler and Richie Supa, and they included an instance of the saying.[14]

Life's a journey not a destination
And I just can't tell just what tomorrow brings

In the 2006 movie *Peaceful Warrior*, character Dan Millman is led on a three-hour trek to a remote location by his mentor, a wise character named Socrates. Millman is excited and happy during the trip because he expects to be shown something important. When shown a nondescript rock, he is initially disappointed. But, after reflection, Millman says the following to Socrates:[15]

> The journey. The journey's what brings us happiness . . . not the destination.

Many of the examples above conform to the following flexible phrasal template: "X is a journey, not a destination." Linguists refer to such a phrase as a "snowclone."[16]

Notes:

Thanks to Jack Herring for his query on this topic. This question was constructed by **QI** based on his inquiry. Also, thanks to Dan Goncharoff for noting the relevant quotation due to Ralph Waldo Emerson.

1.   Ralph Waldo Emerson, "Essay II: Experience," in *Essays: Second Series*, 2nd ed. (Boston: James Munroe, 1844), 65. Accessed in Google Books, https://goo.gl/gQHboV.

2.   Charles Clay Doyle, Wolfgang Mieder, and Fred R. Shapiro, eds., *The Dictionary of Modern Proverbs* (New Haven, CT: Yale University Press, 2012), 142. Verified in hard copy. Phrase in cited volume is as stated: "Life is a journey, not a destination."

3.   "Page for the Young: The Midnight Feast and Its Lesson," *Sunday at Home: A Family Magazine for Sabbath Reading,* December 7, 1854, 512. Accessed in HathiTrust, https://goo.gl/sctT7f.

4.   John Cumming, *The End: or, The Proximate Signs of the Close of This Dispensation* (London: John Farquhar Shaw, 1855), 392. Accessed in Google Books, https://goo.gl/6YVZKo.

5.   John Bate, ed., *A Cyclopaedia of Illustrations of Moral and Religious Truths*, 2nd ed. (London: Elliot Stock, 1865), 535. Accessed in Google Books, https://goo.gl/g5JCZ3.

6.   Lynn H. Hough, "The Sunday School Lesson: First Quarter—Lesson IX," *Christian Advocate*, February 29, 1920, 266. Accessed in Google Books, https://goo.gl/Bu2DYg.

7.   Ralph Delahaye Paine, *Roads of Adventure* (Boston: Houghton Mifflin, 1922), 404. Accessed in Google Books, https://goo.gl/wva2GT.

8.   "You Said It, Marceline" [freestanding verse in "Flights of Fancy"], *Richmond Times Dispatch* (Richmond, VA), August 27, 1926, 6. Accessed in GenealogyBank.

9. "Convent School Wins New Prize by Wide Margin: Third Prize Winning Essay by Irene Wadlington," *Times-Picayune* (New Orleans, LA), May 12, 1929, 26. Accessed in GenealogyBank.

10. "Yale Professor to Give Address," *Springfield Republican* (Springfield, MA), February 12, 1930, 8. Accessed in GenealogyBank.

11. Inez Wallace, "Shadows in Paradise," *Cleveland Plain Dealer* (Cleveland, OH), January 25, 1935, 8. Accessed in GenealogyBank.

12. Millicent Taylor, review of *I Knew Them in Prison* by Mary B. Harris, *Christian Science Monitor*, May 27, 1936, 14. Accessed in ProQuest.

13. "Civic Unit Warned of Dishonest Business," *San Diego Union* (San Diego, CA), December 8, 1937, 7. Accessed in GenealogyBank.

14. "Aerosmith–Amazing," YouTube video, 6:50, copyright 1994, posted by "AerosmithVEVO," December 24, 2009, https://www.youtube.com/watch?v=zSmOvYzSeaQ. Quote is sung at 02:04.

15. Kevin Bernhardt, *The Peaceful Warrior* (screenplay), 2006, http://www.veryabc.cn/movie/uploads/script/PeacefulWarrior.txt.

16. *Wikipedia*, s.v. "Snowclone," last modified July 2, 2016, https://en.wikipedia.org/wiki/Snowclone.

11. "640K [of computer memory] ought to be enough for anyone."

—Bill Gates

These days a computer's memory is tens of thousands of times larger than 640 kilobytes. The 640K limitation was once a real headache for programmers and users. The above quote is notorious among computer enthusiasts and is typically dated to 1981, to the early days of personal computing, but Bill Gates has denied that he ever said it.

During the 1990s Gates wrote a syndicated newspaper column in which he answered questions from the public. When asked in 1996 about the saying, he replied:[1]

> I've said some stupid things and some wrong things, but not that. No one involved in computers would ever say that a certain amount of memory is enough for all time.

The need for memory increases as computers get more potent and software gets more powerful. In fact, every couple of years the amount of memory address space needed to run whatever software is mainstream at the time just about doubles. This is well known.

However, the computer periodical *InfoWorld* did attribute several statements to Gates that expressed acceptance or satisfaction regarding the 640K computer memory limitation, including the earliest version of the quotation being credited to Gates:[2]

When we set the upper limit of PC-DOS at 640K, we thought nobody would ever need that much memory.

—William Gates, chairman of Microsoft

These words appeared at the beginning of an editorial written by James E. Fawcette published in the April 29, 1985, issue of *InfoWorld*. But the piece gave no precise reference, and the words did not occur as part of an interview.

An insight into the mindset of many computer enthusiasts in the 1980s is displayed in a passage from the 1986 book *Windows: The Official Guide to Microsoft's Operating Environment*. The author, Nancy Andrews, who was knowledgeable about PCs, discussed her own belief that even 128 kilobytes of memory was "all the memory we'd ever need." Yet, she quickly recognized that more computer memory was needed to accomplish tasks of increasing sophistication:[3]

> When the IBM PC-1 was introduced in 1981, it came equipped with 64K of memory. Those of us who upgraded our systems to 128K thought we had all the memory we'd ever need. At first, there were very few programs available that needed as much as 128K. But as more and more software became available, the complexity of the programs increased and so did their memory requirements.

In July 1987 the computer columnist and prominent science fiction author Jerry Pournelle expressed a similar sentiment. In an article titled "Law of Expanding Memory: Applications Will Also Expand Until RAM Is Full" in *InfoWorld*, he wrote:[4]

> My first microcomputer had 12K of memory. When I expanded to a full 64K, I thought I had all the memory I'd ever need. Hah. I know better now.
>
> For a while it was just an annoyance, but the memory-resident software situation is now getting completely out of hand.

In February 1988 the computer columnist Steve Gibson ascribed the belief that 640K was enough memory to the designers of the IBM PC collectively. The term "Visicalc" used below referred to a popular spreadsheet application:[5]

Unhappily, the original designers of the IBM PC felt that 640K of RAM would be more than anyone would ever need. After all, Visicalc operated usefully on a mere 48K Apple II!

In November 1988 another computer columnist with *InfoWorld*, George Morrow, commented about memory limitations. He attributed a version of the opinion under investigation to Bill Gates. Morrow did not give a specific reference and did not place the words inside quotation marks:[6]

Microsoft Corp. chairman Bill Gates once said 640K of memory was more than anyone needed. He was wrong.

In 1989 Bill Gates delivered a recorded speech about microcomputers to the computer science club at the University of Waterloo. He presented his recollections concerning the size of memory:[7]

I have to say that in 1981, making those decisions, I felt like I was providing enough freedom for 10 years. That is, a move from 64k to 640k felt like something that would last a great deal of time. Well, it didn't—it took about only 6 years before people started to see that as a real problem.

In January 1990, an issue of *InfoWorld* attributed to Bill Gates the version of the quotation that is now commonplace on the Internet and in the mass media. The quotation occurs in a timeline showing the development of the PC industry in the 1980s. However, the periodical does not provide a precise reference, so it is not clear when Gates was supposed to have made the remark:[8]

IBM introduces the PC and, with Microsoft, releases DOS ("640K ought to be enough for anyone" —Bill Gates)

In November 1995 the *Washington Post* published an article that contained a collection of quotations labeled "If They Only Knew." The sayings were selected to present their speakers as foolish or wrongheaded. Below are three examples. Note that the date of 1981 was assigned to the words attributed to Gates. This date is often paired with the remark now:[9]

"Computers in the future may weigh no more than 1.5 tons."

—*Popular Mechanics*, forecasting the relentless
march of science, 1949

"We don't like their sound, and guitar music is on the way out."

—Decca Recording Co. rejecting the Beatles, 1962

"640K ought to be enough for anybody."

—Bill Gates, 1981

In 1996, as discussed earlier, Gates denied that he made the remark. He also questioned the existence of any solid reference for the statement:[10]

Meanwhile, I keep bumping into that silly quotation attributed to me that says 640K of memory is enough. There's never a citation; the quotation just floats like a rumor, repeated again and again.

The quotation credited to Gates was given further circulation by the 1998 book *The Experts Speak: The Definitive Compendium of Authoritative Misinformation*, where it appeared with a footnote justification. However, the footnote simply pointed to the 1995 *Washington Post* article mentioned above:[11]

640K ought to be enough for anybody.

—Remark attributed to Bill Gates (Founder and
CEO of Microsoft), 1981

QI feels the evidence linking this quotation to Bill Gates is mixed. The first-known citation occurred in 1985, despite the claim that the comment was made in 1981. Indeed, there does not appear to be any direct support for the 1981 date beyond the fact that IBM introduced the PC in that year. It is not clear when or where Gates made the statement given in the 1985 *InfoWorld* article. Perhaps its writer, James E. Fawcette, knows more about the circumstances. The 1985 and 1990 remarks appeared in quotation marks, but they were not part of interviews.

On the other hand, the comments by Nancy Andrews and Jerry Pournelle show that a common mindset of the period was compatible with informal hyperbolic remarks of this type. The 1989 speech by Gates presented a more sophisticated analysis of the growth of computing power and memory.

Since Gates has denied the quotation and the evidence is not compelling, **QI** would not attribute it to him at this time.

Notes:

1. Bill Gates, "Computer Industry Offers Wealth of Career Options," *Daily News of Los Angeles*, January 22, 1996, business section, B1. Accessed in NewsBank.
2. James E. Fawcette, "Give Me Power," *InfoWorld* 7, no. 17 (April 29, 1985): 5. Accessed in Google Books, https://goo.gl/ggtODN. Fred R. Shapiro located this important citation.
3. Nancy Andrews, *Windows: The Official Guide to Microsoft's Operating Environment* (Redmond, WA: Microsoft, 1986), 268. Verified in hard copy.
4. Jerry Pournelle, "A User's View: Law of Expanding Memory: Applications Will Also Expand Until RAM Is Full," *InfoWorld* 9, no. 30 (July 27, 1987): 46. Accessed in Google Books, https://goo.gl/FjbnpX.
5. Steve Gibson, Tech Talk, *InfoWorld* 10, no. 8 (February 22, 1988): 34. Accessed in Google Books, https://goo.gl/juaqhp.
6. George Morrow, "Bus Wars," *InfoWorld* 10, no. 46 (November 14, 1988): 60. Accessed in Google Books, http://goo.gl/n1lNxk. Fred R. Shapiro located this important citation.
7. "1989 Bill Gates Talk on Microsoft," speech by Bill Gates to the Computer Science Club at the University of Waterloo, audio file, 1:33:52, http://goo.gl/X17tia. Quote occurs around 22:25.
8. "The Wonder Years: How the PC Industry Grew Up in the '80s," *Infoworld* 12, no. 1 (January 1 1990): 4. Accessed in Google Books, https://goo.gl/MtIJUC.

9. Evan Roth, "Cybersurfing: If They Only Knew," *Washington Post*, November 16, 1995, style section, D7. Accessed in NewsBank.

10. Gates, "Computer Industry Offers Wealth of Career Options."

11. Christopher Cerf and Victor S. Navasky, *The Experts Speak: The Definitive Compendium of Authoritative Misinformation*, rev. ed. (New York: Villard Books, 1998), 231. Verified in hard copy.

12. "Be kind; everyone you meet is fighting a hard battle."

—Plato

The websites ThinkExist, the Quotations Page, and BrainyQuote list this quotation under the august name of Plato, as do myriad tchotchkes, coffee mugs, inspirational posters, and various generically inoffensive ephemera of the late twentieth century.

QI was able to trace the saying back more than one hundred years to its likely origin. To **QI**'s surprise, the original aphorism did not use the word "kind."

The citations below are a select subset in reverse-chronological order. A 1995 book of daily meditation topics contains an epigraph that credits the saying to a figure whose name does not sound ancient:[1]

> Day 198: Charity
> Be kind; everyone you meet is fighting a hard battle.
>
> —John Watson

John Watson is a relatively common name, so this attribution is of limited help without further information. Continuing backward in time, in 1984 a newspaper in Seattle, Washington, contained a quote that is somewhat similar to the target:[2]

> Ian MacLaren, a noted Scotsman, author of "Beside the Bonnie Brier Bush," cared deeply about those around him. His oft-quoted words offer wise counsel: "Be kind. Everyone you meet is carrying a heavy burden."

Ian Maclaren was the pen name of Reverend John Watson. Some-times the last name of the pseudonym appears as "MacLaren," but the earliest citations use "Maclaren." His book *Beside the Bonnie Brier Bush* was a bestseller in the 1890s.

In 1965, in the *Chicago Tribune,* the words attributed to Ian Maclaren are a close match to the quotation **QI** is tracing:[3]

> Most of us are acutely aware of our own struggles and we are pre-occupied with our own problems. We sympathize with ourselves because we see our own difficulties so clearly. But Ian MacLaren noted wisely, "Let us be kind to one another, for most of us are fighting a hard battle."

In 1957 a curious letter appeared in the *Trenton Evening Times* in New Jersey:[4]

> Sir—A thought to help us through these difficult times: Be kind, for everyone you meet is fighting a hard battle.
>
> —Ian MacLaren

This provides more evidence that the quote of interest is associated with Ian Maclaren. But the Scottish author died in 1907, so the writer who signed the letter with his name was perhaps reusing the old pseudonym. In 1947 the syndicated columnist Robert Quillen shared the following:[5]

> Not until trouble and heartache and sorrow came into my own life could I fully comprehend the words of Ian McLaren: "Let us be kind, one to another, for most of us are fighting a hard battle."

The next instance appears in a letter in a Canadian newspaper in 1932, but the meaning of the quotation given is not obvious to most modern readers. The excerpt mentions the Great War. This is a reference to World War I, as World War II began in 1939. In the quote, Maclaren urges people to be empathetic to one another by using the now uncommon denotation of the word "pitiful" to mean "compassionate":[6]

> Years before the Great War and all the problems that have hurtled down on us poor mortals in consequence thereof, Ian Maclaren wrote: "Be pitiful, for everyone is fighting a hard battle."

The word "pitiful" is used in a way that is infrequent today. Here is the historical definition from the *Oxford English Dictionary*:[7]

> *pitiful*, A. adj. 1. Full of or characterized by pity; compassionate, merciful, tender. Now rare.

An extended discussion of the theme of the aphorism is present in a book published under Maclaren's real name, John Watson, in 1903. The book section is titled "Courtesy":[8]

> This man beside us also has a hard fight with an unfavouring world, with strong temptations, with doubts and fears, with wounds of the past which have skinned over, but which smart when they are touched. It is a fact, however surprising. And when this occurs to us we are moved to deal kindly with him, to bid him be of good cheer, to let him understand that we are also fighting a battle; we are bound not to irritate him, nor press hardly upon him nor help his lower self.

The next citation skips all the way back to 1898. A Boston, Massachusetts, periodical, *Zion's Herald*, contains a story about a Christmas message from Maclaren. This article is dated January 1898, but it seems likely that the message was published in England before December 25, 1897:[9]

> "IAN MACLAREN," along with other celebrities, was asked to send a Christmas message to an influential religious weekly in England. He responded by sending the short but striking sentence: "Be pitiful, for every man is fighting a hard battle." No message is more needed in our days of stress and storm, of selfish striving and merciless competition.

Another citation in 1898 identifies the publication in Britain that published the message:[10]

"Be pitiful, for every man is fighting a hard battle," was the tender Christmas message sent by Ian Maclaren to the readers of *The British Weekly*.

Notes:

Thanks to Glossolalia Black and Fred R. Shapiro for the question.

1. Harville Hendrix and Helen Hunt, *The Personal Companion: Meditations and Exercises for Keeping the Love You Find* (New York: Simon and Schuster, 1995), "Day 198." Accessed in Google Books, https://goo.gl/goBt4k.

2. Dale Turner, "Quiet Wounds: Be Kind, The Pain is Heavy," *Seattle Times* (Seattle, WA), July 21, 1984, A8. Accessed in GenealogyBank.

3. Harold Blake Walker, "Living Faith," *Chicago Tribune* (Chicago, IL), September 17, 1965, B10. Accessed in ProQuest Historical Newspapers.

4. "Letters: Urges Kindness," *Trenton Evening Times* (Trenton, NJ), January 3, 1957, 10 (or possibly 16). Accessed in GenealogyBank.

5. Robert Quillen, "Kindness Triumphs over Cruelty, for It Wins the Hearts of Men Who Hate Tyranny," Robert Quillen Says, *Indianapolis Star* (Indianapolis, IN), November 27, 1947, 19. Accessed in Newspapers.com.

6. Housewife, "Letter to the Editor: City Teachers and the Lawrence Lecture," *Winnipeg Free Press* (Winnipeg, MB), March 12, 1932, 16. Accessed in NewspaperARCHIVE.com.

7. *Oxford English Dictionary Online*, s.v. "pitiful," accessed August 12, 2016.

8. John Watson, *The Homely Virtues* (London: Hodder and Stoughton, 1903), 168. Accessed in Google Books, http://goo.gl/CZGQ21.

9. "Be Pitiful," *Zion's Herald* (Boston, MA) 76, no. 4 (January 26, 1898): 101. Accessed in ProQuest American Periodicals.

10. "In Brief," *Congregationalist* (Boston, MA) 83, no. 1 (January 6, 1898): 9. Accessed in ProQuest American Periodicals.

13. "The purpose of life is to discover your gift. The meaning of life is to give your gift away."

—William Shakespeare
—Pablo Picasso

In August 2014 the actress Reese Witherspoon briefly posted an erroneous quotation to her Instagram account:

Those who were quick to scold her before she deleted the post complained that the influential painter Pablo Picasso was the man responsible. If one were not meticulous and only searched social networks like Facebook and Pinterest, one might confirm Picasso as the true author. However, **QI** has learned the hard way not to trust places like Facebook or Pinterest when it comes to fragments of literature, or what was once called "recorded history." (Now it's all recorded, even the phony or fishy stuff). To boot—**QI** has found no substantive evidence linking this expression to either Shakespeare or Picasso.

An interesting, thematically related statement to this quote was included in an 1843 essay titled "Gifts" by the prominent lecturer Ralph Waldo Emerson. In the piece, Emerson argued that a gift is only worthwhile if it is integrally related to the gift giver:[1]

> Rings and jewels are not gifts, but apologies for gifts. The only gift is a portion of thyself. Thou must bleed for me. Therefore the poet brings his poem; the shepherd, his lamb; the farmer, corn; the miner, a stone; the painter, his picture; the girl, a handkerchief of her own sewing.

A century and a half later, in 1993, David Viscott published *Finding Your Strength in Difficult Times: A Book of Meditations*. Viscott was a psychiatrist who hosted a pioneering radio talk show in the 1980s and 1990s during which he provided counseling to callers. Viscott's statement in his book was composed of three parts instead of two:[2]

> The purpose of life is to discover your gift.
> The work of life is to develop it.
> The meaning of life is to give your gift away.

In January 1994 the religion section of the *Seattle Times* included a stream-lined version in a column by Dale Turner. No attribution was given, and this iteration omitted the middle element.[3]

> As the new year begins, I will share with you some of my collection. Some items were recorded 50 years ago and others just this week. I hope one or more of them will be interesting or useful to you . . .
>
> —The purpose of life is to discover your gift and the meaning of life is in giving it away.

A year later, Turner published additional sayings from his personal assemblage in the *Seattle Times*.[4]

> Today, I am responding to requests that have come to me to share more items from my collection. I hope one or more will be interesting or useful to you this first week of a new year . . .
>
> —The purpose of life is to discover your gift, and the meaning of life is in giving it away.

In May 1995, in New Jersey, the keynote speaker at a meeting designed to encourage young people to enter the teaching profession employed an instance of the dictum.[5]

> "Keep growing professionally," she emphasized. "The purpose of life is to discover your gift; the meaning of life is giving it away."

The connection to Viscott was not forgotten. In 1997 the *Chattanooga Times Free Press* of Tennessee placed the adage at the beginning of an article about a successful painter:[6]

The purpose of life is to discover your gift; the work of life is to develop it; and the meaning of life is to give your gift away.

—David Viscott

In March 2006 the *San Francisco Chronicle* published a profile of a mathematician working at a Hewlett-Packard laboratory. The journalist noticed the saying posted on a wall. No ascription was given, and the words "meaning" and "purpose" were swapped. Also, the word "find" was used instead of "discover:"[7]

A note on the wall says, "The meaning of life is to find your gift; the purpose of life is to give it away."

In May 2006 an article in the *Daily Press* of Newport News, Virginia, described a scene in a documentary called *Master of the Flame* about a local glass artist named Emilio Santini. The artist mentioned the adage.[8]

At one point, Santini summarizes his philosophy: The meaning of life is to find your gift, and the purpose of life is to give it away.

Also in 2006, a book titled *Just Do It! The Power of Positive Living* used the saying as an epigraph for a chapter. The words were ascribed to Joy Golliver, who has written and lectured about community service and caregiving:[9]

The meaning of life is to find your gift.
The purpose of life is to give it away.

—Joy J. Golliver

In conclusion, David Viscott published an instance of the saying in 1993, and **QI** believes he should receive credit for originating the adage. This ascription is based on current knowledge, and it may change in the future as digital archives expand. The most popular modern instance is a simplified version of Viscott's three-part statement. Others employed the adage after it was in circulation. Neither Picasso nor Shakespeare said it.

Notes:

Great thanks to Lucinda Critchley, Laurelyn Collins, and Obsidian Eagle, whose inquiries led **QI** to formulate this question and perform this exploration.

1. Ralph Waldo Emerson, "Gifts," *Dial: A Magazine for Literature, Philosophy and Religion* 4, no. 1 (July 1843): 93. Accessed in Google Books, https://goo.gl/TTXDVb.

2. David S. Viscott, *Finding Your Strength in Difficult Times: A Book of Meditations* (Chicago: Contemporary Books, 1993), 87. Verified in scans.

3. Dale Turner, "Others' Insights Can Help as We Look Ahead to New Year," *Seattle Times* (Seattle, WA), January 1, 1994, A14, http://goo.gl/G4uZxg.

4. Dale Turner, "A Positive Thought Can Go a Long Way in Halting Despair," *Seattle Times* (Seattle, WA), January 7, 1995, A12, http://goo.gl/PwiMrj.

5. Diane D'Amico, "Young Teachers Program Encourages Teenagers to Go into Teaching," *Press of Atlantic City* (Atlantic City, NJ), May 10, 1995, C1. Accessed in NewsBank.

6. Ann Nichols, "Taking a Look Back," *Chattanooga Times Free Press* (Chattanooga, TN), February 16, 1997, J1. Accessed in NewsBank.

7. Benjamin Pimentel, "Challenges—and Solutions—HP Mathematician Cited for Years of Work Helping Others," *San Francisco Chronicle* (San Francisco, CA), March 19, 2006, J1. Accessed in NewsBank.

8. Marty O'Brien, "An Eclectic and Versatile Player," *Daily Press* (Newport News, VA), May 14, 2006, C1. Accessed in NewsBank.

9. Eray Honeycutt, *Just Do It! The Power of Positive Living* (Bloomington: AuthorHouse, 2006), 201. Accessed in Google Books, https://goo.gl/npshVs.

14. "We do not inherit the Earth from our ancestors; we borrow it from our children."

—Chief Seattle

In 1971 the influential environmental activist Wendell Berry published a book titled *The Unforeseen Wilderness: An Essay on Kentucky's Red River Gorge*. Berry emphasized the desirability of preserving natural areas and adopting a long-range perspective about the environment.[1]

> We can learn about it from exceptional people of our own culture, and from other cultures less destructive than ours. I am speaking of the life of a man who knows that the world is not given by his fathers, but borrowed from his children who has undertaken to cherish it and do it no damage, not because he is duty-bound, but because he loves the world and loves his children . . .

The wording in the passage above does not exactly match the saying in its modern circulation, but this citation is the earliest evidence known to **QI**. Later expressions may have been derived directly or indirectly from the words above.

In May 1971 Berry published an essay in *Audubon* magazine titled "The One-Inch Journey," which was based on the second chapter of *The Unforeseen Wilderness*. The excerpt above was reprinted in the essay, and thus it achieved wider dissemination. **QI** notes that this appearance also linked the saying to the Audubon Society.[2]

In 1973 a member of a conservation group based in Martha's Vineyard, Massachusetts, named Carleton H. Parker submitted a statement to a subcommittee of the US Senate that met in July. Parker's statement was placed into the official record, and it contained a version of the saying attributed to the Audubon Society. Parker employed the phrase "true conservationist" although it was placed outside of the quotation marks in the following excerpt.[3]

> I like Audubon Society's definition of a true conservationist as "a man who knows that the world is not given by his fathers but borrowed from his children."

In August 1973 a newspaper in Cape Girardeau, Missouri, printed an instance without ascription that was similar to the version above, but the phrase "true conservationist" was now blended into the saying:[4]

> A true conservationist is a man who knows that the world is not given by his father, but borrowed from his children.

On November 13, 1974, the Australian minister for the environment and conservation gave a speech in Paris at a meeting of the Organisation for Economic Co-operation and Development. The minister's name was Moses Henry Cass, and his address to the environment committee included an instance of the saying. The version Cass spoke was longer and clumsier than modern instances. He used the word "inherited" instead of "given."[5]

> We rich nations, for that is what we are, have an obligation not only to the poor nations, but to all the grandchildren of the world, rich and poor. We have not inherited this earth from our parents to do with it what we will. We have borrowed it from our children and we must be careful to use it in their interests as well as our own. Anyone who fails to recognise the basic validity of the proposition put in different ways by increasing numbers of writers, from Malthus to The Club of Rome, is either ignorant, a fool, or evil.

In July 1975 a version of the saying appeared as part of an article titled "The Land Is Borrowed from Our Children" by Dennis J. Hall that was published in the periodical *Michigan Natural Resources*. Hall worked for the state of Michigan's office of land use. The above article title was listed in the table of contents, but the beginning of the article presents a different title. A compact version of the adage was placed between quotation marks and printed in a large font at the start of the piece. Hence, the adage functioned as an alternative title:[6]

"We have not inherited the land from our fathers, we have borrowed it from our children . . ."

—Dennis J. Hall, Office of Land Use

QI believes that the quotation marks signaled that Hall was not claiming authorship of the saying. He was simply using it as a label for his essay, but this usage was certainly confusing, and some later citations credited Hall with the saying.

An article in the proceedings of a transportation conference held in Germany in September 1975 mentioned the adage. The article author, Jorg K. Kuhnemann, credited the Australian minister of the environment, and this lengthy version was similar to the statement by Moses Henry Cass.[7]

There is only one world and, as was pointed out by the Australian Minister of the Environment at the OECD Ministerial Conference on the Environment last November, we have not inherited the earth from our fathers and are hence entitled to use it according to our wishes. We have rather borrowed it from our children and have to maintain it properly until they can take over.

In January 1976 an Illinois monthly called the *Common Bond* printed the maxim in an editorial about school funding. No individual was credited.[8]

We have no excuse. Someone once said; "We did not inherit our future from our ancestors, we have borrowed it from our children."

In May 1976 a New York newspaper printed the saying as the final paragraph of an article about the environment. The words were attributed to Dennis Hall:[9]

We have not inherited the land from our fathers, but have borrowed it from our children.

—Dennis Hall

Also in May 1976, the journal *Liberal Education* published the remarks of the incoming chairman of the Association of American Colleges, which included the quotation. The saying was credited, almost correctly, to Wendell Berry.[10]

> I prefer Wendell Berry's phrase that we must act as "a man who knows that the world is not given by his fathers but borrowed from his children."

In May 1978 a Pittsburgh, Pennsylvania, newspaper attributed an instance of the saying to someone named John Madson:[11]

> A true conservationist is a man who knows that the world is not given by his fathers, but borrowed from his children.
>
> —John Madson

In 1980 the United Nations Environment Programme published an annual review for the year 1978. Hence, there was a delay between the execution of the review and the publication of the results. The back cover of this document displayed an instance of the maxim without an ascription:[12]

> We have not inherited the earth from our fathers. We have borrowed it from our children.

In March 1980 Lee M. Talbot of World Wildlife Fund International spoke before the Royal Society of Arts in the United Kingdom about "A World Conservation Strategy." Talbot employed the maxim in his talk, and when it was printed, it was placed between quotation marks. No attribution was given.[13]

> "We have no right to destroy any other life form," "We have the capability to destroy other forms of life, therefore, we have the responsibility to see that they are not destroyed," or "We have not inherited the earth from our parents, we have borrowed it from our children."

In September 1980 a poem titled "Where Silkwood Walks" by Ezekiel Limehouse was published in the *Lake Street Review*, and a contributor's note about Limehouse mentioned the prominent physician and activist Helen Caldicott. The adage was labeled a principle of Caldicott's.[14]

> His hymn "Where Silkwood Walks" is indebted to William Blake's
> "And Did Those Feet in Ancient Time" and was written in the spirit
> of Dr. Helen Caldicott's principium: "We did not inherit the earth
> from our ancestors; we borrowed it from our descendants."

In May 1981 an article in the *Bulletin of the Atomic Scientists* by Paul Ehrlich and Anne Ehrlich included the adage as an epigraph. The words were associated with an environmental organization and not an individual.[15]

> "We have not inherited the Earth from our parents, we have bor-
> rowed it from our children."
>
>   —International Union for the Conservation of
>   Nature, World Conservation Strategy.

In January 1983 a congressman writing in the *Christian Science Monitor* attributed the maxim to the prominent environmentalist Lester Brown.[16]

> The time to act is now. As Lester Brown of the Worldwatch Institute
> says, "We have not inherited the earth from our fathers, we are bor-
> rowing it from our children."

In March 1983 a reviewer of Lester Brown's work *Building a Sustainable Society* noted that the adage appeared on the cover of the book.[17]

> "We have not inherited the Earth from our fathers, we are bor-
> rowing it from our children." —so proclaims the cover of Lester
> Brown's latest book.

In 1985 the *Los Angeles Times* published a story that included a profile of the influential environmentalist David Brower, who expressed some confusion when he was given credit for the maxim.[18]

> Brower picked up a book with a jacket quote which, he said, rather pleased, had been attributed to him, although "I don't remember when I said it." It reads: "We have not inherited the Earth from our fathers. We are borrowing it from our children."

In 1986 an adviser to the International Union for Conservation of Nature in Gland, Switzerland, employed the adage without attribution.[19]

> Taghi Farvar, a senior adviser to the IUCN, said the ultimate message of the environmentalists today is that "you can have your cake and eat it." With proper development, the environment needed in making a living can be maintained and used again. "We have not inherited the world from our parents," says Dr. Farvar. "We have borrowed it from our children."

In 1988 a piece in the *Los Angeles Times* described the adage as an "Amish saying":[20]

> "We have not inherited the land from our parents, we are borrowing it from our children."
>
> This Amish saying is quoted by a Glacier Bay National Park ranger in an open letter of tribute to John Muir in this 150th anniversary year of the pioneer naturalist's birth.

In 1989 *Backpacker* magazine presented a version of the quotation spoken by David Brower that supplemented the adage with an additional barbed comment.[21]

> Remember, we don't inherit the earth from our fathers, we borrow it from our children. And if you borrow something you don't have the capability of paying back, you are actually stealing.

In 1990 then US secretary of state James Baker ascribed the maxim to the famous transcendentalist Ralph Waldo Emerson.[22]

> Emerson, the 19th century American essayist and poet, put it this way: "We do not inherit the Earth from our ancestors, we borrow it from our children."

In 1991 a report from the US Council on Environmental Quality ascribed the saying to the famous Native American Chief Seattle and suggested that the words were quite old. No supporting citation was given.[23]

> The same thought was expressed over a century ago in timeless language by the Native American Chief Seattle, who said, "We do not inherit the Earth from our ancestors—we borrow it from our children."

In 1993 the quotation expert Ralph Keyes discussed the origin of the adage in the pages of the *Washington Post*.[24]

> When James Baker was Secretary of State, he quoted Emerson as having said, "We have not inherited the earth from our fathers, we are borrowing it from our children." Emerson didn't say that. Who did? A Celestial Seasonings tea box calls this an "Amish belief." The saying is more often called a "Native American proverb." Neither is likely. The maxim is a little too perfectly tailored to today's headlines. Its origins remain a mystery.

The 1994 book *Talking on the Water: Conversations About Nature and Creativity* printed an interview with David Brower, who stated that fellow environmentalist Lester Brown had ascribed the increasingly popular expression to Brower.[25]

> On the cover of the book *Building a Sustainable Society*, by Lester Brown, is the quote, "We do not inherit the earth from our fathers,

we are borrowing it from our children." Lester says he got that quote from me, though I don't remember having said it.

In 1995 David Brower published a book that contained a description of a conversation he had with Lester Brown many years earlier. Brown had told Brower that the statement, "We do not inherit the Earth from our fathers, we are borrowing it from our children" was carved in stone at the National Aquarium, and that the words were credited to Brower. Although Brower was pleased, he was also puzzled:[26]

> At home in California, I searched my unorganized files to find out when I could have said those words. I stumbled upon the answer in the pages of an interview that had taken place in a North Carolina bar so noisy, I could only marvel that I was heard at all. Possibly, I didn't remember saying it because by then they had me on my third martini.

Brower does not give the date of the North Carolina interview.

In conclusion, **QI** would tentatively assign credit to Wendell Berry for crafting the first version of this statement, which has been evolving for decades. Moses Henry Cass employed the word "inherited" instead of "given," which appeared in Berry's phrasing. Now the most popular modern expressions use "inherited" or "inherit." This section represents a snapshot of what **QI** has found so far based on currently available information.

Notes:

Many thanks to Andy Behrens, who told **QI** about the crucial 1971 Wendell Berry citation. Great thanks to George Marshall, whose inquiry about this saying led **QI** to formulate the question and perform this exploration.

1. Wendell Berry, *The Unforeseen Wilderness: An Essay on Kentucky's Red River Gorge* (Lexington, KY: University Press of Kentucky, 1971), 26. Verified in hard copy.
2. Wendell Berry, "The One-Inch Journey," *Audubon*, May 1971, 9. Verified in hard copy.

3. *Hearing Before the Subcommittee on Parks and Recreation of the Committee on Interior and Insular Affairs on Bill S. 1929, to Establish the Nantucket Sound Islands Trust*, 93rd Cong., 1st sess. (July 16, 1973), (statement of Carleton H. Parker, Concerned Citizens of Martha's Vineyard, Inc., West Tisbury, Massachusetts), 204. Accessed in HathiTrust, https://goo.gl/smXo61.

4. Field and Stream Notes, *Southeast Missourian* (Cape Girardeau, MO), August 31, 1973, 9. Accessed in Google News Archive.

5. Moses Henry Cass, speech on environmental policy, Ministerial Meeting of the OECD Environment Committee, Paris, November 13, 1974, text in *Australian Government Digest* 2, no. 4 (October 1, 1974–December 31, 1974): 1145. Verified in scans. Special thanks to John McChesney-Young and the UC Berkeley Library.

6. Dennis Hall, "The Land Is Borrowed from Our Children," *Michigan Natural Resources* 44, no. 4 (July–August 1975): 3. Verified in hard copy.

7. Jorg K. Kuhnemann, "Better Towns with Less Traffic," in Peter Stringer and H. Wenzel, eds., *Transportation Planning for a Better Environment*, NATO Conference Series (New York: Plenum, 1976), 5. Verified in hard copy.

8. "Building the Future for East Moline?" *Common Bond* (East Moline, IL), January 1976, 4. Accessed in GenealogyBank.

9. Bill Roden, Adirondack Sportsman, *Warrensburg-Lake George News* (Warrensburg, NY), May 13, 1976, 4. Accessed in Old Fulton NY Post Cards, fultonhistory.com.

10. "Remarks of the Incoming Chairman by Theodore D. Lockwood," *Liberal Education* 62 (May 1976): 317. Verified in hard copy.

11. "Rambling Afield: Birds of a Feather, Huh?" *Pittsburgh Press* (Pittsburgh, PA), May 28, 1978, D10. Accessed in Google News Archive, https://goo.gl/EVBkog.

12. United Nations Environment Programme, *UNEP Annual Review 1978* (Nairobi: United Nations Environment Programme, 1980), back cover. Accessed in Google Books, http://goo.gl/mOv7hW.

13. "A World Conservation Strategy by Lee M. Talbot, Director of Conservation and Special Scientific Advisor, World Wildlife Fund International," text of speech delivered on March 19, 1980, *Journal of the Royal Society of Arts* 128, no. 5288 (July 1980): 495. Verified in hard copy.

14. "Notes on Contributors: Ezekiel Limehouse," *Lake Street Review* 9 (Summer 1980): 41. Verified in scans. Thanks to Dennis Lien and the University of Minnesota Libraries.

15. Paul Ehrlich and Anne Ehrlich, "The Politics of Extinction," *Bulletin of the Atomic Scientists* 37, no. 5 (May 1981): 26. Accessed in Google Books, https://goo.gl/WggHi4.

16. Ed Jones, "Saving the Soil—by Private Initiative," *Christian Science Monitor*, January 5, 1983, 23. Accessed in ProQuest.

17. Anne H. Ehrlich, review of *Building a Sustainable Society*, by Lester R. Brown, *Bulletin of the Atomic Scientists* 39, no. 3 (March 1983): 40. Accessed in Google Books, https://goo.gl /E1xsWU.

18. Beverly Beyette, "Concern over Movement's Direction: Environmentalists: Three Who Believe," *Los Angeles Times*, June 6, 1985, E1. Accessed in ProQuest.

19. David R. Francis, "New Environmental Tack: Development + Conservation = Growth," *Christian Science Monitor*, June 12, 1986, 12. Accessed in ProQuest.

20. Frank Riley, "John Muir's Legacy Still Strong in Glacier Country," *Los Angeles Times*, August 14, 1988, 5. Accessed in ProQuest.

21. David Brower, "Wilderness Shows Us Where We Came From," *Backpacker* 17, no. 4 (June 1989): 25. Accessed in Google Books, https://goo.gl/Cn4wjF.

22. "Diplomacy for the Environment," (text of address by Secretary of State [James] Baker to the National Governors Association, February 26, 1990, Washington, DC), Current Policy no. 1254, February 1990, 4. Accessed in HathiTrust, https://goo.gl/cFyi8t.

23. *Environmental Quality [1990]: The Twenty-First Annual Report of the Council on Environmental Quality Together with the President's Message to Congress*, (Washington, DC: Executive Office of the President, Council on Environmental Quality, 1991), 4. Accessed in HathiTrust, https://goo.gl/Lc5vMo.

24. Ralph Keyes, "Some of Our Favorite Quotations Never Quite Went That Way: Did They REALLY Say It?" *Washington Post*, May 16, 1993, L10. Accessed in ProQuest.

25. "David Brower: The Archdruid Himself," in Jonathan White, *Talking on the Water: Conversations About Nature and Creativity* (San Francisco: Sierra Club, 1994), 47. Verified in hard copy.

26. David R. Brower and Steve Chapple, *Let the Mountains Talk, Let the Rivers Run: A Call to Those Who Would Save the Earth* (San Francisco: HarperCollins West, 1995), 1, 2. Verified in hard copy; Ralph Keyes, *The Quote Verifier: Who Said What, Where, and When* (New York: St. Martin's, 2006), 98, 298, 299. Verified in hard copy.

15. "If you love someone, set them free. If they come back they're yours."

—Richard Bach

On his first solo album in 1985, the musician Sting included a song called "If You Love Somebody Set Them Free." A client of **QI** heard a more elaborate quotation along these lines and wondered if there were some connection:

> If you love something, let it go. If it returns, it's yours; if it doesn't, it wasn't.

> If you love someone, set them free. If they come back they're yours; if they don't they never were.

These statements are often attributed to Richard Bach, author of the enormously popular inspirational novel from the 1970s, *Jonathan Livingston Seagull*. **QI** has found no substantiation that Bach created or used the phrases above.

In 1951 *Esquire* magazine published a short story titled "The Tyranny of Love" by Harry Kronman. The piece contained a quotation that prefigured part of the saying under investigation:[1]

> I mean, if you love something very much, you've got to go easy with it—give it some room to move around. If you try to hold it tight like that, it'll always try to get away.

The earliest known version of the precise saying appeared in a book titled *I Ain't Much Baby—But I'm All I've Got* by Jess Lair, which was privately published in 1969. Lair was a teacher, and he asked his students to create short writing samples. Ahead of each class meeting, a student was asked to write "some comment, question or feeling" on a three-by-five-inch card and place it on a table at the front of the classroom. Lair then read the short texts and made comments at the beginning of the class. The following was written on one card:[2]

> If you want something very, very badly, let it go free. If it comes back to you, it's yours forever. If it doesn't, it was never yours to begin with.

Lair stated that about half of the cards were unsigned, and he did not identify the person who submitted the expression above. Here are three other examples from his college students:

1. I heard a very profound statement last night. Unfortunately I've forgotten it.
2. No guts—no glory.
3. Laughter is the song of the angels.

Lair did not require the words to be original, and he did not request attributions. So the student may have acquired the quotation of interest from another unknown person.

Top quotation expert Fred R. Shapiro, editor of *The Yale Book of Quotations*, obtained a copy of the 1969 book and verified the presence of the passage.[3]

In 1972 a compact version of the expression appeared as the caption of a one-panel comic by the graphic artist Peter Max, who was part of the 1960s and 1970s zeitgeist. The phrasing of Max's version was closer to the modern variants. Max did not claim authorship; instead, he used the label "Unknown":[4]

> If you love something, set it free. If it comes back, it is yours. If it doesn't, it never was.

> —Unknown

The comic was part of a syndicated series called *Meditation*, for which Max prompted his readers to send in quotations by asking the following question— "What words of wisdom guide your life?" Max indicated that the words above were sent in by "Chantal Sicile, Staten Island, N.Y." But Sicile did not claim authorship, apparently. The reward for a published quote was a poster auto-graphed by Max.

In April 1975 the *Oregonian* newspaper published a profile of basketball player Bill Walton in its Sunday magazine section. The article noted a picture that displayed a different phrasing for the saying:[5]

> In the office of Bill Walton's San Francisco attorney, there's a picture
> that is captioned:
>
>> If you love something very much
>> Let it go free.
>> If it does not return, it was not meant to be yours.
>> If it does return, love it as hard as you can for the rest of your
>> life.

Apparently, Walton's attorney wasn't the only one living by the maxim. For several years the actor Lee Majors was married to the actress and iconic beauty Farrah Fawcett. In 1978 an interviewer for the United Press International news service asked Majors about this relationship, and he said the following:[6]

> I have an old saying framed in my office. It goes like this, "If you
> love something, set it free. If it comes back to you, it's yours. If it
> doesn't, it never was." That's how I feel about a marriage partner.

By the 1990s the expression had implausibly been assigned to the author Richard Bach. Here is an example message from the Usenet distributed discus-sion system in 1994:[7]

> In summary, I'd like to add something I read by Alan Dean Foster:
> "If you love something, set it free. If it comes back, it is yours for-
> ever. If it doesn't, then it never was yours at all."
> Actually it was Richard Bach, but Foster is a great author too!

By 1999 a comical remark had been appended to the maxim, as seen in this Usenet message:[8]

But, if it just sits in your living room,
messes up your stuff, eats your food,
uses your telephone, takes your money,
and doesn't appear to realize that you had set it free . . .
You either married it or gave birth to it.

In conclusion, the creator of this general saying is not known. Jess Lair helped to popularize one version starting in 1969. An anonymous student gave him the statement. Peter Max helped to popularize another shorter version in 1972. He was sent the expression by Chantal Sicile.

Notes:

Many thanks to Randi, who asked about this quotation and inspired the construction of this query and reply.

1. Harry Kronman, "The Tyranny of Love," *Esquire*, February 1951, 30. Verified in hard copy.
2. Jess Lair, *I Ain't Much Baby—But I'm All I've Got* (Privately published: 1969), 98. Verified in hard copy by Fred R. Shapiro; Jess Lair, *I Ain't Much Baby—But I'm All I've Got* (Garden City, NY: Doubleday, 1972), 203. Verified in hard copy. Note that this published edition is different from the privately published one in endnote 2.
3. Fred R. Shapiro, *The Yale Book of Quotations* (New Haven: Yale University Press, 2006), 440. Verified in hard copy.
4. Peter Max, *Meditation* [cartoon panel], *Cleveland Plain Dealer* (Cleveland, OH), September 16, 1972, 19B. Accessed in GenealogyBank; Peter Max, *Meditation* [cartoon panel], *News Journal* (Mansfield, OH), September 16, 1972, 3. Accessed in NewspaperARCHIVE .com. This newspaper mentioned Chantal Sicile and the request for quotations.
5. Judy Hughes, "At Home with Bill Walton," *Northwest Magazine* in *Oregonian* (Portland, OR), April 20, 1975, 12. Accessed in GenealogyBank.
6. United Press International, "Lee Majors Is No Mr. Fawcett," *Nashua Telegraph* (Nashua, NH), July 5, 1978, 15. Accessed in Google News Archive, https://goo.gl/anKFlo.
7. Rob Geraghty, "Re: What Do Women Want??? I Need a Woman's Advice!!" in reply to Michael Aulfrey, alt.romance.chat Usenet newsgroup, April 26, 1994. Accessed in Google Groups, https://goo.gl/a5aG19.

8. Bbaylarry, "OTP: Joke—If You Love Something," alt.support.arthritis Usenet newsgroup, August 23, 1999. Accessed in Google Groups, http://goo.gl/naC3Lo.

PROVERBIAL WISDOM

16. "Give a man a fish, and you feed him for a day. Teach a man to fish, and you feed him for a lifetime."

—Maimonides

The origin of this thought is highly contested. **QI** has recorded claims that the adage is Chinese, Native American, Italian, Indian, or biblical. It has been variously linked directly, if falsely, to Lao-tzu, Mao Tse-tung, and Maimonides.

The general principle of alleviating poverty by facilitating self-sufficiency has a long history. The twelfth-century philosopher Maimonides wrote about eight degrees in the duty of charity. In 1826 an explication of the eighth degree was published in a journal called the *Religious Intelligencer*.[1]

> Lastly, the eighth and the most meritorious of all, is to anticipate charity by preventing poverty, namely, to assist the reduced brother, either by a considerable gift or loan of money, or by teaching him a trade, or by putting him in the way of business, so that he may earn an honest livelihood and not be forced to the dreadful alternative of holding up his hand for charity . . .

So **QI** has found a conceptual match in a summary of the writings of Maimonides, but no vivid fishing metaphor. In 1885 a statement that did refer to fishing and partially matched the modern adage appeared in the novel *Mrs. Dymond* by the popular novelist Anne Isabella Thackeray Ritchie. As the daughter of the prominent writer William Makepeace Thackeray, she was continuing the family tradition of a life of letters. The second half of Ritchie's statement did not directly refer to the act of being fed, however.[2]

> He certainly doesn't practise his precepts, but I suppose the Patron meant that if you give a man a fish he is hungry again in an hour. If you teach him to catch a fish you do him a good turn. But these very elementary principles are apt to clash with the leisure of the cultivated classes.

The novel was serialized in leading periodicals like *Macmillan's Magazine* of London and *Littell's Living Age* of Boston, Massachusetts, in 1885.[3] (This important citation in *Mrs. Dymond* was mentioned by top quotation researcher Ralph Keyes in the reference work *The Quote Verifier*.[4])

The adage continued to evolve for decades. In 1911 a collection of essays called *The Common Growth* by M. Loane included an "oft quoted saying" that did not refer to consumption or the act of being fed.[5]

> It is an oft quoted saying, and one full of social wisdom: "Give a man a fish, and he will be hungry again to-morrow; teach him to catch a fish, and he will be richer all his life."
>
> Nevertheless, this does not settle all possible questions as to the right method of helping our neighbours. Suppose, to continue the figure of speech, that the man had never tasted fish, and seriously doubted whether it was a palatable or wholesome form of nourishment; would it be practicable to induce him to make the exertion necessary to acquire the art of fishing, unless you previously caught and killed and cooked a fish for him, presented it to him, and overcame his reluctance to eat it?

In 1945 a Wisconsin newspaper printed an instance similar to the text above. The writer was a public health nurse, and she labeled the expression "an old Indian proverb."[6]

> In every public health program, the aim is not only to perform a given service but to teach the individual positive attitudes toward

health which will benefit him throughout life. The purpose is well stated in an old Indian proverb.

"If you give a man a fish, he will be hungry tomorrow. If you teach a man to fish, he will be richer forever."

In November 1961 a newspaper in Rockford, Illinois, presented the testimony of missionary Fred Nelson, who had worked in Taiwan and mainland China. When discussing foreign aid, Nelson molded a modern version of the saying and called it a "Chinese proverb."[7]

Foreign aid—"You give a poor man a fish and you feed him for a day. You teach him to fish and you give him an occupation that will feed him for a lifetime."

—Chinese proverb

In October 1962 the *Winnipeg Free Press* of Winnipeg, Manitoba, noted that Miss Anna Speers spoke the phrase during a meeting of the Winnipeg Council of Women while discussing her work on the Canadian Freedom from Hunger Committee. Speers suggested a Chinese origin for the expression.[8]

As a fitting motto for the Committee's work, Miss Speers quoted a Chinese proverb: "If you give a man a fish, you feed him for a day—if you teach him to fish, you feed him for many days."

In May 1963 the adage appeared in the *Sunday Gleaner* of Kingston, Jamaica, as an epigraph to an article titled "Tackling World Hunger." The paper suggested the quotation was Italian.[9]

GIVE A MAN a fish and you feed him for a day. Teach him how to fish and you feed him for his life time.

—Italian proverb

In May 1963 a newspaper in Van Buren, Missouri, printed the saying and indicated that it had been spoken during a convention held in Melbourne, Australia.[10]

> A quotation from one convention speaker was, "Give a man a fish and you feed him one meal. Teach him to fish and he can feed himself for many meals."

In November 1963 a speaker at a meeting of the National Council of Jewish Women in Waco, Texas, employed the saying and labeled it a "Chinese proverb."[11]

> Since I am speaking in international terms I remind you of a Chinese proverb, "give him a fish and he can eat but teach him to fish and he can eat many days."

In 1970 Susan Whittlesey's book *VISTA: Challenge to Poverty*, affiliated with a volunteer service organization, suggested that the saying was "an old Navajo proverb":[12]

> "One of the hardest things about being a VISTA," explains Mary, "is that we're never allowed to do anything for people directly, not even fill out forms. This isn't always easy, but it's the only way."
> There is an old Navajo proverb which VISTAS must often remind themselves of:
>
> > Give a man a fish, and you feed him for a day. Teach a man to fish, and you feed him for a lifetime.

A 1976 public policy book, *Africa: From Mystery to Maze*, linked a version to Lao-tzu and Mao Tse-tung.[13]

> To paraphrase Lao-tse and Chairman Mao, can the American people understand that it is better to teach a man to fish than to give him a fish? Hero's finding that the American public strongly

supports technical assistance to transfer American know-how suggests that they can.

In 1986 an article about bodywork in *Yoga Journal* ascribed the saying to Lao-tzu.[14]

Lao Tsu said that if you give a hungry man a fish, you feed him for a day, but if you teach him how to fish, you feed him for a lifetime.

QI feels that current knowledge on this subject is incomplete. Based on current evidence, Anne Isabella Thackeray Ritchie deserves credit for formulating a striking adage that uses fishing as the ultimate mode of self-sufficiency. The saying has evolved over time and becomes more memorable by mentioning the ability to eat for a lifetime. The claim that the adage was an old proverb from China, Italy, India, or the early Americas is unsupported by the evidence, **QI** concludes.

Notes:

Great thanks to Michael Becket, whose inquiry led **QI** to formulate this question and perform this exploration. Additional thanks to researchers Ralph Keyes and his book *The Quote Verifier*, Fred R. Shapiro and his book *The Yale Book of Quotations*, and Barry Popik and his website, The Big Apple. Also thanks to the mailing-list discussants George Thompson and Victor Steinbok.

1. Nathan Whiting, "Ladder of Benevolence," *Religious Intelligencer* 10, no. 43 (March 25, 1826): 681. Accessed in Google Books, https://goo.gl/Inv3ij.

2. Miss Thackeray (Mrs. Richmond Ritchie) [Anne Isabella Thackeray Ritchie], *Mrs. Dymond* (London: Smith, Elder, 1885), 342. Accessed in Google Books, https://goo.gl/s952Ai.

3. Mrs. Ritchie, *Mrs. Dymond* [serialized version of novel], *Macmillan's Magazine* 52 (May 1885), 246. Accessed in Google Books, https://goo.gl/Eot2bu; Mrs. Ritchie, *Mrs. Dymond* [excerpted from *Macmillan's Magazine*], *Littell's Living Age* no. 2150 (September 5, 1885), 602. Accessed in Google Books, https://goo.gl/k8Z5BY.

4. Ralph Keyes, *The Quote Verifier: Who Said What, Where, and When* (New York: St. Martin's, 2006), 65. Verified in hard copy.

5. M. Loane, *The Common Growth* (New York: Longsmans, Green, 1911), 139. Accessed in Google Books, https://goo.gl/nfoji9.

6. Leone Norton, "Promoting Positive Health Stressed by County Public Health Program, Says Nurse," *Wisconsin Rapids Daily Tribune*, December 24, 1945, 5. Accessed in NewspaperARCHIVE.com.

7. Jack Nelson, "Missionary from Formosa Warns of Communist Threat, Special Report," *Rockford Register-Republic* (Rockford, IL), November 11, 1961, 4. Accessed in GenealogyBank.

8. "New Threat: Hunger," *Winnipeg Free Press* (Winnipeg, MB), October 23, 1962, 18. Accessed in NewspaperARCHIVE.com.

9. John Baker White, "World Spotlight: Tackling World Hunger," *Sunday Gleaner* (Kingston, Jamaica), May 5, 1963, 8. Accessed in NewspaperARCHIVE.com.

10. "Hawkins Day Here Well Attended by Extension Club Women," *Current Local* (Van Buren, MO), May 23, 1963, 1. Accessed in Newspapers.com.

11. "NCJW Officer Gives Talk for Council," *Waco News-Tribune* (Waco, TX), November 8, 1963, B3. Accessed in Newspapers.com.

12. Susan Whittlesey, *VISTA: Challenge to Poverty* (New York: Coward-McCann, 1970), 39. Verified in hard copy.

13. Helen Kitchen, ed., *Africa: From Mystery to Maze*, Critical Choices for Americans (Lexington, MA: Lexington Books, 1976), 391. Verified in hard copy.

14. Joseph Heller and William A. Henkin, "Bodywork: Choosing an Approach to Suit Your Needs," *Yoga Journal*, no. 66 (January–February 1986): 56. Accessed in Google Books, https://goo.gl/7uaJ3c.

17. "Choose a job you love and you will never have to work a day in your life."

—Confucius

In the years after the death of Confucius circa 479 BC, a compilation of his teachings and aphorisms was constructed and is now referred to as the *Analects*. One passage instructs a benevolent ruler on how to rule—the potentate should select tasks for his populace that are appropriate and constructive, and these proper choices should result in subjects who have no reason to be unhappy and complain.[1]

> Tsze-chang said, "What is meant by being beneficent without great expenditure?" The Master replied, "When the person in authority makes more beneficial to the people the things from which they naturally derive benefit—is not this being beneficent without great expenditure? When he chooses the labours which are proper, and makes them labour on them, who will repine? When his desires are set on benevolent government, and he realizes it, who will accuse him of covetousness?

The above is perhaps a starting point but only faintly related to the modern saying. The ruler, not the job seeker, was making the choices. In addition, passion or love was not the goal—propriety was. Nevertheless, **QI** includes this citation for the sake of completeness, and to illustrate how Confucius may fit into the quote's history.

The earliest match of the precise saying located by **QI** was published in a 1982 issue of the *Princeton Alumni Weekly*. Professor of philosophy Arthur Szathmary attributes the words to an anonymous "old-timer."[2]

> An old-timer I knew used to tell his students: "Find something you love to do and you'll never have to work a day in your life."

QI suspects that earlier instances exist that use a different phrasing, but this is where the modern game of telephone started. In June 1985 the trade journal *Computerworld* printed the saying as an epigraph to an article by the journalist Glenn Rifkin, who attributed the words to Confucius. This is the first linkage to the luminary known to **QI**:[3]

> Choose a job you love, and you will never have to work a day in your life.
>
> —Confucius

Also in 1985 a self-help guidebook titled *How to Start, Expand and Sell a Business* by James C. Comiskey described the saying as an "Oriental proverb."[4]

> As an Oriental proverb quite aptly states, "Choose a job you love and you will never have to work a day in your life."

In August 1986 a piece in the *Boston Globe* quoted an art teacher named Janet Lambert-Moore using an instance of the aphorism.[5]

> The outgoing, former art instructor in the Dracut school system took time out from a poster of Ellis Island to explain her philosophy: "If you love your job, you never have to work a day in your life. I'm here most of the day. I probably could get a lot more accomplished without the interruptions." She steps out of the way so two elderly tourists can take a look at her hand-watercolored prints. "But I like the contact."

In February 1989 a book reviewer in *Jet* magazine employed the saying while analyzing the biography of a famous musician.[6]

> "Choose a job you love, and you will never have to work a day in your life," Confucius once said. If this is true, one of America's giants of jazz, trumpeter/scat singer Louis "Satchmo" Armstrong never worked a day in his 40-year musical career.

In May 1989 the US military newspaper *Stars and Stripes* printed a short item that included a quotation from the motivational speaker Harvey Mackay.[7]

> A person is never too old to achieve success, said the 56-year-old Mackay, who will address the subject of aging in the new book.
> "I don't believe in age," he said. "Find something you love to do, and you'll never have to work a day in your life. You find people like that at any age level. Age doesn't limit people one-tenth of 1 percent."

In conclusion, the earliest citation in 1982 located by **QI** is anonymous. The linkage to Confucius appears to be spurious. Harvey Mackay helped to popularize the adage, but he was not the originator. Researchers have found no substantive support for the claim that Confucius made this statement, and neither has **QI**.

Notes:

Special thanks to top researcher Barry Popik for the research performed on this topic, which is presented on his website.[8]
Great thanks to Vic Goddard, Andrew Old, Nina Gilbert, and Kat Caverly, whose inquiries led **QI** to formulate this question and perform this exploration. Thanks to Brian Whatcott, who helpfully pointed to the passage from Confucius containing the partial match. Thanks also to the Project Wombat discussants and the forum participants at the Straight Dope website.

1. James Legge, *The Chinese Classics with a Translation, Critical and Exegetical Notes, Prolegomena, and Copious Indexes*, vol. 1, *Confucian Analects, the Great Learning, and the Doctrine of the Mean* (Hong Kong: London Missionary Society, 1861), 216–17. Accessed in Google Books, https://goo.gl/I8odqO.
2. Ann Woolfolk, "Toshiko Takaezu," *Princeton Alumni Weekly*, October 6, 1982, 32. Accessed in Google Books, https://goo.gl/L8csT5.
3. Glenn Rifkin, "Finding and Keeping DP/MIS Professionals," Update, *Computerworld*, June 3, 1985, 3 (epigraph). Accessed in Google Books, https://goo.gl/kSnNtC.

4. James C. Comiskey, *How to Start, Expand and Sell a Business: The Complete Guidebook for Entrepreneurs*, 3rd print., rev. ed. (San Jose, CA: Venture Perspectives, 1986), 25. Verified in scans.

5. Tom Long, "Lowell: Where the Past Powers the Present," *Boston Globe*, August 21, 1986, 10. Accessed in ProQuest.

6. "Satchmo's Jazz Genius Hits High Note in New Revealing Book on Him," *Jet* 75, no. 20: 31. Accessed in Google Books, https://goo.gl/LDQoxw.

7. "Mustachioed Michael a Suspicious Shopper," Faces 'n' Places, *Stars and Stripes*, May 4, 1989, European edition, 12. Accessed in NewspaperARCHIVE.com.

8. Barry Popik, "Choose a Job You Love, and You Will Never Have to Work a Day in Your Life," The Big Apple, May 20, 2012, http://www.barrypopik.com/index.php/new_york_city /entry/choose_a_job_you_love_and_you_will_never_have_to_work_a_day_in_your_life.

18. "A bird doesn't sing because it has an answer, it sings because it has a song."

—Chinese proverb
—Maya Angelou

In 2015 the US Postal Service released a commemorative stamp featuring the prominent author Maya Angelou that displayed the following words:

> A bird doesn't sing because it has an answer, it sings because it has a song.

Credit: USPS

Angelou's best-known work is titled *I Know Why the Caged Bird Sings*, and the expression above seems to be thematically connected; however, **QI** can confirm that the words were not originally crafted by Angelou.

The earliest match known to **QI** appears in *A Cup of Sun: A Book of Poems* by Joan Walsh Anglund, a popular children's book author. The collection was published in 1967, and the following verse is printed by itself on a single page. **QI** notes that the phrasing differs slightly from the words on the stamp:[1]

> A bird does not sing because he has an answer.
> He sings because he has a song.

By 1984 the quotation was being passed for a Chinese proverb. In 1995 it was reascribed to someone named Howard Clemmons, and by 2001 it was reassigned to Maya Angelou.

QI wishes to examine the bird.

Speculations and pronouncements about the internal wellsprings of avian desire, and about the motivations of singing birds, have a long and variegated history.

In 1818 the influential British literary and art critic William Hazlitt published an article about opera in the London journal *Yellow Dwarf.* Hazlitt compared the divergent purposes of an opera star and a singing bird.[2]

> [T]he thrush that awakes at day-break with its song, does not sing because it is paid to sing, or to please others, or to be admired or criticised. It sings because it is happy; it pours the thrilling sounds from its throat, to relieve the overflowings of its own heart—the liquid notes come from, and go to the heart, dropping balm into it, as the gushing spring revives the traveller's parched and fainting lips.

In 1850 the British poet Alfred, Lord Tennyson published *In Memoriam A. H. H.*, a poem about his late friend Arthur Henry Hallam, who had died in 1833 at the young age of twenty-two. In verse, Tennyson fears that critics will condemn the elegy as a showy "parade of pain," designed for his own gain, and he preempts the complaint by invoking the way a bird sings—because it has to:[3]

> Behold, ye speak an idle thing:
> Ye never knew the sacred dust:
> I do but sing because I must,
> And pipe but as the linnets sing:

In 1886 the *Biblical Recorder* of Raleigh, North Carolina, employed a hydraulic analogy when discussing the impetus of the singing bird.[4]

> A fountain doesn't flow because of a sense of duty, but because it is full; and of its fullness it overflows. A bird doesn't sing because it

has to, but because of the inward thrill that must find vent in the outward trill.

In 1889 a religious book sharpened the spur:[5]

A bird sings because it has a song and must sing it.

In 1902 a column in the *Brooklyn Daily Eagle* of Brooklyn, New York, suggested that duty was not the key motivator.[6]

> The spring does not pour forth because it is its duty, the little bird does not sing because of duty, but because its little heart would burst if it did not sing.

In 1949 a biographical work called *The Sage of the Hills* highlighted the importance of having a song in the heart.[7]

> It should be remembered that the Nightingale does not sing just because we listen; it sings because it has a song in its heart.

In 1950 the *Richmond Times Dispatch* in Virginia printed the following about why a bird sings.[8]

> The import of it, is, simply this—the bird is asked why it sings and replies, "I know not, I know not, my heart is so full of song I can't help it!" Jenny forgets herself, and becomes the bird, and sings as the bird sings, because she can't help it.

In 1967 Joan Walsh Anglund published a book of poems that included the following verse, as noted previously:

> A bird does not sing because he has an answer.
> He sings because he has a song.

But the familiarity of the quotation has seemed to always cause confusion. In February 1970 a Chillicothe, Missouri, newspaper mentioned an educational and musical organization called Up With People. A version of the saying was employed by someone who was a member of the group. No attribution to Anglund was given:[9]

> Thoughts from the "Up With People" friends included:
>
>> "The bird sings not because he has an answer, but because he has a song."

Also in February 1970, a speaker at a garden club meeting in Georgia used the expression without attribution.[10]

> Mrs. Riddle began her program by saying "A bird doesn't sing because he has the answer, he sings because he has a song."

In 1973 a columnist named Jimmie Allison in a Mexia, Texas, newspaper used the saying without attribution:[11]

> A bird does not sing because he has an answer; He sings because he has a Song.

In 1974 the connection between Anglund and the quotation was recalled in a St. Petersburg, Florida, newspaper:[12]

> A bird does not sing
> Because he has an answer.
> He sings
> Because he has a song.
>
> FROM "A CUP OF SUN"
> J. W. ANGLUND

And nine years later, *Mademoiselle* obscured it anew, in an astrology column called Starcast that implausibly asserted that the lines were a Chinese proverb.[13]

> Your year ahead can be summed up by a lovely Chinese proverb: "A bird does not sing because it has an answer, it sings because it has a song."

In 1988 a newspaper in Kuala Lumpur, Malaysia, also asserted that the saying was a Chinese proverb.[14]

> Reminds one of the Chinese proverb: A bird does not sing because it has an answer. It sings because it has a song.

In 1990 an interview with Maya Angelou was published in the *Paris Review*. She stated emphatically that her metaphorical singing was a difficult task.[15]

> Of course, there are those critics—New York critics as a rule—who say, Well, Maya Angelou has a new book out and of course it's good but then she's a natural writer. Those are the ones I want to grab by the throat and wrestle to the floor because it takes me forever to get it to sing. I work at the language.

In May 1995 a newspaper in Mobile, Alabama, printed a section of a high school campus newspaper that included the saying with an attribution to "Angland," a misspelled instance of Anglund.[16]

> This week's quote is from Angland. It is, "A bird doesn't sing because it has an answer, it sings because it has a song."

In June 1995 a commentator in a Granbury, Texas, newspaper shared the saying with readers without attribution:[17]

How 'bout It? Howard
A bird does not sing because he has an answer—He sings because
he has a song!

—Howard Clemmons

In 1997 the collection *Reader's Digest Quotable Quotes: Wit and Wisdom for All Occasions* included the following:[18]

A bird does not sing because it has an answer. It sings because it
has a song.

—Chinese proverb

By 2001 the version of the saying using "it" had been reassigned to Maya Angelou. For example, the Quotes section of the *Index-Journal* of Greenwood, South Carolina, included the following instance:[19]

A bird doesn't sing because it has an answer, it sings because it has
a song.

—Maya Angelou

In 2003 a Knoxville, Tennessee, newspaper credited the saying to a prominent football coach.[20]

TAKE NOTE

"A bird doesn't sing because it has an answer. It sings because it has
a song."

—Lou Holtz, University of South Carolina football
coach

A Greek website for blues music enthusiasts published an article dated 2013 called "Dr. Maya Angelou: A Muse in Our Midst." The text appears to be an interview with Angelou. A remark about her famous memoir included an instance of the quotation, but Angelou does not claim credit for coinage.[21]

> I would like to start with the book "I Know Why Cage Birds Sings [*sic*]." Why do people write poetry and play music?
>
> Dr. Angelou: They write because they have something to say, something about life, sometimes something about pain, something about love, even something about laughter. I wrote the book because "Bird Sings Why The Caged I Know" is a song. A bird doesn't sing because it has an answer, it sings because it has a song.

In April 2015, after the text of the quotation on Angelou's commemorative stamp was announced, a journalist at the *Washington Post* described uncertainty regarding the provenance of the saying.[22]

> Jabari Asim, associate professor of writing, literature and publishing at Emerson College in Boston, was excited. Until he read the quote on the Angelou stamp:
>
> > "A bird doesn't sing because it has an answer, it sings because it has a song."
>
> Funny thing, he had always thought the quote came from Joan Walsh Anglund, the prolific children's book author.

A few days later the *Washington Post* reported that the eighty-nine-year-old Anglund had claimed credit for the quotation.[23]

> "A bird doesn't sing because it has an answer, it sings because it has a song," the Angelou "Forever" stamp reads.
> "Yes, that's my quote," Anglund said Monday night from her Connecticut home. It appears on page 15 of her book of poems "A

Cup of Sun," published in 1967. Only the pronouns and punctuation are changed, from "he" in Anglund's original to "it" on the stamp.

In conclusion, **QI** believes that Joan Walsh Anglund should be credited with the words she wrote in 1967. The close variant saying using "it" instead of "he" was derived from Anglund's expression. A large number of precursor statements about singing birds circulated in the 1800s and 1900s, but **QI** has not found a stronger match than Anglund's verse.

Notes:

Great thanks to the anonymous individuals who contacted me as this story was unfolding back in April 2015. Thanks also to Ben Zimmer, Stephen Goranson, Jay Dillon, and other discussants for early heads-ups, feedback, and research. Top researcher Barry Popik located valuable citations for this topic and shared them with **QI**.

1. Joan Walsh Anglund, *A Cup of Sun: A Book of Poems* (New York: Harcourt, Brace, 1967), 15. Verified in scans.
2. W. H. [William Hazlitt], "The Little Hunch-Back," *Yellow Dwarf: A Weekly Miscellany*, no. 21 (May 23, 1818): 166. Accessed in Google Books, https://goo.gl/mqR4g3.
3. Alfred Tennyson, *In Memoriam A. H. H.*, 3rd ed. (London: Edward Moxon, 1850), 36. Accessed in Google Books, https://goo.gl/kHzMJW.
4. The Dead Point, *Biblical Recorder* (Raleigh, NC), January 27, 1886, 1. Accessed in Newspapers.com.
5. John B. Robins, *Christ and Our Country: Or, A Hopeful View of Christianity in the Present Day*, 2nd ed. (Nashville: Publishing House of the M. E. Church, 1889), 133. Accessed in Google Books, https://goo.gl/QZYsKw.
6. "Progress the Keynote of Sermons in Many of the Churches—Dr. P.S. Henson on Pressing Onward," *Brooklyn Daily Eagle* (Brooklyn, NY), January 6, 1902, 12. Accessed in Newspapers.com.
7. J. M. [Jesse Marvin] Gaskin, *The Sage of the Hills: Life Story of the Reverend W. G. "Bill" Lucas* (Shawnee, OK: Oklahoma Baptist University Press, 1949), 36. Accessed in HathiTrust, https://goo.gl/owiEqd.

8.   "Jenny Lind Sang Here 100 Years Ago and the Memory Is Still Prodigious," *Richmond Times Dispatch* (Richmond, VA), December 17, 1950, A7. Accessed in GenealogyBank.

9.   "After Chillicothe, 'Up with People' to Paris, White House," Letters from Two Girls, *Chillicothe Constitution-Tribune* (Chillicothe, MO), February 9, 1970, 9. Accessed in Newspapers.com.

10.   "Mrs. Spencer Speaks on Birds at Laurel Garden Club Meeting," *Rome News-Tribune* (Rome, GA), February 22, 1970, 6D. Accessed in Google News Archive, https://goo.gl /xak98S.

11.   Jimmie Allison, Tehuacana News, *Mexia Daily News* (Mexia, TX), May 24, 1973, 3. Accessed in NewspaperARCHIVE.com.

12.   [Filler item], *St. Petersburg Times* (St. Petersburg, FL), August 19, 1974, *Pinellas Times* section, 2. Accessed in Google News Archive, https://goo.gl/8Qir00.

13.   Maxine Lucille Fiel, "Happy Birthday, Capricorn!" Starcast, *Mademoiselle* 91 (January 1985), 144. Verified in microfilm.

14.   Mani Le Vasan, "CALL Learning Environment—the Present and Future," MCCE Bulletin section, *New Straits Times* (Kuala Lumpur, Malaysia), December 15, 1988, 3. Accessed in Google News Archive, https://goo.gl/E1rYBi.

15.   George Plimpton, "Maya Angelou: The Art of Fiction No. 119," Interviews, *Paris Review*, no. 116 (Fall 1990), http://www.theparisreview.org/interviews/2279/the-art-of-fiction -no-119-maya-angelou.

16.   Brannan Pedersen, "Campus News: Baldwin County High," *Press Register* (Mobile, AL), May 5, 1995, 10. Accessed in NewsBank.

17.   Howard Clemmons, How 'Bout It? Howard, *Hood County News* (Granbury, TX), June 10, 1995, 1. Accessed in Newspapers.com.

18.   *Reader's Digest Quotable Quotes: Wit and Wisdom for All Occasions* (Pleasantville, NY: Reader's Digest, 1997), 177. Verified in hard copy.

19.   Quotes, *Index-Journal* (Greenwood, SC), September 16, 2001, 4D. Accessed in Newspapers.com.

20.   "Take Note," *Knoxville News Sentinel* (Knoxville, TN), April 11, 2003, home and garden section, E1. Accessed in NewsBank.

21.   Michalis Limnios, "Dr. Maya Angelou: A Muse in Our Midst," Michalis Limnios Blues @ Greece's Blog (blog), June 1, 2013, http://blues.gr/profiles/blogs/interview -with-dr-maya-angelou-a-muse-who-captivates-audiences.

22. Lonnae O'Neal, "The Maya Angelou Stamp Features a Beautiful Quote—That Someone Else May Also Have Written," *Washington Post*, April 4, 2015. Accessed in ProQuest National Newspapers Premier.
23. Lonnae O'Neal, "Whose Words? Author Lays a Claim to Angelou Quote," *Washington Post*, April 7, 2015, C1. Accessed in ProQuest National Newspapers Premier.

II
READER ERROR

TEXTUAL PROXIMITY * REAL-WORLD PROXIMITY * SIMILAR NAMES

1. "An eye for an eye will make the whole world blind."
2. "Money can't buy love, but it improves your bargaining position."
3. "Any idiot can face a crisis; it's this day-to-day living that wears you out."
4. "The cure for boredom is curiosity. There is no cure for curiosity."
5. "The mind is not a vessel that needs filling, but wood that needs igniting."
6. "Today a reader, tomorrow a leader."
7. "Time you enjoy wasting is not wasted time."
8. "Somewhere, something incredible is waiting to be known."
9. "There are things known, and things unknown, and in between are the doors."
10. "Do good anyway" and the Paradoxical Commandments.
11. "What lies behind us and what lies before us are tiny matters compared to what lies within us."
12. "Sometimes, I'm terrified of my heart, of its constant hunger for whatever it is it wants."
13. "The more sand has escaped from the hourglass of our life, the clearer we should see through it."
14. "The secret of change is to focus all of your energy, not on fighting the old, but on building the new."

TEXTUAL PROXIMITY

1. "An eye for an eye will make the whole world blind."

—Mahatma Gandhi

One of the world's top quotation experts, Fred R. Shapiro, editor of *The Yale Book of Quotations*, has examined the question of the above quotation:[1]

> "An eye for an eye leaves the whole world blind" is frequently attributed to M. K. Gandhi. The Gandhi Institute for Nonviolence states that the Gandhi family believes it is an authentic Gandhi quotation, but no example of its use by the Indian leader has ever been discovered.

Shapiro notes that an important biographer of Gandhi, Louis Fischer, used a version of the expression when he wrote about Gandhi's approach to conflict. However, Fischer did not attribute the saying to Gandhi in his description of the leader's life. Instead, Fischer used the expression himself as part of his explanation of Gandhi's philosophy. **QI** thinks some readers may have been confused and decided to directly attribute the saying to Gandhi based on a misreading of Fischer's works.

The epigram is a twist on a famous biblical injunction in the Book of Exodus: "Eye for eye, tooth for tooth." These words appear in the King James English translation.[2] There is a more elaborate version of the clever maxim based on these two phrases:

An eye-for-eye and tooth-for-tooth would lead to a world of the blind and toothless.

QI has located relevant variants for this longer expression. In 1914 a member of the Canadian parliament named Mr. Graham argued against the death penalty. He mentioned the well-known verse from the Book of Exodus and then employed it in a trope about the members of the parliament:[3]

> Mr. GRAHAM: We can argue all we like, but if capital punishment is being inflicted on some man, we are inclined to say: 'It serves him right.' That is not the spirit, I believe, in which legislation is enacted. If in this present age we were to go back to the old time of 'an eye for an eye and a tooth for a tooth,' there would be very few hon. gentlemen in this House who would not, metaphorically speaking, be blind and toothless.

In 1944 Henry Powell Spring used a version of the maxim in his book of aphorisms, *What Is Truth*. The work's acknowledgment section indicated that Spring was a follower of Rudolf Steiner and a spiritual philosophy called "anthroposophy":[4]

> The Spirit and Beings continue unselfishly to maintain life upon our planet, restoring us nightly, and forgiving us our wilful blindnesses far beyond our spiritual or bodily capacity of repayment. If the Spirit, Who is Life, exacted an eye for an eye, or a tooth for a tooth, this world would indeed be peopled with the blind and the toothless.

The 1947 book *Gandhi and Stalin* by Louis Fischer contrasted Gandhi with another archetypal figure, Joseph Stalin. The work contained a version of the saying mentioning eyes (but not teeth) that is often attributed to Gandhi today. Fischer used the phrase while discussing Gandhi and his approach to conflict resolution, but he did not attribute the words to him. This is the earliest citation located by **QI** that connects Gandhi with the saying:[5]

The shreds of individuality cannot be sewed together with a bay-onet; nor can democracy be restored according to the Biblical injunction of an "eye for an eye" which, in the end, would make everybody blind.

Another important early biography by Fischer, *The Life of Mahatma Gandhi*, was published in 1950.[6] Fischer used the maxim again while explaining the concept of Satyagraha, but he did not attribute the words to Gandhi. This citation appears in *The Yale Book of Quotations*:

Satyagraha is peaceful. If words fail to convince the adversary perhaps purity, humility, and honesty will. The opponent must be "weaned from error by patience and sympathy," weaned, not crushed; converted, not annihilated.

Satyagraha is the exact opposite of the policy of an-eye-for-an-eye-for-an-eye-for-an-eye which ends in making everybody blind.

You cannot inject new ideas into a man's head by chopping it off; neither will you infuse a new spirit into his heart by piercing it with a dagger.

In 1958 Martin Luther King Jr., who was influenced by Gandhian ideals, used the aphorism in his book *Stride Toward Freedom: The Montgomery Story*:[7]

Violence as a way of achieving racial justice is both impractical and immoral. It is impractical because it is a descending spiral ending in destruction for all. The old law of an eye for an eye leaves everybody blind. It is immoral because it seeks to humiliate the opponent rather than win his understanding; it seeks to annihilate rather than to convert.

Ralph Keyes writing in *The Quote Verifier* mentioned the above citation.[8] Keyes also noted that the 1971 movie version of the popular musical *Fiddler on the Roof* contained the longer saying. This production debuted on Broadway in 1964 and is based on stories by Sholem Aleichem. Here is an instance of the saying in a script published in 1970:[9]

FIRST MAN: We should defend ourselves. An eye for an eye, a tooth for a tooth.

TEVYE: Very good. And that way, the whole world will be blind and toothless.

In modern times, the Oscar-winning 1982 biopic *Gandhi* helped to popularize the connection between Gandhi and the saying. The film depicted the Jallianwala Bagh massacre and the ensuing violent riots. Gandhi and a close political ally exchanged the following dialogue:[10]

Mohammed Ali Jinnah: After what they did at the massacre? It's only an eye for an eye.

Mahatma Gandhi: An eye for an eye only ends up making the whole world blind.

In conclusion, Mahatma Gandhi may have used the expression, but no conclusive evidence for this has yet been discovered. It is also possible that the ascription is inaccurate, and the books of Louis Fischer may have inadvertently helped to establish the attribution.

Notes:

1. Fred R. Shapiro, *The Yale Book of Quotations* (New Haven: Yale University Press, 2006), 269-70. Verified in hard copy.
2. Exod. 21:24 (King James Bible), http://www.kingjamesbibleonline.org/Exodus-21-24.
3. Transcript of Mr. Graham speaking, *Official Report of the Debates of the House of Commons of the Dominion of Canada*, 3rd sess., 12th parliament, vol. 113 (Ottawa, ON: J. De L. Tache, 1914), 496. Accessed in HathiTrust, https://goo.gl/4T3QeZ.
4. [Henry] Powell Spring, *What Is Truth* (Winter Park, FL: Orange Press, 1944), 10. Verified in hard copy.
5. Louis Fischer, *Gandhi and Stalin: Two Signs at the World's Crossroads* (New York: Harper, 1947), 61. Verified in hard copy.

6. Louis Fischer, *The Life of Mahatma Gandhi* (New York: Harper, 1950), 77. Verified in hard copy.

7. Martin Luther King Jr., *Stride Toward Freedom: The Montgomery Story* (New York: Harper, 1958), 213. Verified in hard copy.

8. Ralph Keyes, *The Quote Verifier: Who Said What, Where, and When* (New York: St. Martin's, 2006), 74–75. Verified in hard copy.

9. *Best Plays of the Sixties*, ed. Stanley Richards (Garden City, NY: Doubleday, 1970), s.v. "Fiddler on the Roof," 322.

10. "Eye for an Eye" scene from *Gandhi* (1982, directed by Richard Attenborough), 1:51, WingClips, http://www.wingclips.com/movie-clips/gandhi/eye-for-an-eye. Line is said at :30.

2. "Money can't buy love, but it improves your bargaining position."

—Christopher Marlowe

QI received an urgent plea for help:

> Christopher Marlowe was a brilliant poet and dramatist of the
> 1500s whose works influenced the luminary William Shakespeare.
> I was astonished to find the following statement attributed to him,
> "Money can't buy love, but it improves your bargaining position."
>
> In my opinion, this expression is not from the 1500s and credit-
> ing Marlowe is nonsensical. Nevertheless, many websites dedicated
> to quotations present this dubious ascription. Would you please
> explore this quotation? Perhaps you could uncover the source of
> this inanity.

Inanity indeed. The earliest evidence located by **QI** was published in the
twentieth century, not the sixteenth. In 1954 a newspaper in Iowa printed an
instance of the saying in a humor column. The phrasing differed somewhat from
the common modern expression, and no attribution was given:[1]

> Money cannot buy love, but it places one in an excellent bargain-
> ing position.

QI believes that the flawed attribution to Christopher Marlowe originated
with the misreading of an influential book of quotations that was compiled by
Laurence J. Peter and published in 1977.

Christopher Marlowe, who died in 1593, did compose a well-known poem
about love called "The Passionate Shepherd to His Love," but the work did not
discuss money or bargaining. The following two verses are from a 1794 edition;
the anomalous spellings are present in the text:[2]

Come live with me and be my love,
And we wil all the pleasures prove
That hils and vallies, dale and field,
And all the craggy mountains yield.
There will we sit upon the rocks,
And see the shepherds feed their flocks,
By shallow rivers, to whose falls
Melodious birds sing madrigals.

Humorous twists on the maxim that "money cannot buy love" have a long history. Here is an example from more than one hundred years ago that was printed in a Canadian newspaper of 1903. The meaning differs from the saying under investigation:[3]

Money, it has been said, cannot buy love, but it often buys such a good counterfeit that it isn't much matter.

In the 1940 collection of aphorisms titled *Meditations in Wall Street* by the stockbroker Henry Stanley Haskins—but published anonymously—the following saying about love appears:[4]

The voyage of love is all the sweeter for an outside stateroom and a seat at the captain's table.

Not a close match at all, but hold that thought. In 1954 the earliest close match for the humorous adage under investigation was published in a newspaper in Elgin, Iowa, as noted previously:[5]

Money cannot buy love, but it places one in an excellent bargaining position.

In 1968 Evan Esar, ever the diligent collector of bon mots, included an instance of the maxim in *20,000 Quips and Quotes*:[6]

Money cannot buy love, but it can put you in a good bargaining position.

In 1977 the popular compendium *Peter's Quotations: Ideas for Our Time* by Laurence J. Peter printed a version of the aphorism in a confusing presentation, melding the quotation from Haskins with a parenthetical comment from Peter, who did not credit his original source. The quotation that followed was from none other than Christopher Marlowe:[7]

> The voyage of love is all the sweeter for an outside stateroom and a seat at the captain's table.
>
> —Henry S. Haskins (Money can't buy love but it improves your bargaining position.)
>
> Come live with me, and be my Love;/And we will all the pleasures prove.
>
> —Christopher Marlowe (1564–1593)

QI hypothesizes that one or more readers of the passage above incorrectly decided to ascribe the expression between parentheses to Marlowe. In addition, some individuals assigned the words to Peter himself.

For example, the 1981 book *Love: Emotion, Myth, and Metaphor* by Robert C. Solomon included the following text:[8]

> Money can't buy love, but it improves your bargaining position.
>
> —Laurence J. Peter

In 2010 *The Mammoth Book of Great British Humor* credited the saying to Marlowe.[9]

In conclusion, this comical remark was in circulation by 1954, and initially it was anonymous. In 1977 Laurence J. Peter employed the adage in a compilation of sayings. Some individuals misread Peter's book and assigned the words to Christopher Marlowe; other readers ascribed the saying to Peter.

Notes:

Great thanks to Tony Fordyce, whose query led **QI** to formulate this question and perform this exploration.

1. "Rich's 'Pipe Dreams,'" *Elgin Echo* (Elgin, IA), March 18, 1954, 2. Accessed in NewspaperARCHIVE.com.
2. Thomas Percy, *Reliques of Ancient English Poetry: Consisting of Old Heroic Ballads, Songs, and Other Pieces of Our Earlier Poets, Together with Some Few of Later Date*, vol. 1, 4th ed. (London: John Nichols, 1794), 234. Accessed in Google Books, https://goo.gl/eV6Sx9.
3. "Surplus of 10,000,000," *Brandon Weekly Sun* (Brandon, MB), June 11, 1903, 5. Accessed in NewspaperARCHIVE.com.
4. [Henry Stanley Haskins], *Meditations in Wall Street* (New York: William Morrow, 1940), 86. Accessed in HathiTrust, https://goo.gl/wJZxcW.
5. "Rich's 'Pipe Dreams.'"
6. Evan Esar, *20,000 Quips and Quotes* (Garden City, NY: Doubleday, 1968), 492. Verified in hard copy.
7. Laurence J. Peter, *Peter's Quotations: Ideas for Our Time* (New York: William Morrow, 1977), 309. Verified in hard copy.
8. Robert C. Solomon, *Love: Emotion, Myth, and Metaphor* (Amherst, NY: Prometheus, 1981), 167. Accessed in Google Books, https://goo.gl/epNgsd.
9. Michael Powell, ed., *The Mammoth Book of Great British Humor* (London: Constable and Robinson, 2010), 351. Accessed in Google Books, https://goo.gl/WKGhPY, and Amazon, https://goo.gl/5ZGXUt.

3. "Any idiot can face a crisis; it's this day-to-day living that wears you out."

—Anton Chekhov

—Clifford Odets

HIGHLY DUBIOUS

A reader wrote to QI complaining that the above quotation had been attributed to Anton Chekhov, the Russian master of short stories and drama, but that he had acquired zero evidence to support this claim. "I even asked my Slavicist friend to look for it in the original Russian works, and she was unable to find it," my client intoned. "Would you please examine its provenance?"

QI believes that this quotation and ascription are mistaken. The statement entered circulation because of a sequence of at least two errors.

The first appearance of a partial match for the quotation was a line spoken by Bing Crosby during the 1954 film *The Country Girl*. Crosby played a character named Frank Elgin who was an alcoholic attempting to return to show business. A self-destructive episode of drinking in Boston almost derailed his comeback attempt, and near the end of the film, the character discussed his probability of achieving success.[1]

> I faced a crisis up there in Boston, and I got away with it. Just about anybody can face a crisis. It's that everyday living that's rough.

The Country Girl movie was based on a play written by Clifford Odets, which was adapted to film by George Seaton. Thus, the line above was connected to Odets, and this was a key step in the multistep process of misattribution as shown by the next citation.

A 1971 anthology of plays entitled *The Tradition of the Theatre*, edited by the educators Peter Bauland and William Ingram, included a translation of Chekhov's *The Cherry Orchard*. The editors wrote an introduction to the play, and the quotation was printed in this preparative text. The statement was ascribed, however, to the American dramatist Odets.[2]

> A character in a Hollywood film of the 1950's casually drops this line: "Any idiot can face a crisis; it's this day-to-day living that wears you out." The screenplay was by Clifford Odets, America's chief inheritor of the dramatic tradition of Anton Chekhov, and in that one line, he epitomized the lesson of his master.

QI conjectures that the quotation above was constructed from a flawed memory of the line in *The Country Girl*. The textbook referred to a screenplay by Odets, but as noted previously, the screenplay was by Seaton, and the play by Odets. **QI** has examined the edition of the play published in 1951, and the line is absent. In addition, the modern quotation is also absent; hence, **QI** would credit Seaton with the line.[3]

Another error contributed to the creation of the misquotation. An inattentive or confused reader might misunderstand the above excerpt and assign the quotation to Chekhov instead of Odets.

The first instance of the misattribution to Chekhov that **QI** has found was printed in a 1981 compilation called *The Fitzhenry and Whiteside Book of Quotations*. No citation was specified for the quotation:[4]

> Any idiot can face a crisis—it's this day-to-day living that wears you out.
>
> —Anton Chekhov

This influential reference work has been released in many editions and revised several times. The same quote is present in the 1986 enlarged edition of *The Fitzhenry and Whiteside Book of Quotations* and in the renamed 1987 edition of the *Barnes and Noble Book of Quotations*.[5] These volumes act as powerful vectors for transmission of the statement coupled with the Chekhov ascription.

In 1985 the quote was used as an epigraph in a syndicated newspaper column covering the game of bridge called The Aces by Bobby Wolff.[6] In 1990 the syndicated columnist Molly Ivins employed the quotation and credited Chekhov in the pages of *Mother Jones* magazine.[7]

> "Wait until we see him face a real crisis," they say in D.C. But as Chekhov once observed, "Any idiot can face a crisis; it is this day-to-day living that wears you out."

In 1999 the *New York Times* published a short profile of an advertising executive who recited the quote during his interview:[8]

> Peter G. Krivkovich finds a small slip of paper on his desk—wedged somewhere between the advertising memorabilia and the Asian artifacts—with a few lines scribbled in red ink. The phrase, he says, comes from Chekhov, and it may be a kind of Dilbertian take on the pressures of everyday business life.
>
> "Any idiot can face a crisis," Mr. Krivkovich, 52, the president and chief executive at the Cramer-Krasselt advertising agency in Chicago, reads aloud. "It's the day-to-day living that can wear you out."

In conclusion, there is no substantive evidence that Chekhov wrote or said the quotation under examination. **QI** believes the error mechanism of textual proximity is to blame, as is simple paraphrasing, as **QI** believes happened with the line from *The Country Girl*.

Notes:

Great thanks to Michael Singer, whose email query on this topic caused **QI** to construct this question and perform this exploration. Many thanks to Frank Daniels, who told **QI** about the important partial match in the script of the movie *The Country Girl*. Daniels also listened to the LA Theatre Works production of the play and examined an online copy of the script of the play. In addition, thanks to Corey Robin, who examined this quotation in an essay at the *Chronicle of Higher Education* website.[9]

1. *The Country Girl* (1955, directed by George Seaton), 1:44. Accessed in Amazon's streaming service, https://www.amazon.com/Country-Girl-Bing-Crosby/dp/B005DNPGBC. Line is spoken at 1:37.

2. Peter Bauland and William Ingram, eds., *The Tradition of the Theatre* (Boston: Allyn and Bacon, 1971), 405. Verified in hard copy.

3. Clifford Odets, *The Country Girl: A Play in Three Acts* (New York: Viking, 1951). Verified in hard copy.

4. Robert I. Fitzhenry, ed., *The Fitzhenry and Whiteside Book of Quotations* (Toronto: Fitzhenry and Whiteside, 1981), 39. Thanks to the librarian at St. Augustine's Seminary in Toronto, Ontario, who visually verified this citation.

5. Robert I. Fitzhenry, ed., *Barnes and Noble Book of Quotations*, rev. and enl. (New York: Barnes and Noble, 1987), 54. Verified in hard copy.

6. Bobby Wolff, "The Aces," *Gettysburg Times* (Gettysburg, PA), July 15, 1985, 18. Accessed in NewspaperARCHIVE.com.

7. Molly Ivins, "Mimic Men," Impolitic, *Mother Jones*, February–March 1990, 57. Accessed in Google Books, https://goo.gl/aaOBot.

8. David Barboza, "Peter G. Krivkovich," *New York Times*, September 5, 1999. Accessed in ProQuest.

9. Corey Robin, "Who Really Said That?" The Chronicle Review, *Chronicle of Higher Education*, September 16, 2013, http://chronicle.com/article/Who-Really-Said-That-/141559.

4. "The cure for boredom is curiosity. There is no cure for curiosity."

—Dorothy Parker

The earliest instance of this quotation known to **QI** appeared in *Reader's Digest* in December 1980 in a column called Quotable Quotes, where the words were ascribed to a person named Ellen Parr:[1]

> The cure for boredom is curiosity. There is no cure for curiosity.
>
> —Ellen Parr

In March 1981 the *Centre Daily Times* of State College, Pennsylvania, attributed the words to Parr:[2]

> 'The cure for boredom is curiosity,' Ellen Parr wrote, adding: 'There is no cure for curiosity.'

In 1984 the saying continued to circulate, and a newspaper in Sitka, Alaska, used it as the solution to a cryptogram puzzle:[3]

> Answer for 2413, The cure for boredom is curiosity. There is no cure for curiosity. (Ellen Parr)

In March 1996 a collection of quotations was shared on a mailing list called "Humor List" in alphabetical order, based on the last name of the ascription. A quotation about checks attributed to Parker was immediately adjacent to the quotation about curiosity from Parr. The following excerpt shows six of the items. The precise format of the message is preserved below.[4]

#The right man, in the right place, at the right time – can steal millions. —Gregory Nunn
#The man who has not anything to boast of but his illustrious ancestors is like a potato – the only good belonging to him is under-ground. —Sir Thomas Overbury
#The two most beautiful words in the English language are: 'Cheque enclosed.' —Dorothy Parker
#The cure for boredom is curiosity. There is no cure for curiosity. —Ellen Parr
#Justice without force is powerless; force without justice is tyran-nical. —Blaise Pascal
#Never tell people 'how' to do things. Tell them 'what' to do and they will surprise you with their ingenuity. —General George S. Patton

An inattentive person scanning the list might link Parker to the contiguous curiosity quotation. Parker died in 1967, and there is no substantive evidence that she employed this saying. However, the quotation can be divided into two phrases, and the second phrase, "There is no cure for curiosity," has been in circulation for more than one hundred years. In 1915 an instance was printed in the *Boston Sunday Post* of Massachusetts.[5]

> There is no cure for curiosity. It must be outgrown or endured. A child is born with its mouth in position to utter the word "Why?" and when, at some later date, it is punished for asking too many questions, it thinks up enough additional questions during its pun-ishment to make the Encyclopaedia Britannica look sick.

The assignment of the quotation to Parker may have seemed plausible to some readers because she used the word "curiosity" in some of her better-known poems and quips. For example, her 1926 collection of verse titled *Enough Rope* included a poem called "Inventory," which featured the following two lines.[6]

> Four be the things I'd been better without:
> Love, curiosity, freckles, and doubt.

In 1966 a gossip columnist stated that when the topic of euthanasia for a cat was discussed, Parker quipped, "Have you tried curiosity?"[7] **QI** hypothesizes that an error of alphabetical ambiguity, together with the plausibility of Parker's authorship, led to this misattribution. By April 1997 the saying had been reassigned to Parker within a message posted to the hfx.general newsgroup of Usenet.[8]

In 2002 an article in a Syracuse, New York, newspaper about the graduating students of Lafayette High School included a remark by the salutatorian crediting the quotation to Parker.[9]

> My advice to my graduating class: "The cure for boredom is curiosity. There is no cure for curiosity." —Dorothy Parker. Forget regret and don't be afraid to take risks.

A newspaper in Evansville, Indiana, printed the saying in 2004 as a "Thought for the Day" while also ascribing it to Parker.[10]

In conclusion, based on current evidence this statement should be credited to Ellen Parr, although that answer has led **QI** to a much more mysterious question: Who is Ellen Parr?

Notes:

Great thanks to Mardy Grothe and Laura Mihaela, whose inquiries led **QI** to formulate this question and perform this exploration. Grothe is the author of several clever and entertaining quotation books such as *Oxymoronica* and *Never Let a Fool Kiss You or a Kiss Fool You.*

1. Quotable Quotes, Reader's Digest 117 (December 1980): 172. Verified in microfilm.
2. "Good Evening! Times Goes Under," Centre Daily Times (State College, PA), March 12, 1981, 1. Accessed in GenealogyBank.
3. Kryptograms from Katlian, Sitka Daily Sentinel (Sitka, AK), July 9, 1984, 2. Accessed in NewspaperARCHIVE.com.
4. "Digest for Monday, March 11, 1996," The Humor List, http://archive.thehumorlist.us/Site1/Digests/H9603110.php. Quote is in message dated March 12, 1996, by Piotr Plebaniak, with message subject "Quotes Part 37/88."

5. "Curiosity," Boston Sunday Post, August 1, 1915, 30. Accessed in NewspaperARCHIVE .com.

6. Dorothy Parker, "Inventory," Life 88 (November 11, 1926), 12. Accessed in ProQuest American Periodicals.

7. Leonard Lyons, "The Lyons Den," Reading Eagle, August 7, 1966, 14. Accessed at https:// news.google.com/newspapers?nid=1955&dat=19660807&id=lrEhAAAAIBAJ&sjid= HJwFAAAAIBAJ&pg=5295,2521338&hl=en.

8. Heather Breeze, "Point Pleasant Nature Walk, May 4," hfx.general Usenet newsgroup, April 30, 1997. Accessed in Google Groups, https://goo.gl/JW5DZ1.

9. "Lafayette Jr./Sr. High School," Post-Standard (Syracuse, NY), June 4, 2002, "Graduation 2002" special section, E5. Accessed in NewspaperARCHIVE.com.

10. Rebecca Coudret, "Getaway Saturday," Evansville Courier and Press (Evansville, IN), June 5, 2004, B9. Accessed in NewsBank.

5. "The mind is not a vessel that needs filling, but wood that needs igniting."

—Socrates X
—Plato
—**William Butler Yeats**

An educator asked **QI** to investigate a series of quotations with muddled attribution, which the educator had seen variously as:

Education is the kindling of a flame, not the filling of a vessel.

—Socrates

Education is not the filling of a pail, but the lighting of a fire.

—William Butler Yeats

Education is not the filling of a pail, but the lighting of a fire.

—Plutarch

The mind is not a vessel that needs filling, but wood that needs igniting.

—Plutarch

QI has located no substantive evidence that Socrates or William Butler Yeats produced one of these sayings. These two attributions apparently are incorrect.

This family of statements probably originated with a passage in the essay "On Listening" in *Moralia* by the Greek-born philosopher Plutarch who lived between AD 50 and 120.[1] The following excerpt was translated by Robin Waterfield for a 1992 Penguin Classics edition.[2]

> For the correct analogy for the mind is not a vessel that needs filling, but wood that needs igniting—no more—and then it motivates one towards originality and instills the desire for truth. Suppose someone were to go and ask his neighbours for fire and find a substantial blaze there, and just stay there continually warming himself: that is no different from someone who goes to someone else to get some of his rationality, and fails to realize that he ought to ignite his innate flame, his own intellect . . .

Here is an alternative translation of the first sentence published in the 1927 Loeb Classical Library edition.[3]

> For the mind does not require filling like a bottle, but rather, like wood, it only requires kindling to create in it an impulse to think independently and an ardent desire for the truth.

Here are additional selected citations in chronological order.

In 1892 the classical scholar Benjamin Jowett published an edition of *The Dialogues of Plato* that he had translated. In the introduction to "The Republic," Jowett wrote the following.[4]

> Education is represented by him, not as the filling of a vessel, but as the turning the eye of the soul towards the light.

This statement partially overlaps the quotation under investigation, and it is possible that the later misattribution to Socrates was facilitated by the existence of this sentence about Plato by Jowett.

In 1966 a version of the saying was credited to Socrates in the *Malaysian Journal of Education*. This excerpt placed the word "education" outside the quotation marks. Some later versions incorporate the word "education" directly into the quote.[5]

Socrates aptly described education as "the kindling of a flame, not the filling of a vessel." With this concept of education in mind, educators bear the responsibility of helping the student to lead a richer and fuller life and developing his mental and spiritual qualities to the utmost.

In 1968 a version of the saying was ascribed to Plutarch in the book *Vision and Image: A Way of Seeing* by James Johnson Sweeney. This instance placed "education" into the quote, and it used the word "pail" instead of "vessel." Interestingly, the Plutarch quotation was immediately adjacent to a quote credited to "W. B. Yeats," also known as William Butler Yeats. One important mechanism for generating misattributions is based on the misreading of neighboring quotations. A reader sometimes inadvertently transfers the ascription of one quote to a contiguous quote. Here is the relevant passage from *Vision and Image*.[6]

William Butler Yeats has expressed the heart of this viewpoint in his statement, "Culture does not consist in acquiring opinions but in getting rid of them" and Plutarch in "Education is not the filling of a pail, but the lighting of a fire."

In 1987 the *Barnes and Noble Book of Quotations* included an aphorism that exactly matched the instance above, but the words were credited to Yeats instead of Plutarch. This reassignment fits the pattern of misattribution just described:[7]

Education is not the filling of a pail, but the lighting of a fire.

—William Butler Yeats

The same statement and attribution was repeated by a North Carolina newspaper in 1997 with additional historical detail:[8]

. . . quoted outside uptown library as part of yearlong celebration of reading.

In conclusion, Plutarch is properly credited with the quotation given near the beginning of this section, in two separate translations. The saying ascribed to William Butler Yeats is stylish, but evidence suggests that the linkage was a mistake. The attribution to Socrates is also unsupported.

Notes:

Thanks to Stephen Fahey and to Andrew Old, whose tweet of inquiry on this topic gave impetus to **QI** to formulate this question and perform this exploration. Also, thanks to the volunteer editors of Wikiquote.

1. *Oxford Dictionary of Philosophy*, 2nd rev. ed., in Oxford Reference Online, s.v. "Plutarch," accessed March 28, 2013, http://www.oxfordreference.com/.

2. Plutarch, *Essays*, trans. Robin Waterfield (New York: Penguin Classics, 1992), 50. Accessed in Google Books, https://goo.gl/EMguaN.

3. "De Auditu by Plutarch as Published in Vol. 1 of the Loeb Classical Library Edition, 1927," Bill Thayer, accessed March 28, 2013, http://penelope.uchicago.edu/Thayer/E/Roman/Texts /Plutarch/Moralia/De_auditu*.html. Webpage note: "The work appears in pp. 201–259 of Vol. I of the Loeb Classical Library's edition of the *Moralia*, first published in 1927." **QI** has not verified this text in hard copy.

4. *The Dialogues of Plato Translated into English with Analyses and Introductions*, trans. Benjamin Jowett, vol. 3, 3rd ed. (London: Oxford University Press, 1892), cci. Accessed in HathiTrust, https://goo.gl/Mn3jNk. The first edition was printed in 1871 and the second edition in 1875. Thanks to Wikiquote editors of the "Socrates" entry for pointing out this citation.

5. Tan Soon Tze, "The Role of Music in Education," *Malaysian Journal of Education* 3, no. 1 (June 1966): 84. Verified in scans. Special thanks to a librarian at the University of Chicago Library.

6. James Johnson Sweeney, *Vision and Image: A Way of Seeing*, Credo Perspectives (New York: Simon and Schuster, 1968), 119. Verified in hard copy. Thanks to the Wikiquote editors of the "Socrates" entry for pointing out this citation.

7. Robert I. Fitzhenry, ed., *Barnes and Noble Book of Quotations*, rev. and enl. (New York: Barnes and Noble, 1987), 112. Verified in hard copy.

8. Quotable, *Charlotte Observer* (Charlotte, NC), July 10, 1997, 14A. Accessed in NewsBank.

6. "Today a reader, tomorrow a leader."

—Margaret Fuller

QI has been unable to find any substantive support for crediting Margaret Fuller with this motto. Fuller is the educator, however, that many websites, classroom resources, and posters have credited. The earliest evidence of the quotation appeared in 1926 in a journal called the *Library*, which published an intriguing report from the Newark Public Library in New Jersey. The head of the library had received a collection of forty-three slogans constructed by students, and the set included the statement under investigation. The creator of the slogan pertinent to the saying was a student named W. Fusselman. Here is an excerpt from the article:[1]

SLOGANS FOR A LIBRARY

Invented by Vocational School Boys

Max S. Henig, of the Essex County Vocational School for Boys, in Irvington, N.J., sends me a list of 43 "library slogans" and says "these slogans were written by the members of my classes at the West Orange Essex County Vocational School. They were originated and used as part of a campaign planned to arouse interest in the growth and use of a school library which some of the boys had created by generous donations of books."

The article noted that the books were lent for four days with a fee of one cent. The expressions were created as part of a classroom exercise, and the journal editors were impressed enough that they reprinted eight of them. Here are the first four together with the names of the students who crafted them:

Today a reader, tomorrow a leader. —W. Fusselman

A library is an education on a shelf. —H. Ohlandt
If you read to learn you're bound to earn. —M. Tremper
A good book read puts you ahead. —Howard Fraebel

Catchphrases using the two words "leaders" and "readers" existed before 1926. For example, in 1917 an advertisement for a bookseller in an Illinois newspaper used a compact expression of three words:[2]

ATTENTION SOLDIERS
LEADERS ARE READERS
MILITARY BOOKS
MOST COMPLETE LINE IN CITY

The slogan printed in the 1926 *Library* article was arguably distinct from "Leaders are readers," and the student ascription was not forgotten. In 1959 a compilation titled *New Treasury of Stories for Every Speaking and Writing Occasion* by Jacob Morton Braude included the following entry in the category "Reading":[3]

Today a reader, tomorrow a leader.

—W. Fusselman

In 1963 an advertisement for a reading program developed by Science Research Associates included the following:[4]

READERS ARE LEADERS . . . LEADERS ARE READERS

In 1987 *Scouting* magazine from the Boy Scouts of America printed another saying with "leader" and "reader":[5]

"If you're going to be a leader," he said, "you've got to be a reader."

In 2001 a newspaper in Ohio reported that the slogan being examined was printed on the side of a bookmobile without attribution:[6]

The driver's side of the van displays the project's motto: Today a reader, tomorrow a leader.

By 2005 the saying had been assigned to Fuller in an Illinois newspaper:[7]

Today a reader; tomorrow a leader.

—Margaret Fuller

Yet, the connection to the student of 1926 was not lost. In the same year, 2005, a Florida newspaper preserved the ascription:[8]

There is much truth to author W. Fusselman's quote: "Today a reader, tomorrow a leader."

In conclusion, based on current evidence, this slogan was probably created during a classroom exercise by a student named W. Fusselman. His teacher then sent the phrase to a journal focused on libraries, where it was printed in 1926 and began to achieve wider distribution.

A follow-up question received by **QI** wondered if there was an explanation for the curious shift of credit from W. Fusselman to Margaret Fuller. Here is one speculative hypothesis for this change. The names Fusselman and Fuller are close to one another in an alphabetical listing. In a small collection of quotations about education or libraries, the sayings from the two individuals might have been placed adjacent to one another. The name Margaret Fuller might have appeared above a quote by W. Fusselman, and an inattentive reader might have assumed that Fuller deserved credit.

Notes:

Thanks to Udo Helms, whose inquiry was used by **QI** to fashion this question.

1. "Slogans for a Library," *Library* 2, no. 4 (April 1926): 56. Verified in scans. Thanks to Dennis Lien and the University of Minnesota Libraries.

2. [Advertisement for H. D. McFarland Co.], *Rockford Morning Star* (Rockford, IL), October 12, 1917, 12. Accessed in GenealogyBank.

3. Jacob M. Braude, *The New Treasury of Stories for Every Speaking and Writing Occasion* (Englewood Cliffs, NJ: Prentice-Hall, 1959), 331. Accessed in https://books.google.com /books?id=n4NZAAAAMAAJ&dq=new+treasure+of+stories+for+every+speaking+and +writing+occasion&focus=searchwithinvolume&q=Fusselman.

4. [Advertisement for Boston Traveler], *Boston Herald* (Boston, MA), March 24, 1963, section IV, 11. Accessed in GenealogyBank.

5. Robert Hood, "Each One Teach One," *Scouting*, September 1987, 52. Accessed in Google Books, https://goo.gl/guInEx.

6. "Greene County Library Fires Up Bookmobile," *Dayton Daily News* (Dayton, OH), April 26, 2001, Z4-1. Accessed in NewsBank.

7. Roland Tolliver, "For Love of Community," *Journal-Standard* (Freeport, IL), March 5, 2005. Accessed in NewsBank.

8. Kathy Marsh, "If Books Are Like Gold, a Library Is Fort Knox," How I See It, *Florida Times-Union* (Jacksonville, FL), July 23, 2005, M14. Accessed in NewsBank.

7. "Time you enjoy wasting is not wasted time."

—Bertrand Russell
—T. S. Eliot
—John Lennon
—Søren Kierkegaard

In addition to John Lennon and Bertrand Russell, the saying above has been attributed to T. S. Eliot, Søren Kierkegaard, Laurence J. Peter, and others. The attribution to Russell was a mistake that was caused by the misreading of an entry in a quotation book compiled by Peter.

The first instance of the phrase located by **QI** was published in 1912, before both Peter and Lennon were born. The expression appeared in the book *Phrynette Married* by Marthe Troly-Curtin. This novel was part of a series by Troly-Curtin that began with *Phrynette* in 1911.[1] An advertisement in *Lippincott's Monthly Magazine* in July 1911 grandly proclaimed that *Phrynette* was "The Most Talked-About Book in London Today."[2]

In the following excerpt from *Phrynette Married*, a character is reproved for wasting the time and energy of others:[3]

> "Your father, for instance, don't you think he would have done three times as much work if it had not been for your—what shall I say—'bringing up'?"

> "He liked it—time you enjoy wasting is not wasted time."

> "Oh, but it was in his case—wasted for him and for many lovers of art."

In December 1912 the saying was printed together with a small set of unrelated aphorisms in a newspaper in Ashburton, New Zealand. The wording exactly matched the phrase in *Phrynette Married*, though no attribution was given. It's possible that the phrase may have been copied from that volume or, alternatively, that the statement may already have been in circulation.[4]

THOUGHTS FOR THE DAY.
Time you enjoy wasting is not wasted time.

In 1920 a close variant of the saying was syndicated in newspapers in Trenton, New Jersey;[5] San Antonio, Texas;[6] Seattle, Washington;[7] and Salt Lake City, Utah. In each case, the phrase appeared without attribution. The *Salt Lake Telegram* published the variant together with several other phrases that the editors deemed humorous. Here are three sample sayings:[8]

> When ignorance is bliss, 'tis folly to confess.
> Time you enjoy wasting isn't always wasted time.
> Man may have his will, but woman will have her way.

In 1924 a newspaper in Kingston, Jamaica, printed a column about love affairs, "a subject which never grows old," written by Rilette, who offered makeup tips and encouragement along with her love advice:[9]

> Be sure you enjoy yourself wherever you are, even if others consider
> you are wasting your time; remember that time you enjoy wasting
> is not wasted time! —Bye,'bye.
>   Your friend, "RILETTE"

In 1927 a theosophical magazine credited an individual named Meredith with employing a curious version of the maxim. This name might be a reference to the noted Victorian novelist and poet George Meredith, but **QI** has not found definitive evidence to disambiguate the moniker:[10]

> Which brings to mind Meredith's words: "Time enjoyed wasted,
> is not wasted time."

In his 1932 essay "In Praise of Idleness," Bertrand Russell said that work hours per week should be dramatically reduced. This essay does not contain the adage. The following excerpt is included simply to suggest why Russell was a plausible candidate for originating the term:[11]

> The war showed conclusively that, by the scientific organisation of production, it is possible to keep modern populations in fair comfort on a small part of the working capacity of the modern world. If, at the end of the war, the scientific organization, which had been created in order to liberate men for fighting and munition work, had been preserved, and the hours of work had been cut down to four, all would have been well. Instead of that the old chaos was restored, those whose work was demanded were made to work long hours, and the rest were left to starve as unemployed.

Being idle would give one plenty of time to "waste." But **QI** has located no direct evidence that Russell ever used the maxim in question. Indeed, the words were attributed to him primarily because of a mistake that involved Laurence J. Peter.

Peter is best known for his 1969 book *The Peter Principle* about management and hierarchies. Several sardonic phrases emerged from his treatise—for example, "In a hierarchy every employee tends to rise to his level of incompetence." But Peter also compiled the aforementioned collection *Peter's Quotations: Ideas for Our Time*. Unfortunately, the format of the book was prone to mislead his readers. Here is the confusing entry for a Bertrand Russell quotation:[12]

> The thing that I should wish to obtain from money would be leisure with security.
>
> —Bertrand Russell (The time you enjoy wasting is not wasted time.)

The parenthetical comment after the name Bertrand Russell was not written by Russell. It was added by Peter. This helps to explain why the saying under investigation is sometimes attributed to Russell and sometimes to Peter. The *Oxford Dictionary of Quotations* uncovered this problem and mentioned it in a valuable section about misquotations.[13]

By 2000 the adage was being credited to the famous musician John Lennon, who died in 1980. An ascription was printed in an astrology column in an Australian magazine:[14]

> As Libran John Lennon noted, "Time you enjoy wasting, was not wasted."

In conclusion, **QI** suggests crediting Marthe Troly-Curtin with this adage, provisionally. She is the author of the earliest currently known instance of the phrase. It is possible that someone used it before her, and future research may uncover earlier examples.

Notes:

1. Marthe Troly-Curtin, *Phrynette* (Philadelphia: J. B. Lippincott, 1911). Accessed in Google Books, http://goo.gl/Yin9ij.

2. [Advertisement for *Phrynette* by Marthe Troly-Curtin], Lippincott's Magazine Advertiser, *Lippincott's Magazine* 88, no. 1 (July–September 1911). Accessed in HathiTrust, https://goo.gl/zlgsCA.

3. Marthe Troly-Curtin, *Phyrnette Married* (London: Grant Richards, 1912), 256. Accessed in Google Books, https://goo.gl/VkBAC8. Verified in hard copy. Thanks to Eric at the Stanford University Information Center for verification of the text in hard copy.

4. Thought for the Day, *Ashburton Guardian* (Ashburton, New Zealand), December 18, 1912, 6. Accessed in Papers Past, http://goo.gl/ZuXmR5.

5. Daily Magazine Page for Everybody, Words of Wise Men, *Trenton Evening Times* (Trenton, NJ), October 27, 1920, 21. Accessed in NewspaperARCHIVE.com.

6. Words of Wise Men, *San Antonio Evening News* (San Antonio, TX), October 27, 1920, 4. Accessed in NewspaperARCHIVE.com.

7. [Filler item], *Seattle Times*, November 12, 1920, 11. Accessed in GenealogyBank.

8. Just Joking: This Week's Wisdom, *Salt Lake Telegram* (Salt Lake City, UT), June 29, 1920, 4. Accessed in GenealogyBank.

9. "Rilette Writes Again to Her Dear Friend Eve," *Daily Gleaner* (Kingston, Jamaica), February 26, 1924, 11. Accessed in NewspaperARCHIVE.com.

10. Emmett Small Jr., "On Looking Up Words in the Dictionary," an address delivered at the William Quan Judge Theosophical Club Meeting, May 27, 1927, in *Theosophical Path* 33,

no. 1 (July 1927). Text is based on a 2003 Kessinger reprint. Verified in a Google Books entry that is no longer viewable.

11. Bertrand Russell, *In Praise of Idleness and Other Essays* (London: Routledge Classics, 2004). Accessed in Google Books, https://goo.gl/tNuqr8.

12. Laurence J. Peter, *Peter's Quotations: Ideas for Our Time* (New York: William Morrow, 1977), 299. Verified in hard copy.

13. Elizabeth Knowles, ed., *Oxford Dictionary of Quotations* in Oxford Reference Online, s.v. "Misquotations," accessed May 2010.

14. Mystic Medusa, *Australian*, October 14, 2000, 62. Accessed in NewsBank.

8. "Somewhere, something incredible is waiting to be known."

—Carl Sagan

The above quotation has been attributed to the popular cosmologist Carl Sagan. However, **QI** has not found any substantive evidence that Sagan crafted this quotation. The erroneous ascription is based on a misreading of *Newsweek* magazine. On August 15, 1977, the magazine published a cover story with an extended profile of Sagan titled "Seeking Other Worlds." Four reporters participated in the creation of the report—David Gelman with Sharon Begley in New York, Dewey Gram in Los Angeles, and Evert Clark in Washington, DC.

The article begins by noting that Sagan in his youth had been entranced by the adventure tales of Edgar Rice Burroughs. The stories were set on a fantastical version of the planet Mars called Barsoom, which featured canals and fifteen-foot-tall green warriors with four arms.

The end of the profile discusses the topic of hypothetical life-forms on other planets. Sagan was in favor of funding a serious search for extraterrestrial life by scanning the skies for electromagnetic signals. He contended that obtaining positive or negative results would be interesting and valuable. The ellipses in the following passage are present in the original printed text:[1]

> "A serious search with negative results says something of profound importance," Sagan argues. "We discover there's something almost forbidden about life . . . if it turns out we really are alone." But clearly, Sagan is looking for a happier result. There may be no galumphing green Barsoomian giants to satisfy the fantasies of a romantic Brooklyn boy. But no doubt, there are even stranger discoveries to be made . . . some totally new phenomenon perhaps . . . Somewhere, something incredible is waiting to be known.

The final sentence was not placed between quotation marks. If Sagan had spoken the final compelling phrase, it would have been placed within such marks. Instead, the final statements were written using a reportorial voice.

On January 13, 2015, **QI** was contacted by Sharon Begley, who worked on the team that created the *Newsweek* article. Begley is now the senior health and science correspondent at Reuters. She stated that the words in the final sentence of the article were her words and not Sagan's. She also told **QI** about a stylistic guideline that was adhered to at the time by the writers at the magazine:[2]

> A nearly ironclad rule at *Newsweek* back then was that it was lazy and unacceptable to end a story with a quote. Writers/reporters were paid to come up with an original, thought-provoking kicker, and that's what we did, or tried to. The words were not Sagan's.

In 1982 a newspaper columnist in Illinois published a diverse group of quotes. He included the one above, which he credited to Sagan without a citation:[3]

> SOMEWHERE, SOMETHING incredible is waiting to be known.
>
> —Carl Sagan

In 1988 a syndicated newspaper feature by the Associated Press called "Today in History" repeated the quotation and credited Sagan without a citation.[4] In October 2009, at a ceremony awarding the National Medal of Science and the National Medal of Technology and Innovation, President Barack Obama delivered a speech that included the saying:[5]

> Carl Sagan, who helped broaden the reach of science to millions of people, once described his enthusiasm for discovery in very simple terms. He said, "Somewhere, something incredible is waiting to be known." (Laughter.) Thank you all for the incredible discoveries that you have made, the progress you've invented, and the benefits you've bestowed on the American people and the world.

The expression remains popular, and in February 2014 it was included in an opinion piece in the *Charleston Gazette* of West Virginia:[6]

> "Somewhere, something incredible is waiting to be known." This quote by Carl Sagan reminds us that what we don't know about the universe exceeds that which we do know.

In conclusion, based on current evidence, Sagan did not create this quotation. Instead, the reporter Sharon Begley constructed the phrase. The quotation has been ascribed to Sagan because the passage at the end of the 1977 *Newsweek* profile article has been misinterpreted.

Notes:

1. David Gelman, Sharon Begley, Dewey Gram, and Evert Clark, "Seeking Other Worlds," *Newsweek*, August 15, 1977, 53. Verified in microfilm.

2. Sharon Begley (writer of 1977 *Newsweek* profile of Carl Sagan), email communication with the author, January 13, 2015.

3. Pat Cunningham, "Thinking Only Leads to Confusion," *Rockford Register Star* (Rockford, IL), March 4, 1982, A8. Accessed in GenealogyBank.

4. Associated Press, Today in History, *Mobile Register* (Mobile, AL), July 29, 1988, 9D. Accessed in GenealogyBank.

5. "President Barack Obama Delivers Remarks at a Ceremony Awarding the National Medal of Science and the National Medal of Technology and Innovation, as Released by the White House" *Congressional Quarterly Transcriptions*, October 7, 2009. Accessed in NewsBank.

6. Jim Borg, "Celebrating Twenty Years of Exploring the Universe," *Honolulu Star-Advertiser*, March 13, 2013. Accessed at http://www.staradvertiser.com/2013/03/13/hawaii-news/celebrating-20-years-of-exploring-the-universe/.

REAL-WORLD PROXIMITY

9. **"There are things known, and things unknown, and in between are the doors."**

> —**William Blake**
> —**Aldous Huxley**
> —**Jim Morrison**

Among the "over 1.5 million" quotes to "inspire, motivate, and make you successful" in the online database QuoteAddicts is this profound piece of wisdom attributed to lead singer Jim Morrison of the famous rock band The Doors.

William Blake's circa 1790 work *The Marriage of Heaven and Hell* contained a quote that famously spoke of perception and metaphorical doorways:

> If the doors of perception were cleansed, every thing would appear
> to man as it is: infinite.

Aldous Huxley wrote a 1954 book called *The Doors of Perception*, which discussed his experiences with psychoactive agents. The title was an allusion to Blake's work. The music played by The Doors is often described as psychedelic rock, and the genesis of the band name has been linked to these two authors. However, **QI** has not located the quotation under examination in the texts of either Blake or Huxley.

In 1967 *Newsweek* published an article about The Doors titled "This Way to the Egress." The magazine noted that the group's debut album had risen to the top of the charts. The piece quoted cofounder Ray Manzarek discussing the name of the band.[1]

"There are things you know about," says 25-year-old Manzarek, whose specialty is playing the organ with one hand and the bass piano with the other, "and things you don't, the known and the unknown, and in between are the doors—that's us. We're saying that you're not only spirit, you're also this very sensuous being. That's not evil, that's a really beautiful thing. Hell appears so much more fascinating and bizarre than heaven. You have to 'break on through to the other side' to become the whole being."

In 1990 an advertisement for a movie about the well-known band, titled simply *The Doors*, displayed an instance of the saying attributed to Morrison:[2]

There are things known and things unknown and in between are the DOORS . . .

—Jim Morrison

Melissa Ursula Dawn Goldsmith wrote a 2007 MA thesis at Louisiana State University titled "Criticism *Lighting His Fire*: Perspectives on Jim Morrison from the *Los Angeles Free Press*, *Down Beat*, and the *Miami Herald*." Goldsmith stated that "Manzarek suggested the link between the name of the band and its purpose and function to *Newsweek*."[3] These words were followed by the Manzarek quotation and a footnote pointing to the *Newsweek* article. This valuable information was used by **QI** to locate and verify the quote on microfilm.

In 2010, however, the quotation website ThinkExist duplicated the movie advertisement's error and credited Jim Morrison with the saying.[4] This same quotation and ascription can be found on websites such as Lifehack, BrainyQuote, AZQuotes, and Goodreads:

There are things known and things unknown and in between are the doors.

In conclusion, **QI** believes that the quotation from 1967 should be attributed to Ray Manzarek.

Notes:

Thanks to Fred R. Shapiro for inspiring this question, and thanks to Gregory McNamee for pointing to the Blake quote.

1. "This Way to the Egress," *Newsweek*, November 6, 1967, 101. Verified in microfilm.
2. [Advertisement for the movie *The Doors*], *Indiana Gazette* (Indiana, PA), June 29, 1990, 10. Accessed in Newspapers.com.
3. Melissa Ursula Dawn Goldsmith, "Criticism *Lighting His Fire*: Perspectives on Jim Morrison from the *Los Angeles Free Press*, *Down Beat*, and the *Miami Herald*" (master's thesis, Louisiana State University, 2007), 1, http://goo.gl/Mx6vhS.
4. "There Are Things Known and Things Unknown and In Between Are the Doors," Jim Morrison quotes, ThinkExist, accessed November 17, 2010, http://thinkexist.com /quotation/there_are_things_known_and_things_unknown_and_in/340186.html.

10. "Do good anyway" and the Paradoxical Commandments.

—Mother Teresa

In 1968 Kent M. Keith published *The Silent Revolution: Dynamic Leadership in the Student Council*. Here are the original expressions given in the pamphlet:[1]

I. People are illogical, unreasonable, and self-centered. Love them anyway.

II. If you do good, people will accuse you of selfish ulterior motives. Do good anyway.

III. If you are successful, you win false friends and true enemies. Succeed anyway.

IV. The good you do today will be forgotten tomorrow. Do good anyway.

V. Honesty and frankness make you vulnerable. Be honest and frank anyway.

VI. The biggest men with the biggest ideas can be shot down by the smallest men with the smallest minds. Think big anyway.

VII. People favor underdogs, but follow only top dogs. Fight for a few underdogs anyway.

VIII. What you spend years building may be destroyed overnight. Build anyway.

IX. People really need help but may attack you if you do help them. Help people anyway.

X. Give the world the best you have and you'll get kicked in the teeth. Give the world the best you have anyway.

In 1972 a revised edition of the pamphlet was published, and it included a collection of commandments that was identical to the original. Keith was listed as the author, and all ten statements were reprinted.[2] Note that Keith has a website that includes a page listing the expressions above, which he calls the "Paradoxical Commandments of Leadership."[3] Keith discusses the origin of the commandments, and his claims are consistent with the documentary evidence that **QI** has located.

These statements evolved during decades of transmission, and multiple variants have been published in newspapers, books, and magazines. For example, in the first commandment, the ordering of the initial three terms varies: "unreasonable, illogical, and self-centered" versus "illogical, unreasonable, and self-centered." Also, the final phrase varies: "Forgive them anyway" versus "Love them anyway."

In the second commandment, the word "kind" is sometimes used instead of "good." The first phrase begins: "If you are kind" or "If you do good." The final phrase begins "Be kind anyway" or "Do good anyway." Occasionally, entire statements have been deleted. But Keith's "Paradoxical Commandments" function as the foundational text, and other sets have been directly or indirectly derived from them.

In December 1972 the commandments, in slightly modified form, were given a new attribution in a syndicated newspaper article. The following excerpt shows the introduction and the first commandment:[4]

Dempsey Byrd has put together ten rules which you can make your own to your eternal profit. We'll tell you who Dempsey Byrd is after you read his rules. They are:

1. People are illogical, unreasonable, and self-centered. Love and trust them anyway . . .

The first statement above ends with the phrase "Love and trust them anyway." Keith's original expression ended with "Love them anyway." The newspaper article listed ten statements in total that were nearly identical to Keith's expressions. It identified Dempsey Byrd as the editor of *Hearsight*, a publication of the Alabama Institute for the Deaf and Blind.

In 1981 the sayings were misattributed again in a profile of a wrestling coach named Howard Ferguson that was published in the *Cleveland Plain Dealer* of Ohio. A sidebar article printed the ten statements with the following introduction:[5]

> These are St. Edward wrestling coach Howard Ferguson's "Paradoxical Commandments of Leadership."

In 1983 the commandments appeared in the widely distributed advice column of Ann Landers with another incorrect ascription. A reader in Ontario sent Landers a collection containing eight of the statements under the title "Thoughts to Ponder" along with the following prefatory comment:[6]

> Occasionally, you print an inspiring poem or an essay by another author. Will you consider this contribution from the Canadian Hemophilia Society? It was written by E. T. Gurney, the executive director.

So the commandments have been incorrectly ascribed to Dempsey Byrd, Howard Ferguson, and E. T. Gurney.

This sequence of reattributions is certainly odd. It's possible that the commandments circulated widely without an attribution, and, when they were reprinted, they were sometimes ascribed to the person who reprinted them because their origin was opaque.

However, the frequent ascription to Mother Teresa stems from the misreading of a 1995 book about the "Blessed Teresa of Calcutta" called *A Simple Path* that was compiled by Lucinda Vardey. The page preceding the appendices was titled "Anyway," and it presented versions of eight of the ten statements under investigation. Statements VI and VII were omitted. A note at the bottom of the page said:[7]

From a sign on the wall of Shishu Bhavan, the children's home in Calcutta.

So the words were not directly attributed to Mother Teresa. Instead, a person at a children's home operated by her charity organization hung a poster with the sayings, and their origin was misconstrued. All the homes operated by the charity organization were linked to Mother Teresa, and all the sayings on the walls were linked to the charity organization. This provided a short route for misunderstanding and for the creation of the misquotation. In addition, there was another avenue for error. The primary subject of *A Simple Path* was Mother Teresa. Thus, all the sayings in the book without clear ascription were linked to her. A reader skimming the book might have reassigned the "Paradoxical Commandments" directly to her.

Following the publication of *A Simple Path,* the words were indeed often reassigned to Mother Teresa herself. For example, in October 1997 a letter in an Illinois newspaper discussed the recent resignation of a fire chief. When the chief stepped down, "he read an inscription that he attributed to Mother Teresa."[8]

By December 1999 a modified version of the sayings under the title "Do It Anyway" was also attributed to Mother Teresa. This version had eight statements and a coda. Here is an excerpt from a Texas newspaper showing the modified eighth statement and the coda:[9]

Give the world the best you have, and it may never be enough; give the world the best you've got anyway.

You see, in the final analysis, it is between you and God; it was never between you and them anyway.

In 2002 a *New York Times* article told the tale of Keith and his crowd-pleasing collection of aphorisms. The article explained that the words had been improperly ascribed to Mother Teresa for several years. Yet, Keith eventually triumphed with a lucrative book deal.[10]

Notes:

Thanks to Gene Torisky, whose email query inspired this question and answer.

1.   Kent M. Keith, *The Silent Revolution: Dynamic Leadership in the Student Council*, 4th ed. (Cambridge, MA: Harvard Student Agencies, 1968), 11. Verified in scans. Many thanks to the librarians of the Olin C. Bailey Library at Hendrix College.

2.   Kent M. Keith, *The Silent Revolution in the Seventies: Dynamic Leadership in the Student Council*, rev. ed. (Washington, DC: National Association of Secondary School Principals, 1972), 8 (also stamped 18). Verified in hard copy.

3.   Kent M. Keith, "The Origin of The Paradoxical Commandments," Anyway: The Paradoxical Commandments, accessed August 16, 2016.

4.   Globe Syndicate, The Way It Is with People, *Robesonian* (Lumberton, NC), December 3, 1972, 4A. Accessed in Google News Archive, https://goo.gl/qVyZJ6.

5.   "Wrestling Is a Way of Life," sidebar "Howard Ferguson's Ten Commandments," *Cleveland Plain Dealer* (Cleveland, OH), March 9, 1981, 8C. Accessed in GenealogyBank.

6.   Ann Landers, "Do It Anyway," *Telegraph-Herald* (Dubuque, IA), May 13, 1983, 6. Accessed in Google News Archive, https://goo.gl/SyJcoD.

7.   Mother Teresa with Lucinda Vardey, *A Simple Path*, (New York: Ballantine, 1995), 185. Verified in hard copy.

8.   Lisa Hopper, letter to the editor, *State Journal-Register* (Springfield, IL), October 8, 1997, 6. Accessed in NewsBank.

9.   John Laird, "Some Lessons Were Just Meant to Be," *El Paso Times* (El Paso, TX), December 26, 1999, 12A. Accessed in NewsBank. Two semicolons were added to the excerpted text.

10. David D. Kirkpatrick, "Good Things for Maxim Writer Who Waited," *New York Times*, March 8, 2002, A1. Accessed in ProQuest.

11. "What lies behind us and what lies before us are tiny matters compared to what lies within us."

—Ralph Waldo Emerson
—Henry David Thoreau

This popular motivational saying has been ascribed to a diverse collection of individuals. Quotation research expert Ralph Keyes wrote in *The Quote Verifier*:[1]

> This quotation is especially beloved by coaches, valedictorians, eulogists, and Oprah Winfrey. It usually gets attributed to Ralph Waldo Emerson. No evidence can be found that Emerson said or wrote these words.

The earliest appearance of this adage located by **QI** is in a 1940 book titled *Meditations in Wall Street* with an introduction by economics writer Albert Jay Nock. The word "before" is used instead of "ahead" in this initial saying:[2]

> What lies behind us and what lies before us are tiny matters compared to what lies within us.

When the book was originally released, the name of the author was kept a mystery, although he was described as a Wall Street financier. However, that did not prevent eager quotation propagators from fabricating attributions. The maxim has been assigned to the introduction writer Nock, the head of the publishing house William Morrow, and even Ralph Waldo Emerson and Henry David Thoreau.

In 1947 the *New York Times* revealed the author's identity—Henry S. Haskins, a man with a colorful and controversial background as a securities trader. **QI** believes that Haskins originated this popular saying which has in modern times been reassigned to more famous individuals.

Earlier, in 1910, the *New York Times* reported in a front-page story that a disciplinary action was taken against the Wall Street trader Henry Stanley Haskins. The firm Lathrop, Haskins, and Company had failed, and a committee report blamed "reckless and unbusinesslike dealing" on the part of Haskins. Understandably, Haskins disagreed and stated that he was being unjustly treated. His defenders claimed that he was a scapegoat:[3]

> The Governing Committee of the Stock Exchange, at a special meeting yesterday, took action which practically amounts to the expulsion from the Exchange of Henry Stanley Haskins, the floor member of Lathrop, Haskins Co., leaders in the Hocking pool, which collapsed on Jan. 19.

In 1940, as earlier mentioned, the book containing the adage under investigation was published, and a short review in the financial magazine *Barron's* commented about its unknown author and its compelling aphoristic content:[4]

> One of the most popular guessing games current in downtown New York is finding an answer to the question, "Who wrote 'Meditations in Wall Street'?" So far there's no authoritative answer, but this little book deserves reading in any case. It is not just about the Street—in fact, very little of it is devoted to affairs of finance. It is the philosophy of a successful business man and financier—or so it's stated in the extremely laudatory preface by Mr. Nock—expressed in aphorisms.

Later, in March 1940, a reviewer on the opposite coast of the United States, in Los Angeles, also commented about the mysterious author:[5]

> Titled "Meditations in Wall Street," this book just published by William Morrow & Co., New York, and reputedly written by an important financier of old New England stock, presents the anomaly of being written in Wall Street by a Wall Street man with nothing in it that deals with Wall Street.

No market theories or advice on how to get rich but only pungent and philosophical aphorisms on various phases of life are served the reader.

Later still in March 1940, the book received a very positive notice in the *New York Times*. The reviewer clearly thought the maxim was original and interesting because he or she reprinted it and remarked on it:[6]

It is a book of meditations on life and humanity and the individual, and if they are terse and pithy they are also farseeing and wise. The author's name is not known to the publishers; Albert Jay Nock has "heard him spoken of vaguely as 'a Wall-Streeter,'" but the precise nature of his occupation even he does not know . . .

With all the philosopher's play of wit and diversity he never weakens his major emphasis: "What lies behind us and what lies before us are tiny matters compared to what lies within us." Or, as quoted by Mr. Nock in the foreword, "It is the brain which does the thinking, not the thought; it is the soul which moves us forward, not ourself."

In May 1940 the *Los Angeles Times* incorrectly speculated about the author of *Meditations in Wall Street*. In a caption beneath a caricature of Albert J. Nock, the paper presented a guess about authorship:[7]

ALBERT JAY NOCK—Is believed to be the author of "Meditations in Wall Street"

The eagerness to learn the identity of the author enhanced the likelihood of an error based on real-world proximity. Nock wrote the introduction, and he was acquainted with the author. Some people who wished to unmask the author were willing to shift the ascription from anonymous to Nock due to this connection. Another misattribution was also based on proximity—the publisher of the work was the company William Morrow; hence, Morrow's name was also tightly coupled to the book. As shown in a citation further below, the adage has been incorrectly ascribed to Morrow.

By 1947 the *New York Times* had identified the author of the book. Thus when the newspaper reprinted an aphorism from the volume, it attributed the words to Haskins:[8]

> Glory lies in the estimation of lookers-on. When lookers-on perish as countless generations have done, glory perishes, as countless glories have done.
>
> —Henry S. Haskins in "Meditations in Wall Street."
> (William Morrow & Co.)

In 1950 the *Chicago Tribune* concurred with the *New York Times* and attributed adages in the book to Haskins:[9]

> "With some whose nerves have a deep covering of fat, happiness is less of a problem than it is an accident of anatomy."
>
> —Henry S. Haskins: *Meditations in Wall Street*

However, in February 1974 *Forbes* magazine erroneously credited the adage to William Morrow, the founder of the company that had published *Meditations in Wall Street*. The saying appeared on a quotation-filled page titled "Thoughts on the Business of Life" that has appeared in every issue of *Forbes* for decades.[10]

In 1980 the president of California State Polytechnic University, Pomona, attributed the saying to Ralph Waldo Emerson:[11]

> Cal Poly president Hugh La Bounty said at the awards banquet that some lines from Ralph Waldo Emerson best summed up the Scolinos philosophy and the team performance that exemplified it:
>
> > "What lies behind us and what lies before us are tiny matters compared to what lies within us."

In 1989 the bestseller *The Seven Habits of Highly Effective People* by Stephen Covey included the quotation and attributed it to Oliver Wendell Holmes.

Covey did not specify whether Holmes junior or senior was supposed to be responsible for the maxim.[12]

By the 1990s a modified and extended version of the saying was being attributed to Thoreau in a book offering spiritual guidance and numerology:[13]

> What lies before us and what lies behind us are small matters compared to what lies within us. And when we bring what is within out into the world, miracles happen.
>
> —Henry David Thoreau

The Walden Woods Project lists this adage on a webpage dedicated to misquotations of Thoreau. The webpage points to Henry Stanley Haskins and the book *Meditations in Wall Street* as the correct provenance for the saying.[14]

In 2001 the celebrity psychologist Phillip C. McGraw used a version of the saying in one of his very popular books. The wording was somewhat different, and the maxim was credited to Emerson:[15]

> As Emerson once wrote, "What lies behind us and what lies in front of us pales in comparison to what lies within us."

In conclusion, **QI** believes that this quotation was crafted by Henry Stanley Haskins, a Wall Street trader with a checkered background. The phrase was misattributed because the true author's name was initially withheld. In addition, the assignment of the maxim to a more prestigious individual—for example, Emerson or Thoreau—made it more attractive and more believable as a nugget of wisdom.

Notes:

Thanks to the members of the Project Wombat group, who inquired about this saying and discussed its provenance.

1. Ralph Keyes, *The Quote Verifier: Who Said What, Where, and When* (New York: St. Martin's, 2006), 253–54. Verified in hard copy.

2. [Henry Stanley Haskins], *Meditations in Wall Street* (New York: William Morrow, 1940), 131. Accessed in HathiTrust, https://goo.gl/YWhCVR.

3. "Stock Exchange Shuts Haskins Out," *New York Times*, February 17, 1910, 1. Accessed in ProQuest.

4. Business Book of the Week, *Barron's* 20, no. 12 (March 18, 1940): 2. Accessed in ProQuest.

5. Wesley Smith, "The March of Finance," *Los Angeles Times*, March 23, 1940, A9. Accessed in ProQuest.

6. "A Salty Philosophy," Miscellaneous Brief Reviews, *New York Times*, March 31, 1940, 96. Accessed in ProQuest.

7. [Caricature image and caption of Albert J. Nock], *Los Angeles Times*, May 5, 1940, C7. Accessed in ProQuest.

8. Treasure Chest: "Glory," *New York Times*, May 11, 1947, BR2. Accessed in ProQuest.

9. A Little Anthology, *Chicago Daily Tribune*, October 22, 1950, 13. Accessed in ProQuest.

10. Thoughts on the Business of Life, *Forbes*, February 15, 1974, 90. Verified in microfilm.

11. David LePage, "NCCA Champions: 5 Broncos Taken in Baseball Draft," *Los Angeles Times*, June 15, 1980, SG1. Accessed in ProQuest.

12. Stephen R. Covey, *The Seven Habits of Highly Effective People* (New York: Fireside, 1990), 96. Verified in Amazon's "Look Inside" feature, https://goo.gl/IJk1D3.

13. Dan Millman, *The Life You Were Born to Live: A Guide to Finding Your Life Purpose*, new millennium ed. (Tiburon, CA: H. J. Kramer, 2000), xi.

14. "The Henry D. Thoreau Mis-Quotation Page," The Walden Woods Project, https://www.walden.org/Library/Quotations/The_Henry_D._Thoreau_Mis-Quotation_Page, accessed January 10, 2011.

15. Phillip C. McGraw, *Relationship Rescue: A Seven-Step Strategy for Reconnecting with Your Partner*, repr. (New York: Hyperion, 2001), 4. Accessed in Google Books, https://goo.gl/oaz8i9.

SIMILAR NAMES

12. "Sometimes, I'm terrified of my heart, of its constant hunger for whatever it is it wants."

—Edgar Allan Poe

In March 2015 **QI** was contacted by a songwriter and musician named Poe. She had released an album called *Haunted* in 2000, and she had spoken the words above on its fifth track:[1]

> Sometimes, I'm terrified of my heart, of its constant hunger for whatever it is it wants; the way it stops and starts.

The songwriter Poe assured me that the words above had been composed by her alone; however, a quick Internet search proved that many people indeed held the mistaken belief that the line was written by none other than Edgar Allan Poe, the great literary master of horror. **QI** could see how someone might make that mistake.

In one of Edgar Allan Poe's most famous short stories, "The Tell-Tale Heart," the unhinged narrator is terrified by the sound of a beating heart that grows louder and louder. But the heart is not his own. Indeed, the aural hallucination precipitates the narrator's breakdown and criminal confession. Imperfect memories of this story may have caused some individuals to link the quotation to Edgar Allan Poe, but the sentences are not present in the text.[2]

In 2010 a member of the Goodreads community posted the quotation and ascribed the words to Edgar Allan Poe. The popular expression had gathered

1,762 likes by March 2015. That number has continued to grow, but the attribution has since been changed to the songwriter Poe.[3]

Skepticism about the linkage to the celebrated macabre short story writer was expressed in a post at a blog called *The World of Edgar Allan Poe* in September 2012. The blog owner, Undine, presented the saying together with its common spurious ascription and then stated the following:[4]

> Wrong Poe, kids. This line is from a song by the living singer-songwriter Poe, ("Terrified Heart") rather than the not-so-living author.

In September 2014 the website of the Edgar Allan Poe Museum of Richmond, Virginia, posted an article titled "Did Poe Really Say That?" The article mentioned the quotation, followed by this corrective commentary:[5]

> This came from a song written by the singer Poe. Con-fusing, yes; however, they are two distinctly different people.

In conclusion, **QI** believes that the passage should be ascribed to the musical artist Poe and not Edgar Allan Poe.

Notes:

Great thanks to the gifted musical artist Poe who notified **QI** about the widespread misattribution. Her message led to the formulation of this question and the initiation of this exploration.

1.   "Terrified Heart Poe," YouTube video, 0:28, posted by "Amanda Johnson," March 12, 2012, https://www.youtube.com/watch?v=512E1JiSr_A. Note that there is a delay before the final word of the lyric is spoken. According to AllMusic.com, "Terrified Heart" appears on Poe's 2000 album *Haunted* (SSR/FEI/Sheridan Square). See http://www.allmusic.com/song/terrified-heart-mt0006351043.

2. Edgar Allan Poe, "The Tell-Tale Heart," *Pioneer*, January 1843. Scans of the magazines were accessed at the Poe Museum website, https://www.poemuseum.org/collection-details .php?id=196. The full text of the story may also be found on the Poe Museum website, https://www.poemuseum.org/works-telltale.php.

3. "Poe > Quotes > Quotable Quote," Goodreads, accessed August 29, 2016, https:// www.goodreads.com/author/show/11072248.

4. Undine, "The Power of (Misusing) Words," *The World of Edgar Allan Poe* (blog), September 18, 2012, http://worldofpoe.blogspot.com/2012/09/the-power-of-misusing -words.html.

5. Kelly, "Did Poe Really Say That?" Edgar Allan Poe Museum, September 10, 2014, https:// www.poemuseum.org/blog/did-poe-really-say-that/.

13. "The more sand has escaped from the hourglass of our life, the clearer we should see through it."

—Niccolò Machiavelli X
—Jean-Paul Sartre

The earliest evidence of this saying located by **QI** appears in a 1795 German novel titled *Hesperus oder 45 Hundsposttage, Eine Biographie* by Johann Paul Friedrich Richter, who used the pen name Jean Paul. *The Oxford Companion to German Literature* describes the work as follows:[1]

> The eccentric sub-title refers to the chapters, which are designated Hundsposttage, and are supposed to have been brought to the author's friend by a Pomeranian dog. Written in Jean Paul's characteristic whimsical style, the book has a complex and absurd plot.

The quotation about a figurative hourglass referred to a single individual named Emanuel in the novel. The statement was later generalized to encompass all people. Here is the relevant passage in German, followed by one possible English translation:[2]

> Emanuel sah ruhig wie eine ewige Sonne, auf den Herbst seines Körpers herab; ja je mehr Sand aus seiner Lebens-Sanduhr herausgefallen war, desto heller sah er durch das leere Glas hindurch.

> Emanuel looked peacefully as an eternal sundown upon the autumn of his body; indeed the more sand had fallen out of his life-hourglass, the clearer he saw through the empty glass.

In 1837 a weekly journal called the *New-York Mirror* printed an article titled "Original Translations: Scraps from Jean Paul," which included a version of the quotation together with other adages from Richter. Here are three examples:[3]

> Our sorrows are like thunder clouds, which seem black in the distance, but grow lighter as they approach.

> The more sand has escaped from the hour-glass of our life, the clearer we should see through it.

> The moon is a light-house on the shore of the other world.

In 1884 the statement continued to circulate and was published in a collection called *Treasury of Thought: Forming an Encyclopedia of Quotations from Ancient and Modern Authors.* The words were credited to Johann Paul Friedrich Richter:[4]

> PERCEPTION.
> The more sand has escaped from the hourglass of our life, the clearer we should see through it.
>
> —Richter

In 1968 *Forbes* magazine included the expression attributed to the pen name Jean Paul in the collection *The Forbes Scrapbook of Thoughts on the Business of Life*:[5]

> The more sand has escaped from the hourglass of our life, the clearer we should see through it.
>
> —Jean Paul

In 1993 the saying was printed in *Phillips' Book of Great Thoughts and Funny Sayings*; however, the words were not ascribed to Richter. Instead, the famous existentialist philosopher Jean-Paul Sartre was named, and **QI** hypothesizes that this misattribution was caused by confusion with the pseudonym "Jean Paul."[6]

> The more sand has escaped from the hourglass of our life, the clearer we should see through it.
>
> —Jean Paul Sartre

In 2011 Don MacDonald, an artist residing in Boston, discussed the quotation and noted that it was often attributed to Niccolò Machiavelli; however, MacDonald had uncovered evidence in an 1893 citation that the proper credit should go to Richter. MacDonald stated the following:[7]

> The quote seems to be from the German Romantic writer Johann Paul Friedrich Richter, better known by his nom de plume Jean Paul. Rev. James Woods attributes the saying to Jean Paul in his *Dictionary of Quotations: from Ancient and Modern, English and Foreign Sources* of 1893, although lacking a source for the quote.

In conclusion, Johann Paul Friedrich Richter deserves credit for providing the seed of this quotation applied to an individual in 1795. His words were altered to yield a general maxim and appeared in English by 1837. Richter's pen name of Jean Paul probably catalyzed the incorrect reassignment to Jean-Paul Sartre. There is no substantive support for the curious ascription to Niccolò Machiavelli.

Notes:

Many thanks to Nina Gilbert, who requested a trace of this quotation when a student expressed a desire to use it in a yearbook. Special thanks to Don MacDonald for his valuable work tracing this quotation, and thanks to S. M. Colowick for locating MacDonald's blog post. Great thanks to W. Brewer and Kat Petersen for providing **QI** with suggestions for the translation of the 1795 passage from German to English.

1. *Oxford Companion to German Literature*, 3rd ed., s.v. "Hesperus oder 45 Hundsposttage, Eine Biographie," 374–75. Verified in hard copy.

2. Jean Paul [Johann Paul Friedrich Richter], *Hesperus; oder, 45 Hundsposttage: Eine Biographie* (Berlin: Drud und Berlag von G. Reimer, 1847), 294. Accessed in Google Books, http://bit.ly/2dhJyu3.

3. "Scraps from Jean Paul," *New-York Mirror* 14, no. 46 (May 13, 1837): 362. Accessed in Google Books, https://goo.gl/wVNob9. Please note that the metadata supplied for this match by Google Books is inaccurate; the data in this citation is based on the page images.

4. Maturin Murray Ballou, *Treasury of Thought: Forming an Encyclopedia of Quotations from Ancient and Modern Authors* (Boston: Houghton, Mifflin, 1884), 387. Accessed in Google Books, https://goo.gl/coKT9k.

5. *The Forbes Scrapbook of Thoughts on the Business of Life* (New York: Forbes, 1968), 214. Verified in hard copy.

6. Bob Phillips, *Phillips' Book of Great Thoughts and Funny Sayings* (Wheaton, IL: Tyndale House, 1993), 118. Verified in scans.

7. "On Machiavelli, Hourglasses, and More Fake Quotes," DonMacDonald, May 14, 2011, http://donmacdonald.com/2011/05/on-machiavelli-hourglasses-and-more-fake-quotes/.

14. "The secret of change is to focus all of your energy, not on fighting the old, but on building the new."

—Socrates

In 1980 the first edition of *Way of the Peaceful Warrior* by the world-class gymnast Dan Millman was released. The book was a fictionalized memoir that explored the series of physical and mental challenges that Millman had faced in his life and the spiritual growth he experienced. The main catalyst of his spiritual journey was an attendant at an all-night gas station who became his mentor in 1966. Millman gave this enlightened counselor the nickname "Socrates," and the quotation above was spoken by the modern fictionalized character and not the ancient Socrates. Here is an excerpt containing the quote in the 1984 edition:[1]

> Back in the office, Socrates drew some water from the spring water dispenser and put on the evening's tea specialty, rose hips, as he continued. "You have many habits that weaken you. The secret of change is to focus all your energy not on fighting the old, but on building the new."

The book was published in multiple editions and made into a 2006 movie with Nick Nolte playing Socrates. Over the years, Millman has been a top athlete, a winning coach, and a popular self-help author. He credits at least part of his success to his oddly named counselor.

The reassignment of the quotation to the Greek luminary was, no doubt, facilitated by confusion between the matching names. This is a known mechanism for misattribution.

The revised 2000 edition of Millman's book was titled *Way of the Peaceful Warrior: A Book that Changes Lives*; it was rereleased in 2006 in conjunction with the movie. The text of the quotation in this edition was modified somewhat:[2]

Back in the office, Socrates drew some water from the springwater dispenser and put on the evening's tea specialty, rose hips, as he continued. "To rid yourself of old patterns, focus all your energy not on struggling with the old, but on building the new."

The previous version of the saying appears to be more popular and is often incorrectly ascribed.

In conclusion, the quotation is from a character named Socrates who was a gas station attendant in a book published in the 1980s by Dan Millman. The quote is not from the renowned Greek philosopher.

Notes:

Great thanks to Christian Higgins, whose inquiry led to the construction of this question and gave impetus to this exploration.

1. Dan Millman, *Way of the Peaceful Warrior: A Book that Changes Lives* (Tiburon, CA: H. J. Kramer, 1984), 113. Verified in hard copy.
2. Dan Millman, *Way of the Peaceful Warrior: A Book that Changes Lives*, rev. ed. (Tiburon, CA: H. J. Kramer, 2000), 105. Accessed in Google Books, https://goo.gl/8p9eZo.

III
AUTHOR ERROR

CONCOCTIONS * HISTORICAL FICTION

1. "For sale: baby shoes, never worn."
2. "Great invention, but who would ever want to use one?"
3. "Able was I ere I saw Elba."
4. "People who like this sort of thing will find this the sort of thing they like."
5. "Half of the town councilors are not fools."
6. "It has become appallingly obvious that our technology has exceeded our humanity."
7. "You can get much further with a kind word and a gun than with a kind word alone."
8. "Hollywood is a place where they'll pay a thousand dollars for a kiss and fifty cents for your soul."
9. "The budget should be balanced; the Treasury should be refilled."

CONCOCTIONS

1. "For sale: baby shoes, never worn."

—Ernest Hemingway

In 1991 a literary agent named Peter Miller authored a book called *Get Published! Get Produced! A Literary Agent's Tips on How to Sell Your Writing*. Miller claimed that almost twenty years prior, in 1974, a "well-established newspaper syndicator" had told him the following story:[1]

> Apparently, Ernest Hemingway was lunching at Luchow's with a number of writers and claimed that he could write a short story that was only six words long. Of course, the other writers balked. Hemingway told each of them to put ten dollars in the middle of the table; if he was wrong, he said, he'd match it. If he was right, he would keep the entire pot. He quickly wrote six words down on a napkin and passed it around; Papa won the bet. The words were "FOR SALE, BABY SHOES, NEVER WORN." A beginning, a middle and an end!

Since 1991 the story above has been repeated by too many creative writing professors the world over, and it has come to represent an entire literary movement called "flash fiction." However, **QI** believes that the story is false.

In the 1980s the playwright John De Groot constructed *Papa*, a one-character play that was first produced in 1989, two years before Miller's book. De Groot included a version of the anecdote, which is the earliest instance in print known to **QI** that connects Hemingway to the expression:[2]

HEMINGWAY: Bet you I can write a complete short story using only 6 words. Any takers? No?

GRINS.

HEMINGWAY: Okay, then.
A short story in 6 words:
"For sale.
Baby shoes.
Never worn."

GRINS, PLEASED WITH HIMSELF.

So what about Miller's "newspaper syndicator" source in 1974? Well, the text of the heartrending very short story evolved over a period of decades, primarily in newspapers, as shown below. By the 1970s someone decided to amplify the power of the text by framing it in a vivid betting anecdote about a famous author. But the identity of this fabulist is uncertain. **QI** has found no evidence that Hemingway ever said or wrote the words "For sale: baby shoes, never worn."

Advertisements closely matching the text appeared in classified sections over the last century and more. Here is an example published in 1906. Intriguingly, this section of short advertisements was labeled "Terse Tales of the Town":[3]

For sale, baby carriage; never been used. Apply at this office.

In 1910 a brief article titled "Tragedy of Baby's Death Is Revealed in Sale of Clothes" was printed in a Spokane, Washington, newspaper. The article described the sorrow of two parents who had recently lost a child and placed a staggering classified ad in the paper, one reminiscent of the 1906 "Terse Tales."[4]

The world is indeed a complication of joys and sorrows, a continuous play made up of tragedy and comedy, and even in every day life, items and experience, small and unusual to us, perhaps, is woven a little story of the heart.

Last Saturday an ad. appeared in a local paper which read: "Baby's hand made trousseau and baby's bed for sale. Never been used." The address was on East Mission street.

This perhaps meant little to the casual reader, yet to the mother who had spent hours and days planning the beautiful things for her tiny baby, it meant a keen sorrow and disappointment.

She had perhaps, dreamed of the time when her little one should be grown up and could, with a source of pride, look back upon its babyhood days and display the handiwork of its mother in the first baby clothes worn and the first trundle bed it had slept in when it first opened its eyes upon the beauties of the world.

But the hand of fate had been unkind and took from the devoted parents the little one which was destined to be the sunshine and light of their life, and the mother, in a desire to forget her sorrow by parting with anything which reminded her of the little one, advertised the garments at a sacrifice.

Note the description of the advertisement as "a little story of the heart," which may have helped the literary allusion gather momentum.

Another precursor reflects the idea of a compressed "short-short" fiction and introduces shoes into the equation in place of the pram. In 1917 a periodical aimed at writers and editors called the *Editor* published a piece by William R. Kane about striving for originality when creating short stories. Kane outlined a tale about a grief-stricken wife who had lost her baby. He suggested using "Little Shoes, Never Worn" as the title and as the key symbol of the narrative.[5]

To give the first example that comes to mind: Our story is one of a wife who has lost her baby, her only possible one, and her grief removes her from the world, and even threatens to estrange her from her husband. Evidently much of her struggle toward normality will be a mental one; the crisis of her struggle certainly will be mental. To bring the story "down-to-the-ground," there must be some concrete symbol of the struggle and the wife's victory.

Suppose this symbol is a pair of "little shoes, never worn." The title of the story might be "Little Shoes, Never Worn." The victory of the wife, her gain to normality, might be symbolized by the giving away of this pair of shoes, over which she has often wept, to a needy babe of another mother. The story I have outlined inclines to the sentimental, but I think it proves my point.

In April 1921 the newspaper columnist Roy K. Moulton printed a brief note that he attributed to someone named Jerry. The note referred to a classified advertisement selling a baby carriage.[6]

> There was an ad in the Brooklyn "Home Talk" which read, "Baby carriage for sale, never used." Wouldn't that make a wonderful plot for the movies? JERRY.

The note achieved national distribution, appearing in newspapers in places such as Janesville, Wisconsin; Eau Claire, Wisconsin;[7] and Port Arthur, Texas.[8]

In June 1921 the magazine *Life* reprinted the following paragraph from a newspaper under the title "Dénouement."[9]

> The great American dramatist will be the man or woman who can write a one-act play as poignant as a seven-word want ad which the Houston Post discovers: For Sale, a baby carriage; never used.
>
> —Louisville Courier-Journal

The next month, the *Boston Globe* printed a paragraph similar to the one above. But the critical analysis was attributed to Avery Hopwood, a popular Broadway playwright in the 1920s.[10]

> "When a dramatist can tell a story as poignantly, as briefly and as dramatically as some of the classified advertisements," declares Avery Hopwood, "then the great American drama will be written."
>
> Mr. Hopwood's inspiration was this advertisement: "For Sale—A baby carriage; never used!"

Also in July 1921, the humor magazine *Judge* published a piece that employed the classified advertisement as a starting point and then transformed its meaning with a twist ending. The story was called "Fools Rush In" by Jay G'Dee. The author began by recounting his emotional reaction to the ad:[11]

> I am an imaginative soul. That is the reason you are reading this; that and the fact that I read this: "For sale, a baby carriage, never used." Merely a classified ad in a Houston paper, but it took hold on me and would not let me alone.
>
> Sympathy is the natural environment of my soul. I re-read the ad. My fancy lingered on the last two words; the pathos of them; the tragedy that was in them.

The author claimed to have searched out the person who placed the ad in order to offer words of condolence. G'Dee found him mowing the front lawn of his house and asked if he might ask his reasons for selling the baby carriage. The man replied:[12]

> "Certainly. You see we figured too low. It's only a single and—" he grinned, damn him—"when the time came we had to get a double-seater."

In 1924 a newspaper in Omaha, Nebraska, presented multiple interpretations for the advertisement.[13]

> There wasn't a "human interest" story in the paper that can compare in human interest with this little want ad: "For Sale—Baby carriage. Never used."
>
> Why was the baby carriage never used? Is the little fellow waiting by himself until the Heavens be no more, or were mother and child buried in the same grave? Or did some old bachelor win the baby carriage at a raffle?

In 1927 the comic strip featuring the character Ella Cinders finally provided the advertisement its literary legacy.[14]

THEY SAY THE GREATEST SHORT STORY IN THE WORLD WAS WRITTEN IN A SEVEN-WORD CLASSIFIED AD: "FOR SALE, A BABY CARRIAGE; NEVER USED!"

In 1992 the Canadian literary figure John Robert Colombo printed part of a letter that he had received from the famous science fiction author Arthur C. Clarke, who was residing in Colombo, Sri Lanka. Clarke was familiar with the Hemingway anecdote and suggested a setting of the 1920s:[15]

> Excerpt from a letter written by Arthur C. Clarke (from Colombo to Colombo). It is dated 11 Oct. 1991 and concerns "short shorts":
>
> > My favourite is Hemingway's—he's supposed to have won a $10 bet (no small sum in the '20s) from his fellow writers. They paid up without a word . . .
> > Here it is. I still can't think of it without crying—
> > FOR SALE. BABY SHOES. NEVER WORN.

In 1993 the *Chicago Tribune* published a series of articles about the deaths of children in Chicago. The journalist Steve Johnson indicated that the baby shoes tale was used as an example by "writing instructors."[16]

> But like the classified advertisement that writing instructors call the shortest short story—"For sale: One pair baby shoes; never used"—each of those paragraphs describing the 57 deaths is its own short story.

In 1997 a piece in the *New York Times* mentioned the yarn with Hemingway. In this variant of the short-short story, the shoes were "Never Used."[17]

> Hemingway once boasted that he could write a compelling short story in six words: "For sale. Baby shoes. Never used." Leaner language doesn't necessarily mean thinner meaning.

In 1998 Arthur C. Clarke retold the tale in an essay published in the UK edition of *Reader's Digest.* The essay was also included in Clarke's 1999 collection *Greetings, Carbon-Based Bipeds!*[18]

> Let me end with the finest example of compressed word power I've ever encountered. Back in the twenties, a young newspaperman bet his colleagues $10—no small sum in those days—that he could write a complete short story in just six words. They paid up . . .
>
> I defy even the wizards of Pleasantville to shorten Ernest Hemingway's shortest and most heartbreaking story:
>
> "For sale. Baby shoes. Never worn."

In 2006 the literary agent Peter Miller told the anecdote about Hemingway again in his new book *Author! Screenwriter! How to Succeed as a Writer in New York and Hollywood.* The setting of the conclave of betting writers was moved from Luchow's restaurant in the 1991 version to the Algonquin Hotel in the 2006 version. Other details were unchanged.[19]

In 2014 the *Journal of Popular Culture* published an article on this topic titled "The Short Story Just Got Shorter: Hemingway, Narrative, and the Six-Word Urban Legend" by Frederick A. Wright. The author noted the paucity of evidence linking Hemingway to the six-word microfiction and concluded that the attribution was spurious.[20]

In 2014 director Simeon Lumgair shared with **QI** a link to his touching film *Abrupt Ending* starring Irene Ng, which was inspired by this six-word tale.[21]

In conclusion, **QI** has located no substantive evidence that Ernest Hemingway composed a six- or seven-word story about an unworn pair of baby shoes or an unused baby carriage. In 1910 the core idea of the story was illustrated by a newspaper account that presented it as nonfiction. In 1917 William R. Kane did write an article that was thematically linked to these short-short tales. The story title Kane suggested was "Little Shoes, Never Worn."

In April 1921 the newspaper columnist Roy K. Moulton credited "Jerry" with pointing out that the advertisement "Baby carriage for sale, never used" embodied the plot of a story. It is possible that this recognition may have been facilitated by a familiarity with Kane's earlier article.

More elaborate claims, for example, that the advertisement was the "greatest short story in the world," probably evolved over time. The Hemingway anecdote was forged from this widely distributed material.

Notes:

Thanks to my very helpful local librarians. Kind thanks to David Haglund, editor of the culture blog at *Slate*, for featuring these results in an article at *Slate*.[22]

1. Peter Miller, *Get Published! Get Produced! A Literary Agent's Tips on How to Sell Your Writing* (New York: Shapolsky, 1991), 27. Accessed in Google Books, https://goo.gl/Xoatol.
2. John de Groot, *Papa: A Play Based on the Legendary Lives of Ernest Hemingway*, 25. (Boise, ID: Hemingway Western Studies Center, Boise State University, 1989). Verified in scans. Myriad thanks to Bonnie Taylor-Blake and University of North Carolina—Chapel Hill Libraries for examining this citation and referring **QI** to the 2014 Wright article in the *Journal of Popular Culture*.
3. Terse Tales of the Town [advertisements], *Ironwood News Record* (Ironwood, MI), April 28, 1906, 5. Accessed in NewspaperARCHIVE.com.
4. "Tragedy of Baby's Death is Revealed in Sale of Clothes," *Spokane Press*, May 16, 1910, 6. Accessed in Chronicling America. A correspondent named Hugo located this important citation.
5. [Untitled article], The Editor's Editor, *Journal of Information for Literary Workers* 45, no. 4 (February 24, 1917): 175–76. Accessed in Google Books, http://goo.gl/KobFNu.
6. Roy K. Moulton, On the Spur of the Moment, *Janesville Daily Gazette* (Janesville, WI), April 13, 1921, 6. Accessed in NewspaperARCHIVE.com.
7. Roy K. Moulton, On the Spur of the Moment, *Eau Claire Leader* (Eau Claire, WI), April 13, 1921, 6. Accessed in NewspaperARCHIVE.com
8. Jerry, As Good As Most of Them, *Port Arthur Daily News* (Port Arthur, TX), April 15, 1921, 6. Accessed in NewspaperARCHIVE.com.
9. "Dénouement," Aut Scissors Aut Nullus, *Life* 77 (June 16, 1921): 884. Accessed in HathiTrust, https://goo.gl/Qiwt4a.
10. "Drama and Pictures: Notes about the Players," *Boston Globe* (July 10, 1921), 55. Accessed in ProQuest.
11. Jay G'Dee, "Fools Rush In," *Judge* 81 (July 16, 1921): 70. Accessed in HathiTrust, https://goo.gl/DHp14c.

12. G'Dee, "Fools Rush In," 70.

13. "News in the 'Ads,' Did You Overlook It?" *Morning World-Herald* (Omaha, NE), February 23, 1924. Accessed in GenealogyBank.

14. Bill Conselman and Charlie Plumb, "Ella Cinders: When in Doubt" [comic strip], *Kokomo Daily Tribune* (Kokomo, IN), November 23, 1927, 17. Accessed in GenealogyBank.

15. John Robert Colombo, *Worlds in Small: An Anthology of Miniature Literary Compositions* (Vancouver, BC: CacaNadaDada, 1992), 9. Verified in scans. Great thanks to Dennis Lien and the University of Minnesota Libraries.

16. Steve Johnson, "Killing Our Children: 57 Children Killed in 1992—First of a Year-long Series on the Murder of Children," *Chicago Tribune*, January 3, 1993, 1. Accessed in ProQuest.

17. Alan Robbins, "Email: Lean, Mean, and Making Its Mark," From the Desk of Alan Robbins, *New York Times*, May 11, 1997, F13. Accessed in ProQuest.

18. Arthur C. Clarke, *Greetings, Carbon-Based Bipeds! Collected Essays 1934–1998*, ed. Ian T. Macauley (New York: St. Martin's, 1998), 354. The book contains the following bibliographic note on p. 543: "The Power of Compression," published as "Words That Inspire," first appeared in *Reader's Digest*, UK, December 1998. Verified in hard copy.

19. Peter Miller, *Author! Screenwriter! How to Succeed as a Writer in New York and Hollywood* (Avon, MA: Adams Media, 2006), 166. Verified in hard copy.

20. Frederick A. Wright, "The Short Story Just Got Shorter: Hemingway, Narrative, and the Six-Word Urban Legend," *Journal of Popular Culture* 47, no. 2 (April 2014): 327–40. Special thanks to Wright for his valuable paper and his pointer to a published version of *Papa*.

21. "Abrupt Ending," Vimeo video, 5:22, posted by "Simon Lumgair," October 11, 2013, https://vimeo.com/76692817.

22. David Haglund, "Did Hemingway Really Write His Famous Six-Word Story?" Browbeat (blog), *Slate*, January 31, 2013, http://goo.gl/S6z8Gq.

2. "Great invention, but who would ever want to use one?"

—Rutherford B. Hayes

QI has been unable to locate any compelling evidence that Rutherford B. Hayes made the infamous skeptical remark about the telephone that dogs his legacy. Both presidents Ronald Reagan and Barack Obama have even repeated the anecdote.[1] The earliest known citation connecting Hayes to the telephone anecdote appeared in a 1982 book titled *Future Mind* about computers. Details are given further below.

Oddly, in 1939 an almost identical anecdote was told about Ulysses S. Grant, who preceded Hayes in the White House. This is the earliest instance of the story located by **QI**. Note that Grant left the White House in 1877, and Hayes left in 1881. So the speech described immediately below was made many years after either man was president.

In 1939 Howard Pew, president of the Sun Oil Company, delivered an address at a meeting of the Congress of American Industry. Pew claimed that several famous individuals had made misguided comments about technology. One of his examples was a supposed remark by Grant that revealed a dramatic lack of foresight regarding the potential of the telephone:[2]

> From history, he recited: George Washington thought the first demonstration of John Fitch's steamboat of too little significance to justify his presence; President Ulysses S. Grant thought the telephone was "very remarkable" but wondered "who in the world would ever want to use one of them."
>
> Napoleon couldn't "see the submarine." Daniel Webster thought frost on the tracks would make it impossible to run trains.

In 1949 the anecdote about Grant's reaction to the telephone appeared in an article by a writer named George Peck that was printed in a Virginia newspaper. The quotation attributed to Grant overlapped the 1939 version:[3]

Then there is the rather humorous episode in connection with the first telephone placed on the White House desk. This was when Ulysses Grant was president. After trial had convinced him that he could actually talk through it and hear the answering voice from the other end, he said: "Yes, it is all very remarkable: but who in the world would ever want to use one of them?"

In 1950 the anecdote about Grant was printed in the *Rotarian*, and Peck received an acknowledgment for disseminating the tale:[4]

Need an anecdote to clinch the point that even wise men can't foretell the future? Here's one from George Peck, executive editor of *Partners*, which concerns Ulysses S. Grant. The telephone had just been invented and an instrument was put on a White House desk. A trial convinced President Grant that he could talk through it to another person and hear the reply.

"Yes," said the man who had led great armies to victory and was at the height of his reputation, "it is all very remarkable. But who in the world would ever want to use one of them?"

In 1974 the tale about Grant and his blinkered view of the telephone appeared in a book entitled *Must History Repeat Itself?*:[5]

A similar episode occurred when General Grant, as President of the United States, was given the opportunity of talking over one of the first telephone lines. Having satisfied himself that the apparatus worked, he sat back and said: 'Yes, it is truly remarkable; but who in the world would ever want to use one of them?'

By 1982 the quotation had been slightly altered, and the words were now attributed to Rutherford B. Hayes instead of Ulysses S. Grant. The version of the anecdote given in the book *Future Mind: The Microcomputer, New Medium, New Mental Environment* by Edward J. Lias provided a setting and a date. But the year 1876 cannot be correct because Hayes did not become president until 1877:[6]

When President Rutherford B. Hayes was handed the first telephone for a trial conversation between Washington and Philadelphia in 1876, he had difficulty thinking of anything to say. After several sentences he disconnected the line and said, "That's an amazing invention, but who would ever want to use one of them?"

In 1984 the first edition of a popular reference work titled *The Experts Speak: The Definitive Compendium of Authoritative Misinformation* was published. The authors Christopher Cerf and Victor S. Navasky included a version of the quotation attributed to Hayes. When *Los Angeles Times* columnist Jack Smith reviewed the volume, he selected and reprinted the words credited to Hayes in his column. Hence, the quote achieved wider distribution:[7]

Of the telephone: "That's an amazing invention, but who would ever want to use one of them?"

—Rutherford B. Hayes, President of the United States, 1876

Once again the date of 1876 was invoked, but Grant was president in 1876, not Hayes. All quotations in *The Experts Speak* have notes that attempt to provide supporting evidence. The note for the saying above states that the information was submitted by the author of a 1983 book called *The Naked Computer: A Layperson's Almanac of Computer Lore, Wizardry, Personalities, Memorabilia, World Records, Mind Blowers, and Tomfoolery*:[8]

Rutherford B. Hayes, quoted from Jack B. Rochester and John Gantz, *The Naked Computer* (New York: William Morrow, 1983). Submitted by Jack B. Rochester.

In 1985 Ronald Reagan used the remark attributed to Hayes as part of a joke about his own longevity:[9]

At a recent ceremony in which technology awards were given, Reagan recalled that President Rutherford B. Hayes once was "shown a recently invented device."

"'That's an amazing invention,' he said. 'But who would ever want to use one of them?' He was talking about a telephone. I thought at the time that he might be mistaken."

In conclusion, **QI** believes that the attachment of the quotation to Hayes is not supported by credible evidence at this time. The attachment of the saying to Grant also appears to be unsupported. Indeed, **QI** has not yet located solid evidence connecting the quotation to any prominent individual.

Notes:

1. Helen Thomas, "President Offers No Security Advice," *Reading Eagle* (Reading, PA), February 24, 1985, B26. Accessed in Google News Archive, https://goo.gl/JFeko9; Glenn Kessler, "Obama's Whopper About Rutherford B. Hayes and the Telephone," *Washington Post*, March 16, 2012, http://goo.gl/5mfoo.

2. "You Can't Plan Progress, Manufacturers Are Told," *Milwaukee Journal*, December 7, 1939, 9. Accessed in Google News Archive. (Since removed.)

3. George Peck, "Government Tyranny," As Seen By Others, *Free Lance-Star* (Fredericksburg, VA), June 17, 1949, 4. Accessed in Google News Archive, https://goo.gl/BsedJ4.

4. Last Page Comment, *Rotarian* 76, no. 2 (February 1950), 64. Accessed in Google Books, https://goo.gl/E4wmPE.

5. Antony Fisher, *Must History Repeat Itself? A Study of the Lessons Taught by the (Repeated) Failure and (Occasional) Success of Government Economic Policy Through the Ages* (London: Churchill Press, 1974), 120. Verified in hard copy.

6. Edward J. Lias, *Future Mind: The Microcomputer, New Medium, New Mental Environment*, Little, Brown Computer Systems (Boston: Little, Brown, 1982), 2. Verified in hard copy. This citation was identified by the editors of Wikiquote, who placed it on the webpage for Rutherford B. Hayes.

7. Jack Smith, review of *The Experts Speak: The Definitive Compendium of Authoritative Misinformation*, by Christopher Cerf and Victor S. Navasky, *Los Angeles Times*, October 2, 1984, F1. Accessed in ProQuest.

8. Christopher Cerf and Victor S. Navasky, *The Experts Speak: The Definitive Compendium of Authoritative Misinformation*, rev. ed. (New York: Villard Books, 1998), 227, 382. Verified in hard copy.

9. Thomas, "President Offers No Security Advice," B26.

3. "Able was I ere I saw Elba."

—Napoleon Bonaparte

A famous palindrome is attributed to the renowned French leader Napoleon Bonaparte, who was once exiled to the island of Elba:

Able was I ere I saw Elba.

Supposedly Napoleon said this reversible phrase to Barry Edward O'Meara, who was his physician during his captivity on the island of Saint Helena. **QI**, however, notes that Napoleon died in 1821, and the earliest appearance of this palindrome located by **QI** was published in a US periodical called *Gazette of the Union* in 1848. The article credited someone with the initials J. T. R. residing in Baltimore, Maryland, with the creation of the palindrome. Here is an extended excerpt from that article discussing three palindromes:[1]

Among other things worthy of note, our friend J.T.R. called our attention to the following ingenious though somewhat antique, arrangement of words by the "water poet," Taylor:

"Lewd did I live & evil I did dwell."

He remarked that this sentence had attracted considerable attention, and that challenges had been frequently given in the papers for the production of a combination of words, that would so perfectly "read backward and forward the same," as this line does.

During some moments of leisure, he had produced the following line. In our opinion it is much more perfect than Taylor's because there are no letters used or dispensed with, which are not legitimate, as in his, in the first and last letters—"lewd" and "dwell:"

"Snug & raw was I ere I saw war & guns."

With the exception of the sign &, which is twice substituted for the properly spelt conjunction, which it represents, the sentence is perfect. By the way, there is couched in the sentence a fact, which many a soldier who has just returned from the battle fields of Mexico will fully appreciate.

But our friend was not satisfied with this near approach to perfection, but determined to produce a line which would require the aid of no sign to justify it as a correct sentence, and the following was the result of his endeavor:

"Able was I ere I saw Elba."

Those who are acquainted with the career of Napoleon will readily recognize the historical force of the sentence in its application to that distinguished warrior. Although our friend has *cut* more than one *figure* in the world, in all of which he brought credit to himself, we know he did not desire to *figure* in our paper to the extent we have caused him to do; he merely submitted the above sentences for our personal amusement, and we take the liberty of giving them to our readers; challenging any of them to produce lines of equal ingenuity of arrangement with the same amount of sense.

According to the text above, Napoleon did not construct the palindrome; however, the person who did craft the phrase employed the historical episode of exile as an inspiration for his wordplay.

Within a decade the palindrome had been reassigned directly to Bonaparte. A condensed version of the July 1848 article in *Gazette of the Union* was published in a Galveston, Texas, newspaper in August 1848. Thus the palindrome was disseminated to additional readers. In this short article, the ascription to "J. T. R." was omitted.[2]

Every one remembers the ingenious arrangement of words by Taylor the water Poet:

"Lewd did I live and evil I did dwell"

The *Golden Rule* gives two examples, even better than that, inasmuch as there is one letter too many in the above when read backward. Here they are:

"Snug & raw was I, ere I saw war & guns."

And

"Able was I ere I saw Elba."

The former, says the *Golden Rule*, will apply very well to some of the Mexico recruits, and the latter those acquainted with the career of Napoleon, will easily recognize.

In April 1851 the condensed article above was printed in the *Adams Sentinel* newspaper of Gettysburg, Pennsylvania. So the palindrome continued to circulate.[3]

In March 1858 the palindrome was attributed directly to Bonaparte in an article published in a Richmond, Virginia, newspaper. This is the earliest citation currently known to **QI** crediting Napoleon, but the linkage is tentative. The article excerpt below states that the palindrome was spoken to "Dr. O'Meara." Barry Edward O'Meara acted as Napoleon's personal physician on Saint Helena. Napoleon was exiled to Elba in 1814 and escaped in 1815. He surrendered to the British and was exiled to the island of Saint Helena in 1815, where he died in 1821:[4]

AN EXTENDED ANAGRAM.—It is said that Napoleon, when he was asked by Dr. O'Meara, if he really thought that he could have invaded England at the time he threatened to do so, answered in the following extended anagram:

"Able was I ere I saw Elba."

Whether this is true or not, we should like to see a more ingenious and extended anagram.

This tale of the palindrome origin was printed in other newspapers, such as the *San Antonio Ledger* of San Antonio, Texas, in April 1858.[5]

In July 1858 a newspaper in New Albany, Indiana, printed two different versions of the same basic palindrome:[6]

NAPOLEON BONAPARTE—The following sentence in reference to the great Napoleon makes sense whether read backwards or forwards, with only a little change of punctuation.

Elba saw I, ere I was able.
Able was I, ere I saw Elba.

In conclusion, based on current evidence, this palindrome should be credited to a person with the initials J. T. R. in Baltimore. The attribution to Napoleon is stimulating, but it appears to be spurious. English was not Napoleon's native language and was thus an unlikely choice for wordplay. **QI** hypothesizes that the ascription to the emperor was fabricated to generate an amusing anecdote. New information may emerge over time as more documents are digitized and more data is gathered.

Notes:

Thanks to American Dialect Society discussants.

1. "Doings in Baltimore," *Gazette of the Union, Golden Rule, and Odd-Fellows' Family Companion* 9 (July 8, 1848): 30. Accessed in Google Books, https://goo.gl/7ZpxWp.

2. [Untitled filler item], *Civilian and Galveston Gazette* (Galveston, TX), August 17, 1848, 2. Accessed in NewspaperARCHIVE.com. The newspaper acknowledged the *Golden Rule* because the full name of the originating periodical was the *Gazette of the Union, Golden*

Rule, and Odd-Fellows' Family Companion. Note that the word "too" instead of "two" is used in the original text.

3. [Untitled filler item], *Adams Sentinel* [Gettysburg, PA], April 28, 1851, 1. Accessed in NewspaperARCHIVE.com.

4. An Extended Anagram, *Daily Dispatch* (Richmond, VA), March 22, 1858. Accessed in Chronicling America, http://goo.gl/UH9kPH. Thanks to Stephen Goranson for finding this citation.

5. An Extended Anagram, *San Antonio Ledger* (San Antonio, TX), April 10, 1858, 1. Accessed in GenealogyBank.

6. "Napoleon Bonaparte," *New Albany Daily Ledger* (New Albany, IN), July 9, 1858, 3. Accessed in NewspaperARCHIVE.com.

4. "People who like this sort of thing will find this the sort of thing they like."

—Abraham Lincoln

A popular anecdote asserts that a friend delivered a prolix lecture about spiritualism to Abraham Lincoln and then eagerly sought his opinion. The president replied with a humorously redundant noncommittal statement designed to be inoffensive. Here are three versions:

> People who like this sort of thing will find this the sort of thing they like.

> For people who like that kind of thing, that is the kind of thing they like.

> For those who like that sort of thing I should think it just the sort of thing they would like.

QI hypothesizes that the seed of this family of expressions was sown by the popular humorist Charles Farrar Browne, known to audiences by his pseudonym Artemus Ward. In 1863 Ward created advertising material for a set of lectures he was performing. He included parodic testimonials from fictional people, and one ersatz supporter was named "O. Abe." The name "Artemus" was misspelled as "Artemas" in the following passage from an October 1863 issue of a Maine newspaper.[1]

> Artemas Ward among other puffs of his lectures has the following from "Old Abe":

Dear Sir–I have never heard any of your lectures, but from what I can learn I should say that for people who like the kind of lectures you deliver, they are just the kind of lectures such people like.

Yours, respectably, O. Abe.

The letter penned by Ward was printed in multiple newspapers. The words became linked to Lincoln because of the suggestive name "Abe." Over time the phrasing evolved, and a variety of anecdotes were constructed to accompany the expression.

Ward also created multiple fake testimonial letters that were called "certificates." When the letter from "O. Abe" appeared in the *American Traveller* of Boston, Massachusetts, in October 1863, it was printed together with a letter from "Amos Pilkins." This note satirized the pseudo-endorsements presented by charlatans selling ineffectual patent medicines:[2]

Artemus Ward: Respected Sir—My wife was afflicted with the pipsywipsy in the head for nearly eight years. The doctors all gave her up. But in a fortunate moment she went to one of your lectures, and commenced recovering very rapidly. She is now in perfect health. We like your lectures very much. Please send me a box of them. They are purely vegetable. Send me another five dollar bill and I'll write you another certificate twice as long as this.

Yours, &c., Amos Pilkins

About a decade later, in 1874, the "O. Abe" letter concocted by Ward was not forgotten; however, it was not remembered accurately. The *New York Tribune* printed an article from a regular correspondent based in Boston, Massachusetts.[3]

I suppose everyone remembers Artemus Ward's story about reading one of his lectures to President Lincoln, and asking the President's opinion of it. According to the showman's version of the interview, the Chief Magistrate answered, with grave deliberation: "For those that like that kind of a lecture I suppose it is just the kind of lecture that such people would like."

The 1863 letter actually stated that "O. Abe" had never heard any of Ward's lectures, which does not comport with the 1874 anecdote above. Thus the quotation and accompanying tale were evolving. Certainly it was possible that Ward presented more than one version of the testimonial. The above item was reprinted in other newspapers such as the *Cincinnati Daily Gazette* of Cincinnati, Ohio.[4]

In 1879 another instance of the story appeared in the *New York Tribune* with further changes. Ward's name was no longer mentioned. Hence, the reader was left unaware that the tale originated with a comedian. Lincoln's friend was reading a "long manuscript" instead of a "lecture."[5]

> President Lincoln once listened patiently while a friend read a long manuscript to him, and then asked: "What do you think of it? How will it take?" The President reflected a little while, and then answered: "Well, for people who like that kind of thing, I think that is just about the kind of thing they'd like."

In 1880 the *Educational Weekly* of Chicago, Illinois, printed the tale with a somewhat clumsy version of the saying.[6]

> Mr. Lincoln once listened to an article, the author of which at the end of the reading asked his opinion of it. "Well," said he, "some people like that kind of thing very much; and for that kind of people, I shouldn't wonder if that article was about the kind of thing they'd like."

In 1888 a book reviewer in the *New York Herald* employed an instance credited to Lincoln and tailored to books.[7]

> We should say of his book what Mr. Lincoln once said of a work on metaphysics—"For those who like that kind of a book, it is just about the kind of a book they would like."

In 1903 the well-known playwright George Bernard Shaw constructed a variant expression and placed it in *Man and Superman: A Comedy and a Philosophy*:[8]

TANNER: . . . You despise Oxford, Enry, don't you?

STRAKER: No, I don't. Very nice sort of place, Oxford, I should think, for people that like that sort of place. They teach you to be a gentleman there. In the Polytechnic they teach you to be an engineer or such like. See?

Max Beerbohm's 1911 novel *Zuleika Dobson* included a distinctive version of Clio, the ancient Greek muse of mythology. Beerbohm assigned an instance of the saying to this incarnation of Clio. His intent was humorous, but the Greek rendition and the linkage to Clio caused some temporal confusion:[9]

> But when, one day, Pallas asked her what she thought of "The Decline and Fall of the Roman Empire" her only answer was ὅστις τοῖα ἔχει εν ἡδονῇ ἔχει ἐν ἡδονῇ τοῖα (For people who like that kind of thing, that is the kind of thing they like).

The acclaimed poet Carl Sandburg wrote a Pulitzer Prize–winning, multivolume biography of Abraham Lincoln. He examined the quotation and its attribution in volume two of *Abraham Lincoln: The War Years*, released in 1939. Sandburg presented a version of the anecdote featuring Robert Dale Owen, who was an influential proponent of spiritualism. Yet, Sandburg also recognized that Ward was the likely source of the saying.[10]

> He had told Robert Dale Owen, it was said, when Owen had read to him a long paper on an abstruse subject akin to spiritualism, "Well, for those who like that sort of thing, I should think it is just about the sort of thing they would like." He may have said this to Owen or it may have been attributed to him with slight changes

out of a certificate of endorsement which Artemus Ward fabricated and published as follows:

> Dear Sir–
> I have never heard any of your lectures, but from what I can learn I should say that for people who like the kind of lectures you deliver, they are just the kind of lectures such people like.
> Yours respectfully,
> O. Abe

In 1961 the *New Yorker* published Muriel Spark's story "The Prime of Miss Jean Brodie." The popular and critically praised work was also released as a book that same year and made into a film in 1969. The story describes a charismatic teacher named Jean Brodie who strongly influences the lives of a small group of impressionable young female students. Spark used the saying in the conversation of her character Miss Brodie.[11]

> Behind them, Miss Brodie was being questioned on the subject of the Brownies and the Girl Guides, for quite a lot of the other girls in the Junior School were Brownies.

> "For those who like that sort of thing," said Miss Brodie in her best Edinburgh voice, "that is the sort of thing they like."

> So Brownies and Guides were ruled out.

In conclusion, Artemus Ward should be credited with the saying within his comical letter fictitiously ascribed to "O. Abe" from 1863. **QI** believes that later instances in this family of sayings were derived directly or indirectly from the words of Ward. **QI** also believes that Lincoln probably did not employ the expression.

George Bernard Shaw, Max Beerbohm, and Muriel Spark did write versions of the quip. But the saying was already in circulation, and their expressions were not completely original.

Notes:

Great thanks to top researcher Bill Mullins, whose comment on this topic led **QI** to formulate this question and perform this exploration. Special thanks to Ralph Keyes, who discussed this quotation in *The Quote Verifier* and presented citations for George Bernard Shaw and Max Beerbohm.[12]

1. [Untitled item], *Daily Eastern Argus* (Portland, ME), October 23, 1863, 4. Accessed in GenealogyBank.

2. "Artemus Ward Advertises," *American Traveller* (Boston, MA), October 31, 1863, 1. Accessed in GenealogyBank.

3. L. C. M., "Boston: Literary Notes," *New York Tribune*, July 15, 1874, 6. Accessed in GenealogyBank.

4. "An Old Story Retold" [acknowledgment to *New York Tribune* correspondent in "Boston: Literary Notes" dated July 15, 1874; see endnote 3 above], *Cincinnati Daily Gazette*, July 17, 1874, 2. Accessed in GenealogyBank.

5. [Untitled filler item], *New York Tribune*, March 27, 1879, 2. Accessed in GenealogyBank.

6. Review of *Four Lectures on Early Child Culture*, by W. N. Hailmann, *Educational Weekly* 7 (April 22, 1880): 285. Accessed in Google Books, https://goo.gl/IbA9go.

7. "A New York Club Man's Ideas," *New York Herald*, October 28, 1888, 14. Accessed in GenealogyBank.

8. George Bernard Shaw, *Man and Superman: A Comedy and a Philosophy* (Westminster: Archibald Constable, 1903), 50. Accessed in Internet Archive, http://bit.ly/2cstyDT.

9. Max Beerbohm, *Zuleika Dobson* (New York: Boni and Liveright, 1911), 187. Accessed in Google Books, https://goo.gl/jJ6obF.

10. Carl Sandburg, *Abraham Lincoln: The War Years*, vol. 2 (New York: Harcourt, Brace, 1939), 306. Verified in hard copy.

11. Muriel Spark, "The Prime of Miss Jean Brodie," *New Yorker*, October 14, 1961, 64. Verified in *New Yorker* online database.

12. Ralph Keyes, *The Quote Verifier: Who Said What, Where, and When* (New York: St. Martin's, 2006), 124–25, 305–6. Verified in hard copy.

5. "Half of the town councilors are not fools."

—Benjamin Disraeli X

The first instance of the above jape found by **QI** was printed in a July 1927 newspaper story set in an unnamed town near Uppsala, Sweden. A government official reportedly lost his temper and rebuked his fellows.[1]

> A municipal councilor . . . remarked that certainly half of his colleagues were fools. An apology was demanded. He promised to make reparation and caused bills with the following correction to be posted on boardings in the town: "I said that half of the town councilors are fools. I now declare that half of the town councilors are not fools."

Over the years the jest has evolved and has been aimed at a variety of politicians, including town councilors, aldermen, cabinet members, and members of the UK House of Commons.

Here are additional selected citations in chronological order.

This tale appeared in multiple newspapers in 1927, such as the *Altoona Mirror* of Pennsylvania, as quoted above; the *Syracuse Herald* of New York;[2] and the *Milwaukee Journal* of Wisconsin.[3]

By 1930 a variant of the anecdote was circulating in Australia as recounted in the *Sydney Mail*. The item was printed on the newspaper's humor page, "In Lighter Vein." In this case, the coerced apology was extracted from a journalist instead of a politician.[4]

> Feeling was very high in the little country town and the editor of the local newspaper bluntly wrote in the columns that "half the aldermen were fools."

There was an outcry and the aldermen demanded a withdrawal. He did as they requested in his next issue. It read: "I wish to apologise and say that half the aldermen are not fools."

In 1933 the *Montreal Gazette* printed a version that closely matched the instance from 1927. The item appeared in a column called A Little Nonsense, and no location was specified for the comical incident.[5]

The 1958 *An Encyclopaedia of Parliament* by Norman Wilding and Philip Laundy attributed a version of the quip to Benjamin Disraeli while asserting that the event was famous.[6]

Many an anecdote can be related involving the use of an unparliamentary expression. One of the most famous concerns the occasion when Disraeli was called to order for declaring that half the Cabinet were asses. "Mr. Speaker, I withdraw," he apologized, "half the Cabinet are not asses!"

QI has searched the electronic repository of the UK parliamentary transcripts, which is called the Hansard database, and he has not yet found evidence of this humorous retraction. The word "asses" may have been censored. **QI** has also searched for variant expressions using words such as "fools," "knaves," and "idiots." If the remark was spoken, then its phrasing has proved elusive.

The 1963 book *In the Fiery Continent* was written by Tom Hopkinson, the editor of *DRUM* magazine of Johannesburg, South Africa. The work contains excerpts from *DRUM*, including a passage written by Casey Motsisi depicting a humorous fictional event.[7]

A leading official had just remarked that half the members of the Opposition were asses, whereupon someone asked him to withdraw. He withdrew by saying that half the members of the Opposition were NOT asses, whereupon he was roundly congratulated for being the first person to withdraw a remark instead of stamping out of the house like a bull.

In 1964 the *New York Times* discussed words and phrases that were disallowed in the UK Parliament and presented the Disraeli version of the anecdote.[8]

> Speakers have decided, for example, that "jackass" is unparliamentary but "goose" is acceptable and that "dog," "rat" and "swine" are out of order, but "halfwit" and "Tory clot" are in order . . .
>
> Some insults bear the stamp of greatness. Disraeli was called to order once for declaring that half the Cabinet members were asses. "Mr. Speaker, I withdraw," he said. "Half the Cabinet are not asses."

In 1967 a volume of linguistic history titled *The Story of the English Language* discussed restrictions on unparliamentary language and referred to the quip.[9]

> But there are ways of circumventing the prohibitions. Disraeli once remarked that "half the Cabinet members are not asses," while Aneurin Bevan, at a later date, used the banned words in quotations from literary sources.

In 1968 a former US congressman and governmental administrator named Brooks Hays published a memoir that included an instance of the quip.[10]

> A member of the Israeli Parliament tried a different tactic. During a hot debate he was called to order for declaring that half the cabinet were asses. "Mr. Speaker, I withdraw the remark," he said, "half the members are not asses."

In 1981 a British politician named Dennis Skinner, speaking in the UK House of Commons, complained that another member had not been attending committee meetings conscientiously:[11]

> Mr. Skinner: The Liberal spokesman was not there half the time.

The member who was criticized disagreed and asked for the comment to be withdrawn:

Mr. Alton: I can assure him that what he said is certainly not the case, and I hope that he will withdraw that comment immediately.

Skinner then employed a quip that was partially analogous to the remark under investigation.

Mr. Skinner: The hon. Member for Edge Hill seems a bit upset about my saying that he was not there half the time. Will he settle for my agreeing that he was there the other half? That is an advance.

In 1985, *Leo Rosten's Giant Book of Laughter* presented a version of the tale. The punch line was delivered by an "English columnist, noted for the sharpness of his pen" and used the word "idiots" instead of "fools" or "asses":[12]

A spate of angry mail from readers has denounced the author of this column for saying that half the members of the House of Commons are idiots. I have been urged to apologize for so harsh and incorrect a statement. Herewith, my apology, I am happy to correct my observation: half the members of the House of Commons are not idiots.

In 1991 a textbook designed for aspiring journalists presented an instance of the anecdote set in a US state legislature that was evenly divided between contending parties:[13]

During a budget session, a lawmaker attacked members of the opposite party and said, "Half the members of this house are fools." Immediately, his opponents objected to the unparliamentary "fools" and urged the member to withdraw his statement. He replied, "I withdraw my statement. Half the members of this house are not fools."

In 2014 a Twitter user posted an image showing politician Dennis Skinner. The superimposed text presented an instance of the joke under investigation:[14]

Dennis Skinner: Half the Tories opposite are crooks.

Speaker: Please retract.

Skinner: OK, half the Tories opposite aren't crooks.

In conclusion, the earliest evidence of the joke in 1927 suggests a Swedish origin with an unnamed protagonist. Because the town and the other participants in the incident were also not specified, the credibility of the anecdote is not high. Over the decades the jest has been retold with modifications to the location and the cast of characters.

Currently, **QI** has been unable to find substantive support for the tale featuring Benjamin Disraeli. Yet, **QI** believes that the 1927 story probably can be antedated and looks forward to hearing about progress by other researchers.

Notes:

Special thanks to Andrew Hickey, who brought a tweet on this topic to the attention of **QI**, which led **QI** to formulate this question and perform this exploration. Thanks also to Twitter user PJM QC (@pjm1kbw) for posting. Great thanks to Ian Preston, who pointed to a comment at the Language Log website by Mark Etherton that identified the 1981 remark by Dennis Skinner.

1. The Better Half, *Altoona Mirror* (Altoona, PA), July 20, 1927, 12. Accessed in NewspaperARCHIVE.com.
2. The Better Half, *Syracuse Herald* (Syracuse, NY), July 21, 1927, 8. Accessed in NewspaperARCHIVE.com.
3. "His Apology Was Not Appreciated," *Milwaukee Journal*, July 27, 1927, Green Sheet page. Accessed in Google News Archive, https://goo.gl/7BhRlw.
4. "Half and Half," In Lighter Vein, *Sydney Mail* (Sydney, Australia), November 26, 1930, 50. Accessed in Google News Archive, https://goo.gl/lEQWNI.
5. A Little Nonsense, *Montreal Gazette*, August 22, 1933, 10. Accessed in Google News Archive, https://goo.gl/1khllp.
6. Norman Wilding and Philip Laundy, *An Encyclopaedia of Parliament* (London: Cassell, 1958), s.v. "unparliamentary expressions," 581. Verified in hard copy.

7. Tom Hopkinson, *In the Fiery Continent* (Garden City, NY: Doubleday, 1963), 83. Verified in hard copy.

8. James Feron, "In Commons, A Lie Is 'Inexactitude': When Briton Slurs Briton, Code Dictates Gentility," *New York Times*, November 8, 1964, 30. Accessed in ProQuest.

9. Mario Pei, *The Story of the English Language*, rev. ed. (Philadelphia: J. B. Lippincott, 1967), 268. Verified in scans.

10. Brooks Hays, *A Hotbed of Tranquility: My Life in Five Worlds* (New York: Macmillan, 1968), 209. Verified in hard copy.

11. "Saving for Things Done Under a License," Commons Sitting, UK Parliament House of Commons, HC Deb 01 April 1981 vol 2 cc433-70, April 1, 1981, (Dennis Skinner speaking). Accessed in Hansard, http://goo.gl/jDtJH1.

12. Leo Rosten, *Leo Rosten's Giant Book of Laughter* (New York: Bonanza, 1989), 457. Verified in scans.

13. William Metz, *Newswriting: From Lead to "30,"* 3rd ed. (Englewood Cliffs, NJ: Prentice-Hall, 1991), 116. Verified in hard copy.

14. PJM QC (@pjm1kbw), Twitter post, April 7, 2014, 11:37 a.m., https://goo.gl/Veipco.

6. "It has become appallingly obvious that our technology has exceeded our humanity."

—Albert Einstein

There is no substantive evidence that Einstein made this statement. It does not appear in the comprehensive collection of quotations *The Ultimate Quotable Einstein* from Princeton University Press.[1]

The earliest evidence of a closely matching quotation known to **QI** occurred in a 1995 movie called *Powder*, which was written and directed by Victor Salva and starred Sean Patrick Flanery as the main character, whose strong paranormal powers drive the plot. Flanery plays Jeremy Reed, who has an albinolike appearance and is given the nickname Powder. Near the end of the film is a dialogue between Reed and a character named Donald Ripley, a physics teacher played by Jeff Goldblum. Ripley delivers the quotation, and Reed immediately ascribes it to Einstein:

Donald Ripley: It's become appallingly clear that our technology has surpassed our humanity.

Jeremy Reed: Albert Einstein.

Donald Ripley: I look at you, and I, I think that someday our humanity might actually surpass our technology.

The statement in this dialogue is not identical to the quote popularly ascribed to Einstein. For example, Ripley's remark uses the words "clear" and "surpassed," while the common Einstein-attributed saying uses "obvious" and "exceeded." But semantically they are quite close.

Albert Einstein did make a famous statement in 1946 that was thematically consonant with the movie *Powder*'s expression. He cautioned mankind about the dangers of the new nuclear age. The *New York Times* reported on May 25, 1946, that Einstein "issued a personal appeal yesterday by telegram to several hundred prominent Americans." Here is an excerpt:[2]

> Our world faces a crisis as yet unperceived by those possessing power to make great decisions for good or evil. The unleashed power of the atom has changed everything save our modes of thinking and we thus drift toward unparalleled catastrophe.

Notes:

Thanks to Álvaro Hernández, whose inquiry inspired **QI** to perform this exploration. Also, thanks to the volunteer editors of Wikiquote, especially Hypnosifl, the pen name of Jesse Mazer, for skillfully tracing Einstein quotations.

1. Alice Calaprice, ed., *The Ultimate Quotable Einstein* (Princeton: Princeton University Press, 2010). Verified in hard copy.
2. "Atomic Education Urged by Einstein," *New York Times*, May 25, 1946, 13. Accessed in ProQuest.

7. "You can get much further with a kind word and a gun than with a kind word alone."

—Al Capone

QI has found no substantive evidence that Al Capone made a remark of this type. The earliest citations found suggest that the line was created by a comedian named Professor Irwin Corey who performed as an eccentric academic spouting parodic erudition.

In 1953 the trade journal *Variety* reported on a radio show broadcast on the NBC network that included Irwin Corey playing an addled ahistorical version of Hamlet:[1]

> I have a simple philosophy which is poignant. Shoot a point, point blank, unsubtle, simple, poignant. My philosophy is you can get more with a kind word and a gun than with just a kind word.

In 1962 the *Seattle Daily Times* of Seattle, Washington, reported on an appearance by Corey at a local venue and described some of the jokes he employed:[2]

> On his campaign to become President—"My slogan was: SOAK THE POOR. I figured we'd better get it from the poor before the rich got it."
>
> On philosophy—"You can get more with a KIND WORD—and a gun—than just with a kind word."

The quip above and other early instances were usually not assigned to any specific individual. However, by 1969 Corey had heightened the humor of the line by attaching the words to Capone. Details for this citation are given further below.

Here are additional selected citations in chronological order.

In 1966 the syndicated column of the *Hollywood Reporter* noted that Ted Bessell, a television actor in a popular sitcom, deployed the quip. The words were not credited to Capone:[3]

> Ted Bessell, on his set of "That Girl," has your thought for the day: You can get more with a kind word—and a gun—than you can with a kind word.

In 1968 a short article printed in a Pennsylvania newspaper reported that an unnamed comic used the expression during a television broadcast. The joke was not yet connected to a gangster in this instance:[4]

> Did you hear the television comic the other night:
> "You can get more with a kind word, and a gun, than you can get with just a kind word."

In July 1969 the popular, widely distributed newspaper supplement *Parade* magazine published "My Favorite Jokes by Professor Irwin Corey," which included a profile of Corey together with a collection of humorous remarks. This article is the first located by **QI** that tentatively and satirically assigns the jest to Capone:[5]

> I think it was Al Capone who once said: "You can get more with a kind word and a gun than with just a kind word."

In August 1969 a variant of the expression was printed in a Brooklyn, New York, periodical. The ascription to Capone was treated seriously:[6]

> It is said of Al Capone that he always claimed that the best way to get along was with a "kind word and a gun, especially a gun."

In October 1970 a newspaper in Iowa printed the statement and credited Capone:[7]

It was Al Capone who once said, "You can get more with a kind word and a gun than with just a kind word."

In November 1970 the expression was published with a tentative ascription to Capone in a Wisconsin newspaper:[8]

I think it was Al Capone who said "You can get more with a kind word and a gun than with just a kind word."

In 1972 *Time* magazine quoted an economist using the expression. The topic was wage and price controls, and Capone was credited:[9]

Says Walter Heller, a member of TIME'S Board of Economists: "Things will never be the same again. Even after controls are lifted, there will be the threat of their reimposition. As Al Capone put it: 'You can get so much farther with a kind word and a gun than with a kind word alone.'"

A 1974 *Parade* piece by comedy team Jim Gannon and Wil Gerstenblatt mentioned a variant of the jest attributed to Capone:[10]

We leave you with some of Al Capone's wisdom: You can always get somewhere with a kind word and a gun.

In 1977 a Boston, Massachusetts, newspaper quoted the economist Walter Heller, but in this case he used the word "smile" instead of the phrase "kind word":[11]

Commenting on Carter's potential coercive powers for dealing with the spiral, Heller quoted the depression era gangster Al Capone, "You can go further with a smile and a gun, than with a smile alone."

In 1979 the language maven William Safire wrote in the *New York Times* that the saying was used by an economic adviser who ascribed the words to Capone:[12]

One of Mr. Kennedy's eminent economic advisers, when in a facetious mood on the subject of incomes policy, likes to recall an aphorism attributed to the gangster Al Capone: "You get a lot more from a kind word and a gun than from a kind word alone."

The 1987 film *The Untouchables* dramatized the conflict between Capone and a team led by government agent Eliot Ness. During a scene with journalists, Al Capone, played by Robert DeNiro, replied to a question about his reputation for using violence with these words:[13]

I grew up in a tough neighborhood, and we used to say you can get further with a kind word and a gun, than you can with just a kind word; and in that neighborhood it might have been true.

The important reference work *The Yale Book of Quotations* includes a note of commentary about this quotation. The editor, Fred R. Shapiro, points out that a 1980 book had linked the statement to the entertainer Irwin Corey:[14]

Usually associated with Capone, but Paul Dickson, *The Official Explanations* (1980), attributes to Irwin Corey, "You can get more with a kind word and a gun than you can with a kind word."

In conclusion, **QI** hypothesizes that this quip was crafted by the humorist Professor Irwin Corey by 1953. Further, **QI** believes that Corey fabricated the ascription to Capone by 1969 to enhance the comical effect and with no real intention to deceive. Nevertheless, the attribution was taken seriously, and today the expression is often incorrectly attributed to Capone.

Notes:

1. "Survey of Humor," *Variety*, July 29, 1953, 51. Thanks to Barry Popik who found this citation.
2. Jack De Yonge, "Impeccable Educator: Prof. Irwin Corey Hits Kennedy Steel Stand!" *Seattle Daily Times*, July 3, 1962, 7. Accessed in GenealogyBank.

3. Mike Connolly's Staff, "Beatty Makes Hit in Dallas," Hollywood Reporter, *Arizona Republic*, December 14, 1966, 36. Accessed in NewspaperARCHIVE.com.

4. "Is Foreign Policy Comic?" *Leader-Times* (Kittanning, PA), April 3, 1968, 6. Accessed in NewspaperARCHIVE.com.

5. Irwin Corey, My Favorite Jokes, *Parade*, July 13, 1969, 18, as found in *Sunday Advocate* (Baton Rouge, LA), July 13, 1969. Accessed in GenealogyBank.

6. John P. Quinn, "Our Own Past Shows that for Well-Being the Control of Production Is Necessary," *Weekly People* (Brooklyn, NY), August 30, 1969, 5. Accessed in Old Fulton NY Post Cards, fultonhistory.com.

7. Thoughts While Viewing, *Waterloo Sunday Courier* (Waterloo, IA), October 4, 1970, 43. Accessed in NewspaperARCHIVE.com.

8. Emilie Russert, "Look to Good, Clean Land: The Notebook," *Oshkosh Daily Northwestern* (Oshkosh, WI), November 21, 1970, 12. Accessed in NewspaperARCHIVE.com.

9. Donald Morrison, "The Future of Free Enterprise," *Time*, February 14, 1972, http://goo.gl/7Hf6jG.

10. Jim Gannon and Wil Gerstenblatt, My Favorite Jokes, *Parade*, September 1, 1974, 12, as found in *Springfield Union* (Springfield, MA), September 1, 1974. Accessed in GenealogyBank.

11. "Carter Adviser Outlines Steps to Halt Inflation," *Boston Herald American*, January 8, 1977, 8. Accessed in GenealogyBank.

12. William Safire, "Rejected Counsel Returns," *New York Times*, September 24, 1979, A19. Accessed in ProQuest.

13. "The Untouchables (1/10) Movie CLIP - A Kind Word and a Gun (1987) HD," YouTube video, 2:13, posted by "Movieclips," October 6, 2011, https://www.youtube.com/watch?v=KdNSlyrbcDY. Quote starts at 1:12.

14. Fred R. Shapiro, *The Yale Book of Quotations* (New Haven: Yale University Press, 2006), 130. Verified in hard copy.

HISTORICAL FICTION

8. "Hollywood is a place where they'll pay a thousand dollars for a kiss and fifty cents for your soul."

—Marilyn Monroe

QI notes the controversial nature of this quote because it was printed in an autobiography of Monroe titled *My Story* that was first published, posthumously, in 1974, twelve years after her tragic death in 1962. Some critics believe that the text does not reflect the actual words of the celebrity. Here is a longer excerpt:[1]

> In Hollywood a girl's virtue is much less important than her hair-do. You're judged by how you look, not by what you are. Hollywood's a place where they'll pay you a thousand dollars for a kiss, and fifty cents for your soul. I know, because I turned down the first offer often enough and held out for the fifty cents.

Following the release of *My Story*, the *Los Angeles Times* book editor critically evaluated the work. The source of the memoir was a typewritten manuscript from a former photographer of Monroe named Milton Greene. The publisher Stein and Day did not attempt to check or research the text. The executors of the Monroe estate shared profits from sales of the book with Greene and the publisher. The newspaper wrote the following:[2]

> This "new" autobiography covers the same ground—most of it word for word—as a series of luridly illustrated articles published 20 years ago in the *London Empire News* between May 9 and Aug 1,

1954. The collaborator/ghost writer of that series was apparently screenwriter Ben Hecht.

Extended passages of identical text from the memoir and the *London Empire News* were displayed in sidebars of the article in the *Los Angeles Times*.

In 1975 the book reviewer in the *Spectator* of London expressed incredulity regarding the authorship of the memoir because of its prose style:[3]

> Which brings us to *My Story* which is supposed to be by Marilyn Monroe. We are asked to believe that she wrote sentences like, "All your hungry days and hysterical nights step up to the headlines and take a bow . . ."
> Try this on for size: "Automobiles roll down Sunset Boulevard like an endless string of beetles. Their rubber tires make a purring high-class noise."

Yet, the perception of Monroe's intellect is often incomplete. The sexpot persona was her artificial construction, and it successfully catapulted her to stardom. She displayed a sharp wit with responses like the following reported in *Time* magazine:[4]

> She admitted she posed for the [calendar] picture back in 1949 to pay her overdue rent . . . Asked if she really had nothing on in the photograph, Marilyn, her blue eyes wide, purred: "I had the radio on."

In conclusion, the quotation was printed in Marilyn Monroe's memoir, but its provenance is not certain. **QI** does not think the passage is a complete fabrication, but a ghostwriter may have helped to shape the text.

Notes:

1. Marilyn Monroe, *My Story* (New York: Stein and Day, 1974), 47. Verified in hard copy.
2. Digby Biehl, "New Monroe Book from Old Memoirs," *Los Angeles Times*, April 15, 1974, C1. Accessed in ProQuest.

3. Larry Adler, "The Corn Is Greene," *Spectator*, November 29, 1975, 701. Verified in microfilm.

4. "Something for the Boys," Cinema, *Time*, August 11, 1952. Accessed in *Time* online, http://goo.gl/3ErdgY.

9. "The budget should be balanced; the Treasury should be refilled."

X

—Cicero

There is no substantive evidence that Cicero spoke or wrote these words, despite what a host on CNN told you in 2011.[1] In 1965 the bestselling author Taylor Caldwell published the book *A Pillar of Iron*. The subtitle on the cover stated, "A novel about Cicero and the Rome he tried to save." A fictionalized version of the historical figure Cicero was the primary character in the novel, and this imaginative portrayal contained the earliest germane evidence known to **QI**.

A passage in *A Pillar of Iron* depicted the thoughts of the character Cicero while he was conversing with a man named Antonius. Note that Caldwell's Cicero did not actually speak the following words in the novel:[2]

> Cicero found himself frequently confounded by Antonius. Antonius heartily agreed with him that the budget should be balanced, that the Treasury should be refilled, that public debt should be reduced, that the arrogance of the generals should be tempered and controlled, that assistance to foreign lands should be curtailed lest Rome become bankrupt, that the mobs should be forced to work and not depend on government for subsistence, and that prudence and frugality should be put into practice as soon as possible.

In the foreword to the book, Caldwell described the extensive research she performed while preparing to write the story:[3]

> I translated many hundreds of letters to and from Cicero and his editor and publisher, Atticus, myself in the Vatican Library in April 1947, and many more from Cicero to his brother, wife, son, daughter, Caesar, Pompey, and other people, in 1962 while again in Rome, and in Greece.

Caldwell also stated that some of the excerpts from letters in the book were based directly on translations of historical documents:

> As few footnotes as possible have been used, but in every place where it is written, "Cicero wrote—Atticus wrote—etc.," the letters are authentic and can be found in many histories in libraries almost everywhere.

Nevertheless, the passage given above about the Roman budget reflected the inner views of the character Cicero as imagined by Caldwell. The words were not part of a letter or a speech.

Cicero did deliver a "Speech in Defense of Sestius" that was thematically consonant with part of the quotation under investigation. The volume *As the Romans Did: A Sourcebook in Roman Social History* from Oxford University Press presents excerpts from the speech translated into English. Cicero commented negatively on a legislative proposal made by Gaius Gracchus to "sell a fixed monthly ration of grain at a low and unvarying price to any Roman citizen":[4]

> Gaius Gracchus proposed a grain law. The people were delighted with it because it provided an abundance of food without work. The good men, however, fought against it because they thought the masses would be attracted away from hard work and toward idleness, and they saw that the state treasury would be exhausted.

Taylor Caldwell's 1965 book *Pillar of Iron* contains the first known version of the quotation.

In May 1966 the Louisiana congressman Otto E. Passman employed an instance of the quotation during a congressional subcommittee hearing. The passage in the novel was modified to give it the form of a direct quote. Also, the phrase "arrogance of the generals" was replaced with "arrogance of officialdom." In addition, Passman presented a second quote about a "special right," which is printed in *A Pillar of Iron* a few pages after the first quote:[5]

> Mr. PASSMAN: The committee will come to order.

You know occasionally in our busy and bored lives we run into interesting, well written books of history. The path that we are traveling is a complete duplication of great nations that preceded us in greatness and finally fell by their foolishness.

I would like to quote one or two items for the record. I am quoting them verbatim.

One—

The budget should be balanced, the treasury should be refilled, public debt should be reduced, the arrogance of officialdom should be tempered and controlled, assistance to foreign lands should be curtailed lest Rome become bankrupt, the mob should be forced to work and not depend on government for subsistence, and prudence and frugality should be put into practice.

—Cicero, 58 B.C.

There is another quotation that certainly makes you recognize that we are taking a page from history. It reads like this:

When a civil right invades a domain of the rights of all the people, then it becomes a special right of a special class.

—Cicero again, 58 B.C.

In November 1966 a *Chicago Tribune* columnist reported on the remarks made by Passman and printed an instance of the statement ascribed to Cicero, thus facilitating its further dissemination. The quotation was further trimmed by a simplification of the last sentence:[6]

He is impressed by the parallels he finds between the destruction of the Roman republic and present trends in our own. This selection from Cicero expresses Passman's views on the Great Society:

> "The budget should be balanced, the treasury should be refilled, public debt should be reduced, the arrogance of officialdom should be tempered and controlled, assistance to foreign lands should be curtailed, lest Rome become bankrupt, and the mobs should be forced to work and not depend on government for subsistence."

In 1968 Congressman Passman continued to circulate the expression that he attributed to Cicero. For example, during a subcommittee hearing he repeated the words to Secretary of State Dean Rusk with this introduction:[7]

> Mr. PASSMAN: All right, Mr. Rusk, I have numerous quotations from history, but I think this statement made by Cicero over 2,000 years ago, is quite appropriate to close this hearing . . .

In 1969 a letter from a Los Angeles resident to the editor of the *Christian Science Monitor* included an instance of the quote ascribed to Cicero. The letter writer acknowledged Otto Passman as the source of the statement.[8]

In March 1971 the *Chicago Tribune* printed a letter to the editor that contained an instance of the passage credited to Cicero.[9] In April 1971 the newspaper printed a critical responding letter from John H. Collins, professor of history at Northern Illinois University:[10]

> I shall be glad to contribute $50 to Mr. Connolly's favorite charity if he (or anyone else) can cite chapter and verse for this alleged quotation anywhere in the known writings of Cicero.
>
> Mr. Connolly has been taken in by the "Foreword" of Taylor Caldwell's "Pillar of Iron." She speaks of nine years of study and "perpetual checking of sources" but the unhappy fact is that the great bulk of her quotations are false. The particular quotation above is from page 483 of "Pillar of Iron" and is totally without

documentation. A historical novelist has a perfect right to put invented conversations and anecdotes into a novel, but should not represent these inventions as authentic history.

In 1989 the Congressional Research Service published *Respectfully Quoted: A Dictionary of Quotations*. The saying ascribed to Cicero was examined with the following conclusion:[11]

No evidence has been found to confirm that Cicero said these words, and it is almost certainly spurious.

In 1992 the popular *San Francisco Chronicle* columnist Herb Caen printed a version of the saying that he obtained from a reader who saw it in Brazil. This version used the phrase "public assistance":[12]

QUOTE: "The national budget must be balanced. The public debt must be reduced; the arrogance of the authorities must be moderated and controlled. Payments to foreign governments must be reduced, if the nation doesn't want to go bankrupt. People must again learn to work, instead of living on public assistance." No, not the words of a candidate for president. Marcus Tullius Cicero said that in Rome in 55 B.C., according to a poster on the wall of a public notary's office in Sao Paolo, Brazil.

In conclusion, **QI** believes that the passage under investigation was constructed by Taylor Caldwell for her 1965 novel *A Pillar of Iron*. The words reflected the thoughts of the fictional character Cicero, who was based on Caldwell's conception of the historical figure Cicero. In the novel the character did not actually speak these words, and they have not been found in the speeches or writings of Cicero.

Notes:

Special thanks to Bonnie Taylor-Blake, who located the 1971 *Chicago Tribune* letter from John H. Collins and found the relevant text in *A Pillar of Iron*. She mentioned her finds at the valuable Snopes website in 2008 on a webpage that has since been removed. Thanks to Ariadne, who pointed out the "Speech in Defense of Sestius" in the same Snopes discussion. Great thanks to Professor Jonathan Lighter, who saw the CNN broadcast and discussed this topic on a mailing list. Much thanks to Michael V., who sent a query about this quote. Also, thanks to Lew Eigen, who critically examined this quotation.

1. *Your Bottom Line*, episode transcript, CNN, November 12, 2011, http://transcripts.cnn .com/TRANSCRIPTS/1111/12/ybl.01.html. Excerpt is spoken by program host Christine Romans.

2. Taylor Caldwell, *A Pillar of Iron* (Garden City, NY: Doubleday, 1965), 483. Verified in hard copy.

3. Caldwell, *A Pillar of Iron*, xiv. Verified in hard copy.

4. Jo-Ann Shelton, *As the Romans Did: A Sourcebook in Roman Social History* (New York: Oxford University Press, 1988), 229–30. Quote is found in Cicero's "Speech in Defense of Sestius." Verified in hard copy.

5. *Subcommittee of the Committee on Appropriations, Foreign Assistance and Related Agencies Appropriation Bill for 1967, Hearings Before a Subcommittee of the Committee on Appropriations*, H.R. REP. NO. 89-2045, at 673 and 820 (1966). Accessed in ProQuest. The cited pages refer to remarks made on May 4, 1966, by Louisiana congressman Otto E. Passman; Caldwell, *A Pillar of Iron*, 483, 489. Verified in hard copy. Text similar to the first quote appears on page 483, and text similar to the second quote appears on page 489.

6. Chesly Manly, "Foreign Aid Called 'Stupidest' Program," *Chicago Tribune*, November 16, 1966, 2. Accessed in ProQuest.

7. *Subcommittee of the Committee on Appropriations, Foreign Assistance and Related Agencies Appropriation Bill for 1969, Hearings Before a Subcommittee of the Committee on Appropriations*, H.R. REP. NO. 90, at 753 (1968). Accessed in ProQuest. The cited page refers to remarks made on May 22, 1968, by Louisiana congressman Otto E. Passman.

8. Cynthia W. Ashmun, letter to the editor, *Christian Science Monitor*, February 20, 1969, 18. Accessed in ProQuest.

9. Jerry Connolly, letter to the editor, *Chicago Tribune*, March 29, 1971, 14. Accessed in ProQuest.

10. John H. Collins, letter to the editor, *Chicago Tribune*, April 20, 1971, 10. Accessed in ProQuest.

11. *Respectfully Quoted: A Dictionary of Quotations*, Suzy Platt, ed. (Washington, DC: Congressional Research Service, 1989), s.v. "Marcus Tullius Cicero (106–43 BC)." Accessed in Bartleby.com, http://www.bartleby.com/73/795.html.

12. Herb Caen, The Monday Caenicle, *San Francisco Chronicle*, February 3, 1992, B1. Accessed in NewsBank.

IV

FINDERS KEEPERS

CAPTURE * HOST

1. "You'll worry less about what other people think of you when you realize how seldom they do."
2. "With great power comes great responsibility."
3. "Sports do not build character. They reveal it."
4. "Life is what happens to you while you're busy making other plans."
5. "Heaven for the climate, and hell for the company."
6. "I'm so fast, I hit the light switch in my bedroom and jump into bed before it gets dark."
7. "Not everything that counts can be counted."
8. "Writing about music is like dancing about architecture."
9. "Those who dance are considered insane by those who can't hear the music."
10. "If I had more time, I would have written a shorter letter."
11. "If you want to know what a man's like, look at how he treats his inferiors."
12. "We are made of star-stuff."
13. "Comedy is tragedy plus time."
14. "Easy reading is hard writing."
15. "In the future, everyone will be anonymous for fifteen minutes."
16. "I fear the day that technology will surpass our human interaction."
17. "To be is to do" . . . "To do is to be" . . . "Do be do be do."
18. "Well-behaved women seldom make history."
19. "Nobody goes there anymore; it's too crowded."

20. "If your only tool is a hammer, then every problem looks like a nail."
21. "Better to remain silent and be thought a fool than to speak and remove all doubt."
22. "History does not repeat itself, but it rhymes."

CAPTURE

1. "You'll worry less about what people think of you when you realize how seldom they do."

—David Foster Wallace

The earliest strong match of the above saying known to **QI** appeared in the widely syndicated newspaper column of Walter Winchell in January 1937. The words were credited to a jokesmith named Olin Miller:[1]

> "You probably," [Miller] submits, "wouldn't worry about what people think of you if you could know how seldom they do!"

QI believes that Olin Miller was the most likely originator of this remark. Other individuals such as David Foster Wallace and Ethel Barrett employed the saying after it was already in circulation. The phrasing has varied as the quotation has evolved over the decades. The occasional linkages to Mark Twain and Eleanor Roosevelt appear to be spurious. In 1751 prominent man of letters Samuel Johnson published an intriguing thematic precursor about excessive self-consciousness. Johnson emphasized that most people were preoccupied with their own affairs.[2]

> But the truth is, that no man is much regarded by the rest of the world, except where the interest of others is involved in his fortune. The common employments or pleasures of life, love or opposition, loss or gain, keep almost every mind in perpetual agitation. If any man would consider how little he dwells upon the condition of

others, he would learn how little the attention of others is attracted by himself.

In January 1937 columnist Walter Winchell credited Olin Miller with the adage, as previously mentioned. In December 1938 a slightly different version of the saying was published as a filler item in the *Evening World-Herald* of Omaha, Nebraska, without an attribution:[3]

You wouldn't worry about what people may think of you if you could know how seldom they do.

In February 1939 a Clinton, New York, newspaper reprinted the expression with an acknowledgment to another newspaper:[4]

You wouldn't worry about what people may think of you if you could know how seldom they do.

—*St. Louis Star-Times*

In June 1939 the top-selling magazine *Reader's Digest* printed the aphorism as a filler item with a correct ascription to Olin Miller:[5]

You probably wouldn't worry about what people think of you if you could know how seldom they do!

—Olin Miller

In June 1940 Arch Ward's long-running *Chicago Tribune* column In the Wake of the News printed an instance in a section called Thinkograms and credited "Sonja and Bob," who had probably relayed the remark to Ward:[6]

We probably wouldn't worry about what people think of us if we knew how seldom they do.

—Sonja and Bob

In May 1941 the popular syndicated column Office Cat by Junius published the expression without an attribution:[7]

> You probably wouldn't worry about what people think of you if you could know how seldom they do!

In 1942 the remark was printed in the pages of the *Los Angeles Times* with an acknowledgment to the sender:[8]

> NEEDLESS WORRY Jack Allis sends this comforting thought: "We wouldn't worry so much about what folks think of us if we knew how seldom they do."

In 1945 *Esquire* magazine published the saying together with a collection of miscellaneous quotations and credited someone named Lee Traveler:[9]

> We wouldn't worry about what people think about us if we knew how seldom they do.
>
> —Lee Traveler

The connection to Olin Miller was not forgotten by some careful compilers. In 1955 *The Speaker's Encyclopedia of Stories, Quotations, and Anecdotes* by Jacob Morton Braude included the expression in the same form given by Walter Winchell in 1937 together with the same ascription:[10]

> You probably wouldn't worry about what people think of you if you could know how seldom they do!
>
> —Olin Miller

In 1968 a humorous self-help book titled *Don't Look Now, But Your Personality Is Showing* by Ethel Barrett placed the adage in an ornamented box on the first page without an ascription:[11]

We would worry less about what others think of us, if we realized how seldom they do.

In 1994 a writer in the *St. Petersburg Times* of Florida connected the saying to the quotation magnet Mark Twain.[12]

I was surprised to learn Mark Twain became rather cynical and bitter in his old age. "You wouldn't worry so much about what people think of you, if you knew how seldom they do," he said. I could never have gotten away with saying that to my parents, but it would have been handy to know when I was a kid.

In 1996 David Foster Wallace published the capacious novel *Infinite Jest*, and he included a section about the bits of wisdom one might acquire at a fictional facility for the treatment of alcohol and drug dependence. Wallace's version of the adage starts off in a slightly different construction than Miller's and includes Wallace's trademark voice ("[Y]ou will become way less concerned . . .").[13]

If, by the virtue of charity or the circumstance of desperation, you ever chance to spend a little time around a Substance-recovery halfway facility like Enfield MA's state-funded Ennet House, you will acquire many exotic new facts . . .

That sometimes human beings have to just sit in one place and, like, hurt. That you will become way less concerned with what other people think of you when you realize how seldom they do. That there is such a thing as raw, unalloyed, agendaless kindness. That it is possible to fall asleep during an anxiety attack.

By 2007 a variant of the saying was being attributed to the famous first lady Eleanor Roosevelt, and **QI** notes how the voice has changed:[14]

You wouldn't worry so much about what other people think of you if you realized how seldom they do.

—Eleanor Roosevelt

In 2013 the periodical *Credit Management* printed an instance together with sundry quotations in a sidebar. The saying was ascribed to Ethel Barrett:[15]

> "We would worry less about what others think of us if we realised how seldom they do."
>
> —Ethel Barrett

In conclusion, **QI** believes that it is reasonable to credit Olin Miller with the version given in the 1937 citation. Ethel Barrett and David Foster Wallace helped to popularize the saying as indicated by the citations in 1968 and 1996 respectively.

Notes:

Great thanks to Corina Borsuk, whose query led **QI** to formulate this question and perform this exploration. Special thanks to Frank Lynch, the proprietor of a valuable Samuel Johnson quotation website, who pointed out the 1751 passage by Johnson. Thanks to top quotation researcher Barry Popik, who located the key Winchell citation and other valuable citations.[16]

1. Walter Winchell, On Broadway, *Logansport Pharos-Tribune* (Logansport, IN), January 7, 1937, 8. Accessed in NewspaperARCHIVE.com.
2. Samuel Johnson, [untitled essay], *Rambler*, no. 159 (September 24, 1751): 6. Accessed in Google Books, https://goo.gl/QprmRp.
3. [Freestanding filler item], *Evening World-Herald* (Omaha, NE), December 27, 1938, 14. Accessed in GenealogyBank.
4. "With the Paragraphers," reprinted from Newsdem, *Clinton Courier* (Clinton, NY), February 2, 1939, 1. Accessed in Old Fulton NY Post Cards, fultonhistory.com.
5. [Filler item with quotation], *Reader's Digest*, June 1939, 60. Verified in hard copy.
6. Arch Ward, "Thinkograms," In the Wake of the News, *Chicago Tribune*, June 29, 1940, 15. Accessed in ProQuest.
7. Junius, Office Cat, *Kingston Daily Freeman* (Kingston, NY), May 13, 1941, 6. Accessed in Old Fulton NY Post Cards, fultonhistory.com.

8. Lee Shippey, Lee Side o' L.A., *Los Angeles Times*, March 24, 1942, A4. Accessed in ProQuest.

9. Going the Rounds with *Esquire*, *Esquire* 23 (June 1945): 107. Verified in microfilm.

10. Jacob Morton Braude, *The Speaker's Encyclopedia of Stories, Quotations, and Anecdotes* (Englewood Cliffs, NJ: Prentice-Hall, 1955), 332. Verified in hard copy in third printing of May 1956.

11. Ethel Barrett, *Don't Look Now, but Your Personality Is Showing*, 5th print. (Glendale, CA: G/L Regal Books, 1968), epigraph before title page. Verified in scans of sixth printing of 1973.

12. Louise Andryusky, "Seniority: Politics, Violence, and Waiting by the Phone," *St. Petersburg Times* (St. Petersburg, FL), February 22, 1994, 23X. Accessed in NewsBank.

13. David Foster Wallace, *Infinite Jest* (Boston: Little, Brown, 1996), 200, 203. Verified in hard copy.

14. Michael Olpin and Margie Hesson, *Stress Management for Life: A Research-Based Experiential Approach* (Belmont, CA: Thomson/Wadsworth, 2007), 127.

15. Nigel Risner, "Ten Tips for Becoming Personally Empowered," *Credit Management*, October 2013, 30–31. Accessed in ProQuest ABI/INFORM Complete.

16. Barry Popik, "You Wouldn't Worry About What People May Think of You if You Could Know How Seldom They Do," The Big Apple, September 1, 2013. http://www.barrypopik.com/index.php/new_york_city/entry/you_wouldnt_worry_what_people_may_think_of_you/.

2. "With great power comes great responsibility."

—Spider-Man

—Voltaire

In September 2014 **QI** received an email with a question about the above popular quotation. The words have been attributed to both Voltaire and Spider-Man. However, the genuine provenance of the saying was—at the time of inquiry—uncertain. The message to **QI** ended with a compliment and a challenge: "I won't believe anyone except the Quote Investigator."

Several other researchers had already tackled this topic, and no one had located the expression in the French-language corpus of Voltaire. The earliest known instance in the English language is dated 1854, as reported in *The Yale Book of Quotations*. **QI** performed a preliminary search by querying his private database of references and by searching Google Books together with several newspaper databases. **QI** also attempted to verify an incomplete citation that pointed to a volume of *The Works of Voltaire* in French, but multiple queries based on pertinent French words and phrases revealed nothing—**QI** concluded that the citation was probably faulty. Overall, **QI** was making no progress, so he suspended his research and redirected his efforts toward a different question from the thousands of other pending requests.

In June 2015, however, **QI**'s client emphatically renewed her appeal. Her next email stated that the quotation had been mentioned in a decision recently handed down by the US Supreme Court. The case was *Kimble v. Marvel Entertainment*, and the quotation was attributed to a 1962 issue of the comic book that had debuted the character Spider-Man, created by Stan Lee and Steve Ditko. The client felt that **QI** had missed an important opportunity. Curious about the identity of his interlocutor, **QI** found that her name matched that of a federal judge on the US Court of Appeals.

QI resumed his efforts.

QI found a strong match to the phrase dating to the period of the French Revolution. The following passage appeared with a date of May 8, 1793, in a collection of the decrees made by the French National Convention.[1]

> Les Représentans du peuple se rendront à leur destination, investis de la plus haute confiance et de pouvoirs illimités. Ils vont déployer un grand caractère. Ils doivent envisager qu'une grande responsabilité est la suite inséparable d'un grand pouvoir. Ce sera à leur énergie, à leur courage, et sur-tout à leur prudence, qu'ils devront leur succès et leur gloire.

Here is one possible translation into English:

> The people's representatives will reach their destination, invested with the highest confidence and unlimited power. They will show great character. They must consider that great responsibility follows inseparably from great power. To their energy, to their courage, and above all to their prudence, they shall owe their success and their glory.

Prominent world leaders such as Lord Melbourne, Winston Churchill, Theodore Roosevelt, and Franklin D. Roosevelt made similar statements in later years, prior to Spider-Man.

A thematic precursor appears in a well-known biblical verse—Luke 12:48. However, the meaning is somewhat different because it does not mention power. The New International and King James translations render the verse as follows:[2]

> From everyone who has been given much, much will be demanded; and from the one who has been entrusted with much, much more will be asked.
>
> For unto whomsoever much is given, of him shall be much required: and to whom men have committed much, of him they will ask the more.

In 1793 the following statement appeared in a volume issued by the French National Convention as mentioned previously:

> Ils doivent envisager qu'une grande responsabilité est la suite inséparable d'un grand pouvoir.

Here is a possible English translation:

> They must consider that great responsibility follows inseparably from great power.

In 1817 the UK House of Commons held a debate concerning the suspension of habeas corpus, and a member named William Lamb spoke in favor of suspension. During the following decades, Lamb became a powerful political figure, and ultimately he emerged as prime minister and now is better known as Lord Melbourne. The transcript of Lamb's words in 1817 used quotation marks to enclose the maxim, indicating that the expression was already in circulation. Please note that the modern reader will find the style of the transcript atypical because it was presented from a third-person perspective. The referent "he" is used to identify the speaker Mr. Lamb.[3]

> It was common to speak of the power of the press, and he admitted that its power was great. He should, however, beg leave to remind the conductors of the press of their duty to apply to themselves a maxim which they never neglected to urge on the consideration of government—"that the possession of great power necessarily implies great responsibility." They stood in a high situation, and ought to consider justice and truth the great objects of their labours, and not yield themselves up to their interests or their passions.

In 1854 Reverend John Cumming, a minister of the Scottish National Church, published a religious text that included a thematic statement.[4]

> The order of God's providence, and certainly the law of Christ's Gospel, is, that wherever there is great power, lofty position, there

is great responsibility, and a call to instant duty. If your house is very magnificent in its architectural splendors without, and in its furniture within, it is that you should look around you, and take care that the houses in the lanes behind shall not be so miserable and wretched as they are.

In 1858 a Masonic periodical called the *Ashlar* printed a thematic instance that reordered the sequence of the two key terms.[5]

He cannot act on their judgment, but must be governed by his own. As he has great responsibility, he has great power, and is bound by the strongest obligations to maintain that power and the dignity of his office.

During an 1897 speech, Sir Hercules G. R. Robinson extended the saying by adding "anxiety" as an inescapable addendum:[6]

But great power carries with it great responsibility, and great responsibility entails a large amount of anxiety.

In 1879 a report by the trustees of the Boston Public Library included a statement from former trustee Professor Henry W. Haynes that contained a version of the saying.[7]

The possession of great powers and capacity for good implies equally great responsibilities in their employment. Where so much has been given much is required.

In 1906 statesman Winston Churchill delivered a speech in the UK House of Commons that included an extended instance of the adage.[8]

Where there is great power there is great responsibility, where there is less power there is less responsibility, and where there is no power there can, I think, be no responsibility.

On June 19, 1908, President Theodore Roosevelt wrote a letter to Sir George Otto Trevelyan that included a discussion of his reasons for declining to seek a third term as president.[9]

> I believe in a strong executive; I believe in power; but I believe that responsibility should go with power, and that it is not well that the strong executive should be a perpetual executive.

In 1913 John A. Fitch wrote a commentary that discussed the power of the US Steel Corporation in the journal the *Railroad Trainman*, and he referenced the adage.[10]

> It may be no crime to be possessed of great power. But great power carries with it great responsibility as to the use that is made of it.

The night before Franklin D. Roosevelt died in April 1945, he penned a speech about Thomas Jefferson that he was planning to deliver during a future radio address. Instead, his text was given to journalists after his death and released by the Associated Press.[11]

> Today we have learned in the agony of war that great power involves great responsibility. Today we can no more escape the consequences of German and Japanese aggression than could he avoid the consequences of attacks by the Barbary Corsairs a century and a half before.

The heroic fantasy figure Spider-Man was introduced in August 1962 in the comic book *Amazing Fantasy* #15. This origin story formulated the guiding principle of Spider-Man's actions, and the phrase was expressed here as a caption. However, the words were spoken neither by the main character Peter Parker, nor by his Uncle Ben. Instead, an omniscient narrative voice was employed.[12]

> And a lean, silent figure slowly fades into the gathering darkness, aware at last that in this world, with great power there must also come—great responsibility!

In conclusion, based on current knowledge **QI** would ascribe the saying to the writer of the 1793 passage from the collection of decrees from the French National Convention, but **QI** does not know the precise identity of this writer. Also, it is certainly possible that earlier close matches will be discovered by future researchers.

In addition, major figures such as Lord Melbourne, Winston Churchill, and Franklin D. Roosevelt employed versions of the adage. The creators of Spider-Man, Stan Lee and Steve Ditko, were important vectors for the popularization of the saying.

Notes:

Great thanks to Sandra Ikuta, whose inquiry about this interesting topic led **QI** to formulate this question and perform this exploration. Many thanks to S. M. Colowick and Anton Sherwood for providing translations of the 1793 passage. All errors are the responsibility of **QI**. Also thanks to Kelly Di Donato, Charles Early, and Murl Winters, who pointed to the biblical reference. In addition, thanks to Fred R. Shapiro for identifying the 1854 citation in *The Yale Book of Quotations*. Further thanks to Vaios K., who mentioned the 1817 citation in a response at Yahoo Answers.

1. Collection Générale des Décrets Rendus par la Convention Nationale, May 1793 (Paris: Chez Baudouin, 1793), 72. Accessed in Google Books, https://goo.gl/wdtYSz.

2. "Luke 12:48," Bible Hub, accessed July 23, 2015, http://biblehub.com/luke/12-48.htm.

3. "Habeas Corpus Suspension Bill," Mr. [William] Lamb speaking, June 27, 1817, in Parliamentary Debates from the Year 1803 to the Present Time 36, ["Comprising the Period from the Twenty-Eighth Day of April to the Twelfth Day of July, 1817"], column nos. 1226–27. Accessed in Google Books, https://goo.gl/D90P1a.

4. John Cumming, *Voices of the Dead* (Boston: John P. Jewett, 1854), 121. Accessed in Google Books, https://goo.gl/UZlHlQ. This citation was identified in Fred R. Shapiro, *The Yale Book of Quotations* (New Haven: Yale University Press, 2006), 449. Verified in hard copy.

5. "Duties of the W.M.," *Ashlar* 3, no. 8 (April 1858): 348. Accessed in Google Books, https://goo.gl/gVnH9I.

6. "Vice-Regal Visit to Parramatta: Public Banquet, July 8, 1872," in *Speeches Delivered by His Excellency Sir Hercules G. R. Robinson, G. C. M. G. During His Administration of the*

Government of New South Wales (Sydney: Gibbs, Shallard, 1879), 6. Accessed in Google Books, https://goo.gl/9kMnTf.

7. City of Boston, "Annual Report of the Trustees of the Public Library [Twenty-Seventh Annual Report of the Trustees of the Public Library]," city doc. 69, 12. Accessed in Google Books, https://goo.gl/8Xwrx4.

8. Mr. Winston Churchill speaking, February 28, 1906, in Parliamentary Debates (Authorised Edition), Fourth Series, First Session of the Twenty-Eighth Parliament of the United Kingdom of Great Britain and Ireland 152, ["Comprising the Period from the Thirteenth Day of February to the Second Day of March, 1906"], column no. 1239. Accessed in Google Books, https://goo.gl/si7euZ.

9. Joseph Bucklin Bishop, *Theodore Roosevelt and His Time: Shown in His Own Letters*, vol. 2 (New York: Charles Scribner's Sons, 1920), 94. Accessed in Google Books, https://goo.gl /LZ6Ynw. The excerpt of the letter is dated June 19, 1908.

10. John A. Fitch, "The Labor Policies of Unrestricted Capital," *Railroad Trainman* 30, no. 4 (April 1913): 305. Accessed in Google Books, https://goo.gl/1g8UzD.

11. Associated Press, "Speech Written by Roosevelt on Night Before His Death," *Daily Illinois State Journal* (Springfield, IL), April 14, 1945, 2. Accessed in GenealogyBank.

12. Stan Lee, "Spider-Man!" *Amazing Fantasy* #15 (August 1962), Marvel Comics. The quotation appeared in a caption above a panel showing character Peter Parker walking away down an urban street. **QI** has not seen the original comic book in hard copy. **QI** bases the quotation information on the text seen in two digitized panel images from the issue *Amazing Fantasy* #15 (August 1962) as seen in Kelly Kond, "The Origin of 'With Great Power Comes Great Responsibility' and 7 Other Surprising Parts of Spider-Man's Comic Book History," We Minored in Film, April 22, 2014, https://goo.gl/mYpyAH.

3. "Sports do not build character. They reveal it."

—John Wooden

John Wooden led UCLA to ten national championships and was arguably the greatest basketball coach who ever lived. Since 1977 the best player in the sport has been awarded a trophy named in Wooden's honor. The ceremony for the award takes place at the Los Angeles Athletic Club in downtown Los Angeles, where the basketball court, ringed by framed portraits of past Wooden Award winners, is also named after the man. Hanging above John Wooden Court is a larger-than-life poster of Wooden in black and white pinstripes shouting from the bench of UCLA. Inscribed above him are the words:

Sports do not build character. They reveal it.

—John R. Wooden

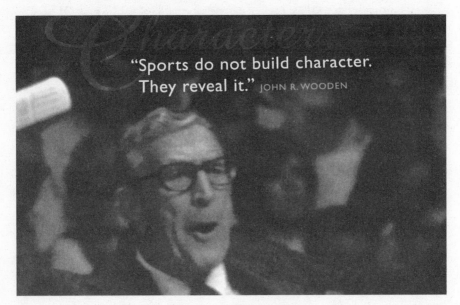

Credit: Los Angeles Athletic Club

QI is dubious.

The earliest citation for the phrase located by **QI** was published in January 1974, the year before Wooden retired, in the *Ames Daily Tribune* of Ames, Iowa. Heywood Hale Broun, an "off-beat sports commentator for CBS television," had recently visited the city and delivered a speech.[1]

> "Anybody who teaches a skill, which coaches do, is admirable. But sport doesn't build character. Character is built pretty much by the time you're six or seven. Sports reveals character. Sports heightens your perceptions. Let that be enough."

Broun expressed this idea more than once, and he employed different phrasings. On May 2, 1974, an article in the *Salina Journal* of Salina, Kansas, reported that Broun was planning to visit the city and present an invited lecture at Kansas Wesleyan University on May 10. The journalist noted that Broun was a sports commentator and a former actor. The article contained a synthesized instance of the quotation; only the second half of the adage was surrounded by quotation marks.[2]

> Sports do not build character, he says. "Sports reveal character and I enjoy writing of sports because, I think, madness—the fierce devotion to succeed competitively—is essential to greatness. I write of people who are interesting and not necessarily those whom I like personally."

Two days after Broun had delivered his speech, on May 12, 1974, the *Salina Journal* published a story noting that more than four hundred people had attended and that Broun had "charmed" the audience. The two phrases of the adage were reversed in this instance.[3]

> "Sports reveals character, it doesn't build it," Broun said. "I do not really think it makes you a better person. It is a means of having a good time."

He quoted Jean-Paul Sartre's observation that man is most free in sports because it's the only place he makes the rules.

In 1976 James A. Michener, well known for creating a series of bestselling novels, decided to examine athletics in a nonfiction work titled *Sports in America*. Michener ascribed the common modern version of the saying to Broun.[4]

> Heywood Hale Broun, who has written much in this field, has said, "Sports do not build character. They reveal it." Darrell Royal, of Texas, phrased it this way: "Football doesn't build character. It eliminates the weak ones." And a comedian has said, "Sport develops not character, but characters."

In 1996 an article in the *Kokomo Tribune* of Kokomo, Indiana, attributed an interesting remark on athletics to Wooden that differed from the one under examination.[5]

> As UCLA basketball legend John Wooden once said, "Yes, sports can build character. But they also can tear down character."

In 2006 the *Hood County News* of Granbury, Texas, printed the aphorism under examination and credited John Wooden, evidently in error:[6]

> Sports do not build character. They reveal it.
>
> —John Wooden

In conclusion, **QI** suspects that the statement was probably streamlined from Heywood Hale Broun's original words. It's not clear when the poster was hung by the Los Angeles Athletic Club above John Wooden Court.

Notes:

Great thanks to Konstantinos Psychas, whose inquiry led **QI** to formulate this question and perform this exploration.

1.   Larry Lockhart, "Broun: 'I Like to See Things Done with Zest,'" *Ames Daily Tribune* (Ames, IA), January 16, 1974, 11. Accessed in Newspapers.com.

2.   "Heywood Hale Broun Will Speak at KW," *Salina Journal* (Salina, KS), May 2, 1974, 12. Accessed in Newspapers.com.

3.   Barbara Phillips, "He Wows Them at K-Wesleyan," *Salina Journal* (Salina, KS), May 12, 1974, 18. Accessed in Newspapers.com.

4.   James A. Michener, *Sports in America* (New York: Random House, 1976), 16. Verified in hard copy.

5.   Terry Mattingly, "Christianity and the Super Bowl Have Some Things in Common," *Kokomo Tribune* (Kokomo, IN), January 27, 1996, A7. Accessed in Newspapers.com.

6.   Forum, *Hood County News* (Granbury, TX), June 24, 2006, 4. Accessed in Newspapers.com.

4. "Life is what happens to you while you're busy making other plans."

—John Lennon

John Lennon composed a song about his son Sean called "Beautiful Boy (Darling Boy)" and released it as part of his 1980 album *Double Fantasy*. The phrase above is contained in the song's lyrics and can be heard at two minutes and sixteen seconds into the track, about halfway through. Lennon sings the following:[1]

Before you cross the street take my hand.
Life is what happens to you while you're busy making other plans.

Ever since, Lennon has been credited with the saying on all sorts of inspirational bric-a-brac. But the general expression can be traced back more than two decades before "Beautiful Boy (Darling Boy)." The first known appearance was in an issue of *Reader's Digest* dated January 1957. The statement was printed together with nine other unrelated sayings in a section called Quotable Quotes:[2]

Allen Saunders: Life is what happens to us while we are making other plans.

—Publishers Syndicate

The newspaper comic strip *Steve Roper* was written by an individual named Allen Saunders and distributed by Publishers Syndicate. It is likely that *Reader's Digest* was referencing that arrangement, though the attribution is slightly inscrutable. Saunders also worked on the comic strips *Mary Worth* and *Kerry Drake*. **QI** has not yet located the saying in any of these comics. Three important reference works list the *Reader's Digest* citation to Saunders—*The Dictionary of Modern Proverbs*,[3] *The Quote Verifier*,[4] and *The Yale Book of Quotations*.[5]

Many of the quotations published in the widely circulated *Reader's Digest* were reprinted in other periodicals. For example, a Charleston, South Carolina, paper reprinted the saying in the same month and year:[6]

> "Life," reads a line of an article in *The Reader's Digest*, "is what happens to us while we are making other plans." How true.
> The trouble is most of us don't realize this except in retrospect and then life has already happened.

In June 1957 the adage appeared in a Texas newspaper as a freestanding filler item. The attribution given was the same as that in *Reader's Digest*—"Allen Saunders, Publishers Syndicate"—but the magazine was not mentioned.[7]

In September 1957 the quote was included in an advertisement for Swanson's, a clothing retailer. The words were listed together with several other sayings and no attribution was provided.[8] In November 1957 the quote appeared in the *Irish Digest* as a filler item. No attribution was listed.[9]

In March 1958 the popular syndicated columnist Earl Wilson published a version of the saying in a subsection titled Earl's Pearls. The words were identical except for the use of the contraction "we're." This time a new person named Quin Ryan received acknowledgment:[10]

> Some people have everything—except fun . . . Life, says Quin Ryan of Chicago, is what happens to us while we're making other plans . . . See no evil, speak no evil, hear no evil—and half the women's clubs would fold up in a hurry.

In April 1958 a slightly modified version of the saying was printed in a column of the *Boston Globe*. The word "when" replaced the word "while," and no credit was given:[11]

> Life is what happens to us when we are making other plans.

In September 1958 a variant of the adage appeared in a *Chicago Tribune* column called A Line O' Type or Two. The statement was credited to Quin Ryan:[12]

PAINFUL TRUTH
Life is what happens to every man's Career while he's making other
plans.

—Quin Ryan

In 1961 the maxim was associated with another person in the pages of the
Los Angeles Sentinel:[13]

Bon vivant, Walter Ward, from somewhere in Italy writes to say,
"Life is what happens to us while we're making other plans."

In 1962 the syndicated columnist Larry Wolters reported on the expression
in Radio TV Gag Bag. This column specialized in collecting jokes and bon mots
that were broadcast on radio and television stations in the United States. Wolters
identified the performer who delivered the line:[14]

Henry Cooke: "A thoughtful man is one who gives his wife a birthday present without mentioning her birthday past."

Also: "Life is what happens to us while we are making other plans."

In 1963 the saying reappeared in the column of Earl Wilson, but this time
the word "busy" was inserted, and the phrase was reassigned to Henry Cooke:[15]

REMEMBERED QUOTE: Life is what happens to us while we
are busy making other plans.

—Henry Cooke

In 1964 the syndicated columnist and quotation collector Bennett Cerf
ascribed a version of the saying to the author Robert Balzer:[16]

Life is what happens to you while you're making other plans.

—Robert Balzer

In 1964 the maxim reappeared in the column of Larry Wolters now called Gag Bag, reassigned to Balzer:[17]

Robert Balzer: "Life is what happens to you while you are making other plans."

In 1965 Earl Wilson decided that the expression was interesting enough to print another time. He assigned the following concise version to someone named L. S. McCandless:[18]

REMEMBERED QUOTE: "Life is what happens while you're making other plans."

—L. S. McCandless.

In 1967 a variant of the adage was printed in the popular Dear Abby column of Pauline Phillips:[19]

Confidential To Del Ray Beachcomber: Yes. See your lawyer about changing your will. Fate is what happens to you while you're making other plans.

In 1979 the work *1,001 Logical Laws*, compiled by John Peers, Gordon Bennett, and George Booth, included the saying and connected it to someone named Knight:[20]

Knight's Law: Life is what happens to you while you're making other plans.

In conclusion, based on currently available evidence, this piece of wisdom can be credited to Allen Saunders. John Lennon also included it in the lyrics of a song many years later. The expression is quite popular and has acquired multiple attributions over the decades.

Notes:

Many thanks to Jay, whose question initiated this exploration.

1. "John Lennon–Beautiful Boy.flv," YouTube video, 4:12, posted by "TheInnerRevolution," November 22, 2009, https://www.youtube.com/watch?v=Z5BBEOjUKrI.
2. Quotable Quotes, *Reader's Digest*, January 1957, 32. Verified in hard copy.
3. Charles Clay Doyle, Wolfgang Mieder, and Fred R. Shapiro, eds., *The Dictionary of Modern Proverbs* (New Haven, CT: Yale University Press, 2012), 145. Verified in hard copy.
4. Ralph Keyes, *The Quote Verifier: Who Said What, Where, and When* (New York: St. Martin's, 2006), 123–24, 305. Verified in hard copy.
5. Fred R. Shapiro, *The Yale Book of Quotations* (New Haven: Yale University Press, 2006), 666. Verified in hard copy.
6. Chlotilde R. Martin, "Beaufort TV Viewer Finds Quiz Programs Distasteful," Lowcountry Gossip, *News and Courier* (Charleston, SC), January 27, 1957, 11B. Accessed in GenealogyBank.
7. R. J. (Bob) Edwards, Round About Town, *Denton Record-Chronicle* (Denton, TX), June 21, 1957, 4. Accessed in NewspaperARCHIVE.com.
8. "A Little of This and That" [quotation within an advertisement for Swanson's], *Titusville Herald* (Titusville, PA), September 24, 1957, 2. Accessed in NewspaperARCHIVE.com.
9. [Freestanding quotation], *Irish Digest* 61 (November 1957): 52. Verified in microfilm.
10. Earl Wilson, Earl's Pearls, *Rockford Register-Republic* (Rockford, IL), March 1, 1958, 2A. Accessed in Genealogy Bank.
11. Joe Harrington, "That Boston Accent . . . What Did He Say?" All Sorts, *Boston Globe*, April 10, 1958, 25. Accessed in ProQuest.
12. A Line O'Type or Two, *Chicago Tribune*, September 18, 1958, 16. Accessed in ProQuest.
13. Paul C. McGee, "Theatricals: The Stem," *Los Angeles Sentinel*, September 14, 1961, C2. Accessed in ProQuest.
14. Larry Wolters, Radio TV Gag Bag, *Chicago Tribune*, August 12, 1962, C28. Accessed in ProQuest.
15. Earl Wilson, Earl Wilson's New York, *Aberdeen American News* (Aberdeen, SD), April 30, 1963, 4. Accessed in GenealogyBank.

16. Bennett Cerf, "Try and Stop Me," *State Times Advocate* (Baton Rouge, LA), January 15, 1964, 10C. Accessed in GenealogyBank.

17. Larry Wolters, Larry Wolters' Gag Bag, *Chicago Tribune*, May 17, 1964, 115. Accessed in ProQuest.

18. Earl Wilson, It Happened Last Night, *Dallas Morning News*, November 19, 1965, A27. Accessed in GenealogyBank.

19. Abigail Van Buren, "Fresh News; Stale Money," Dear Abby, *Cleveland Plain Dealer* (Cleveland, OH), December 8, 1967, 39. Accessed in GenealogyBank.

20. John Peers, Gordon Bennett, and George Booth, eds., *1,001 Logical Laws, Accurate Axioms, Profound Principles, Trusty Truisms, Homey Homilies, Colorful Corollaries, Quotable Quotes, and Rambunctious Ruminations for All Walks of Life* (Garden City, NY: Doubleday, 1979), 81. Verified in hard copy.

5. "Heaven for the climate, and hell for the company."

—Mark Twain

QI has heard the saying phrased in several different ways:

Go to Heaven for the climate, Hell for the company.

I would choose Heaven for climate but Hell for companionship.

Heaven for climate. Hell for society.

J. M. Barrie did use a version of the quip in an 1891 story called "The Little Minister" published in a collection titled *Good Words*.[1] This early usage caused some reference works to credit Barrie with the phrase.

A scholarly multivolume edition of Mark Twain's *Notebooks and Journals* revealed that sometime between May 1889 and August 1890, Twain recorded a version of the joke on one of his writing pads.[2] Thus, Twain's paper trail preceded Barrie's publication, and some reference works attributed the expression to Twain based on this evidence.

However, the earliest citation located by **QI** did not mention Twain or Barrie. Instead, the joke was attributed to "Ben Wade" by a judge named Arthur MacArthur while he was speaking at a National Conference of Charities and Correction in 1885. The context did not provide enough details to uniquely identify Wade, but MacArthur may have been referring to the United States senator Benjamin Franklin "Bluff" Wade:[3]

The effect of that paper reminded me of an anecdote relating to Ben Wade, who was once asked his opinion on heaven and hell. "Well," said Mr. Wade, "I think, from all I can learn, that heaven has the better climate, but hell has the better company."

The second earliest citation located by **QI** also did not refer to Twain or Barrie. An 1886 book titled *Life of Emery A. Storrs: His Wit and Eloquence* credited Storrs with the humorous comment:[4]

> A young man once approached him with, "Mr. Storrs, pardon me, but you are a man who has thought much upon all topics. I wish to ask you for your opinion of Heaven and Hell." Fixing his keen eyes on the enquirer, Mr. Storrs answered "When I think of the beauteous descriptions of the abode of the saints, and when I recollect that many noble, witty, genial souls have died 'unregenerate,' I must answer you, sir, that, while, doubtless, Heaven has the best climate, Hell has the best society."

Between May 1889 and August 1890 Mark Twain wrote the witticism in one of his notebooks. The date he penned the text can be approximated using the date on a nearby entry: February 1, 1890. A footnote to Twain's recorded quip states "Clemens included this anecdote in a political speech of 1901." So Twain later employed the remark before an audience:[5]

> Dying man couldn't make up his mind which place to go to—both have their advantages, "heaven for climate, hell for company!"

In 1891 J. M. Barrie used a version of the jape in a story called "The Little Minister" as mentioned earlier. The tale is written using a dialect that alters the spelling of some words:[6]

> "Maybe you've ower keen an interest in the devil, Tammas," retorted the atheist, "but, ony way, if it's heaven for climate, it's hell for company."

In July 1908 the humor magazine *Life* printed a cartoon depicting a devil sentinel watching some of the denizens of hell. Beneath the figures was the following caption:[7]

Garson O'Toole

"HEAVEN FOR CLIMATE—HELL FOR COMPANY."

—Mark Twain

The *Boston Evening Transcript* drew attention to the cartoon and attempted to provide a full listing of the prominent figures who the *Life* cartoonist felt might be present in Twain's version of hell:[8]

> Life's special eschatologist, Mr. Young, has committed a cartoon illustrating Mark Twain's maxim, "Heaven for climate—hell for company." It gives one a glimpse of the infernal regions with a parade of notables filing by. Partly by their verisimilitude [*sic*], partly by their initials, I recognize Napoleon, Goethe, Charles Darwin, Ralph Waldo Emerson, Robert Ingersoll, P. T. Barnum, Robert Burns, Benjamin Franklin, Brigham Young, Tom Paine and Voltaire. George Sand, Mme. Pompadour and la Du Barry are labelled more clearly. And this is what *Life* calls "company."

In conclusion, J. M. Barrie and Mark Twain both wrote down a version of this humorous expression around 1890. But there are two earlier citations, and currently Ben Wade takes precedence with an attribution in 1885.

Notes:

1. J. M. Barrie, "The Little Minister," *Good Words* 32 (1891), 60. Accessed in HathiTrust, https://goo.gl/qkaXAI.
2. *Mark Twain's Notebooks and Journals*, vol. 3 (1883–1891), ed. Robert Pack Browning, Michael B. Frank, and Lin Salamo (Berkeley, CA: University of California Press, 1979), 538. Accessed in Google Books, https://goo.gl/f1aKpx, and also verified in hard copy.
3. "Minutes and Discussions," *Proceedings of the National Conference of Charities and Correction* 12, Annual Session, Washington, DC, June 4–10, 1885, 500. Citation refers to the transcript of Judge MacArthur speaking on June 10, 1885. Accessed in Google Books, https://goo.gl/b3WdQV.

4. Isaac E. Adams, *Life of Emory A. Storrs: His Wit and Eloquence, as Shown in a Notable Literary, Political and Forensic Career* (Philadelphia: Hubbard Bros., 1886), 795. Accessed in Google Books, https://goo.gl/4vtoeo.

5. *Mark Twain's Notebooks & Journals*, vol. 3 (1883–1891), 538. Verified in hard copy.

6. J. M. Barrie, "The Little Minister," 60.

7. Mr. Young, [Cartoon], *Life* 52, no. 1344 (July 30, 1908): 114. Accessed in Google Books, https://goo.gl/Y4074n.

8. [Untitled], *Boston Evening Transcript*, July 31, 1908, 8. Accessed in Google News Archive, https://goo.gl/66QqWo. Excerpt is located in the left column below the provided link.

6. "I'm so fast, I hit the light switch in my bedroom and jump into bed before it gets dark."

—Muhammad Ali

The earliest instance of the above boast was located by **QI** in a 1917 *Marines Magazine*, a monthly for US Marine Corps personnel. A correspondent from Fort Mifflin, Pennsylvania, using the pseudonym Hablarias employed the jape:[1]

> Corporal Smith is still in training and, believe me, he is some speed merchant. Here is one record he holds: It is 20 feet from the switchboard to his pile of alfalfa and he can switch off the lights and be back in bed before the room gets dark!

In 1919 an article covering the vaudeville circuit in the *Chicago Tribune* stated that the comedy team of Moran and Mack were using a version of the joke:[2]

> "Are you quick?"
> "Am I quick? Why, man, when I go to bed at night and turn out the light I'm in bed before the room is dark."

In 1920 a Kansas newspaper printed the remarkable tale of swiftness. Many individuals still relied on gas lighting rather than electric lighting in that year:[3]

> An Atchison woman: "I'll say my husband is fast. He is so fast that when he turns off the gas light he is in bed before the room gets dark."

In 1937 the tall tale of speed was used in the description of the North American lumberjack character Paul Bunyan as a child. In this instance a candle provided the illumination:[4]

He could tear around all day and then, unlike most boys, he was fast at getting to bed. In fact, he could blow out a candle at the far end of the cabin and be in bed before the room got dark.

In 1943 the *Washington Post* printed a column filled with brainteasers that included the following underhanded question and answer:[5]

Question: Your bed and light switch are situated 12 feet apart. How could you switch off the light and get into bed before the room is dark?

Answer: Simply go to bed in the daytime.

The famous comedy duo Abbott and Costello used a version of the joke in a radio script with a 1945 copyright:[6]

ABBOTT: All right, Costello—that's enough! Now who's going to turn off the lights?

COSTELLO: I will, Abbott! I'm the fastest man here. I can turn off the lights and dive into bed before the room gets dark!

RAFT: Costello, I'd like to see you do that!

COSTELLO: Okay—get into the bed, you guys! All ready? I'll snap out the light and dive right into bed!

[Loud crash.]

In 1969 the prominent baseball pitcher Satchel Paige employed the expression when he complimented fellow pitcher James Thomas "Cool Papa" Bell. Apparently, the reporter or the editor truncated the full description:[7]

Paige claims to be the best pitcher of all time, although not necessarily the fastest. That distinction, he says, belongs to Cool Papa

Bell. "Cool Papa was so fast he could get in bed before the room got dark."

Paige made the remark about Bell on multiple occasions. Here is an example in 1971 in *Jet* magazine:[8]

Satchel Paige described Bell as being so fast that "he could turn the light out and be in bed before the room got dark."

In 1973 a *Washington Post* columnist reapplied the saying to another baseball player:[9]

Like Cool Papa Bell, the fastest man in the old black baseball leagues, Enzo Hernandez can turn off the light and jump into bed before the room darkens. He can outrace a bullet. If he challenged the sun it would never set upon him.

In 1974 a reporter for the *Village Voice* newspaper of New York City recorded and presented the words of the celebrated pugilist Muhammad Ali:[10]

I'm so fast last night I cut the light and hit the switch and was in bed before the room was dark.

In 1975 the *New York Times* printed Ali's humorous grandiloquence:[11]

Why, I'm so fast I could hit you before God gets the news. I'm so fast I hit the light switch in my room and jump into bed before my room goes dark.

In conclusion, this comically exaggerated description of speed was in circulation by 1917. It has been adopted by a variety of comedians and athletes over the decades and continues to circulate.

Notes:

Special thanks to "rone," whose inquiry gave impetus to **QI** to formulate this question and initiate this exploration.

1. Hablarias, "Fort Mifflin, PA," Newsletters from Far and Near, *Marines Magazine*, March 1917, 23. Accessed in HathiTrust, https://goo.gl/3tKUWB.
2. "Majestic," Vaudeville Wit, *Chicago Tribune*, March 9, 1919, D5. Accessed in ProQuest.
3. [Untitled], *Hutchinson News* (Hutchinson, KS), February 25, 1920, 9. Accessed in NewspaperARCHIVE.com.
4. R. D. Handy, *Paul Bunyan and His Big Blue Ox: Stories and Pictures of the Lumberjack Hero of American Folk Lore* (Chicago: Rand McNally, 1937), 12, 14. Accessed in HathiTrust, https://goo.gl/DuuoLr.
5. John Henry Cutler, Try *The Post*'s Mind Teasers, *Washington Post*, November 14, 1943, L4. Accessed in ProQuest.
6. Jack Gaver and Dave Stanley, *There's Laughter in the Air! Radio's Top Comedians and Their Best Shows* (New York: Greenberg, 1945), 135–36. Accessed in HathiTrust, https://goo.gl/FxO7IR.
7. William Gildea, "Paige Admits He's Feeling His Age," On Today's Scene, *Washington Post*, April 29, 1969, D2. Accessed in ProQuest.
8. "White Racism Kept Them Out of Big Leagues; Says They Are Not Bitter," *Jet* 40, no. 17 (July 22, 1971): 48. Accessed in Google Books, https://goo.gl/XNR12n.
9. George Minot, "Padre Hernandez Steals Toward Stardom," *Washington Post*, June 10, 1973, D3. Accessed in ProQuest.
10. Nick Browne, "The Rumble in the Jungle—Ali's Camp: You Can't Get Zaire from Here," *Village Voice*, July 25, 1974, 9. Accessed in Google News Archive, https://goo.gl/aoAwdo.
11. Robert Lipsyte, "King of All Kings: Lonely Man of Wisdom, Champion of the World," *New York Times*, June 29, 1975, 44. Accessed in ProQuest.

7. "Not everything that counts can be counted."

—Albert Einstein

QI suggests crediting William Bruce Cameron instead of Albert Einstein for the above quotation. Cameron's 1963 text *Informal Sociology: A Casual Introduction to Sociological Thinking* contains the following passage.[1]

> It would be nice if all of the data which sociologists require could be enumerated because then we could run them through IBM machines and draw charts as the economists do. However, not everything that can be counted counts, and not everything that counts can be counted.

There are several books that attribute the quote to Cameron and cite this 1963 book. **QI** was unable to find earlier instances of the saying.

The maxim under investigation consists of two parallel and contrasting phrases:

> Not everything that can be counted counts.
> Not everything that counts can be counted.

The position of the two key terms "counted" and "counts" is reversed in the two different phrases. This rhetorical technique is referred to as "chiasmus" or "antimetabole." **QI** hypothesizes that the two phrases were crafted separately and then at a later time combined by Cameron to yield the witty and memorable maxim.

When was the connection with Einstein established? The earliest relevant citation that **QI** could find is dated 1986; however, this is more than thirty years after the death of Einstein in 1955. Thus, the evidence is weak, and the link to Einstein is not solidly supported. The details for this citation are given further below.

First, earlier pertinent findings are presented in chronological order. In 1914 a precursor of one of the phrases appeared in a religious text. The topic was raising money.[2]

> Money is not the thing ultimately or even actually aimed at. Money is not what really counts, though it must be counted.

In 1956 a report published by the United Nations Organization for Education, Science, and Culture (UNESCO) titled *Political Science in the United States of America: A Trend Report* contained a variant of one of the phrases. The words were placed between quotation marks, suggesting that the expression was already in use before 1956.[3]

> There are those who see the movement as diverting political science from important to trivial matters simply because the latter lend themselves to study by the fashionable techniques ("what counts can't be counted").

The phrase "what counts can't be counted" suggests that it is impossible to measure what is important. This statement is an extreme version of "not everything that counts can be counted." The latter phrase states that it is difficult to measure what is important and measurements are likely to be incomplete.

In 1957 a sociology professor named William Bruce Cameron published an article in the *Bulletin of the American Association of University Professors* titled "The Elements of Statistical Confusion, Or, What Does the Mean Mean?" Cameron discussed the difficulty of performing appropriate statistical measurements, and he deployed one of the phrases.[4]

> Equally obvious, 100 evening college students taking one two hour course each are in no meaningful way equivalent to 100 day students, each with a sixteen hour load. The moral is: Not everything that can be counted counts.

In 1958 Cameron wrote another article for the *National Education Association Journal* that included the same phrase.[5]

Counting sounds easy until we actually attempt it, and then we quickly discover that often we cannot recognize what we ought to count. Numbers are no substitute for clear definitions, and not everything that can be counted counts.

In 1963, as mentioned at the beginning of this section, Cameron combined the circulating phrases and used the resulting quotation in his textbook on sociology.[6]

It would be nice if all of the data which sociologists require could be enumerated because then we could run them through IBM machines and draw charts as the economists do. However, not everything that can be counted counts, and not everything that counts can be counted.

In 1966 a version of the saying was printed in the prominent medical journal *JAMA* (*Journal of the American Medical Association*). The article "The Current and Potential Use of Course Examinations" by Jason Hilliard attributed the words to another doctor.[7]

These are best summarized in two propositions which have been neatly articulated by Dr. Stephen Ross, "(1) not everything we count, counts; (2) not everything that counts can be counted."

In 1967 Lord Platt deployed the maxim in the *British Medical Journal*. He cited the 1966 article just mentioned; thus, he also credited Stephen Ross.[8]

Research is supposed to train the mind into channels of scientific (and therefore respectable) thought, but does not this kind of research sometimes encourage the erroneous belief that only that which can be measured is worthy of serious attention? "Not everything we count counts. Not everything that counts can be counted," was wisely said by Dr. Stephen Ross.

In 1968 the adage appeared in the *British Medical Journal* again. But this time the words were attached to Lord Platt, who had used them during a speech.[9]

> He recalled a sentence in Lord Platt's recent Harveian Oration, "Not everything we count counts, and not everything that counts can be counted."

As said at the beginning of this chapter, the earliest citation **QI** could find that associates Einstein with the saying is dated 1986. But the work, *Peak Performers: The New Heroes of American Business*, does not claim that Einstein was responsible for coining the expression. Instead, the business book attributes the saying to George Pickering. Yet, the text also claims that Einstein wrote it on his blackboard.[10]

> Albert Einstein liked to underscore the micro/macro partnership with a remark from Sir George Pickering that he chalked on the blackboard in his office at the Institute for Advanced Studies at Princeton: "Not everything that counts can be counted, and not everything that can be counted counts."

The book does not provide any reference to substantiate this comment, and Einstein died in 1955, more than three decades before the volume was written. Currently, the first appearance known to **QI** for this adage is dated 1963, several years after the death of Einstein.

In 1991 the tale of the writing on Einstein's blackboard was presented in a syndicated newspaper column.[11]

> Albert Einstein once wrote on a blackboard: "Not everything that counts can be counted, and not everything that can be counted counts."

Cameron was not forgotten, and in 1997 a sociology textbook attributed the saying to him and cited the 1963 book mentioned at the start of this section:[12]

As Cameron once said, ". . . not everything that can be counted counts, and not everything that counts can be counted" (1963, p. 13).

A version of the maxim appears in a section titled "Probably Not by Einstein" in the 2010 volume *The Ultimate Quotable Einstein*, which is the most authoritative book about Einstein quotations.[13]

In conclusion, the attachment of this quotation to Einstein is tenuous. There is no evidence that he crafted it, and the evidence that he wrote it on a blackboard is weak.

QI believes that the preponderance of currently available information indicates that William Bruce Cameron combined two phrases to create the adage. Cameron also seems to have coined at least one of the two phrases that were combined. In addition, current evidence suggests that the full two-part adage was created after the death of Einstein.

Notes:

1. William Bruce Cameron, *Informal Sociology: A Casual Introduction to Sociological Thinking*, Random House Studies in Sociology, 6th pr. (New York: Random House, 1967), 13. Verified in hard copy. Researcher John Baker identified this citation, and it appears in the Albert Einstein section of the Internet compendium Wikiquote, https://en.wikiquote.org /wiki/Albert_Einstein.

2. Charles E. Schaeffer, *Our Home Mission Work: An Outline Study of the Home Mission Work of the Reformed Church in the United States* (Philadelphia: Publication and Sunday School Board of the Reformed Church in the United States, 1914), 178. Accessed in Google Books, https://goo.gl/dsuRHB.

3. Dwight Waldo, *Political Science in the United States of America: A Trend Report*, Documentation in the Social Sciences (Paris: UNESCO, 1956), 30. Accessed in Google Books, https://goo.gl/rFBk1K.

4. William Bruce Cameron, "The Elements of Statistical Confusion, Or, What Does the Mean Mean?" *Bulletin of the American Association of University Professors* 43, no. 1 (Spring 1957): 34. Verified in JSTOR.

5. William Bruce Cameron, "Tell Me Not in Mournful Numbers," *National Education Association Journal* 47, no. 3 (March 1958): 173. Verified in hard copy.

6. Cameron, *Informal Sociology*, 13.

7. Jason Hilliard, "The Current and Potential Use of Course Examinations," *JAMA* 198, no. 3 (October 17, 1966): 290. Verified in hard copy.

8. Lord Platt, "Medical Science: Master or Servant?" *British Medical Journal* 4, no. 5577 (November 25, 1967): 442. Verified in JSTOR.

9. "Christian Medical Fellowship," *British Medical Journal* 3, no. 5610 (July 13, 1968): 80. Verified in JSTOR.

10. Charles A. Garfield, *Peak Performers: The New Heroes of American Business* (New York: William Morrow, 1986), 156. Verified in hard copy.

11. L. M. Boyd, "Shy Suffer Hay Fever," This and That, *Ellensburg Daily Record* (Ellensburg, WA), February 11, 1991, 8. Accessed in Google News Archive, https://goo.gl/eT98tK.

12. Chet Ballard, Jon Gubbay, and Chris Middleton, eds., *The Student's Companion to Sociology* (Malden, MA: Blackwell, 1997), 92.

13. Alice Calaprice, ed., *The Ultimate Quotable Einstein* (Princeton: Princeton University Press, 2010), 482. Verified in hard copy.

8. "Writing about music is like dancing about architecture."

—Laurie Anderson
—Frank Zappa
—John Lennon
—Elvis Costello

With the help of some wonderful music librarians and an individual who left a comment on **QI**'s blog post dedicated to this quotation, **QI** can report some revealing citations. The first citation of this saying known to **QI** appears in a magazine dedicated to the history of rock and roll called *Time Barrier Express*. The September–October 1979 issue contains a profile of the group Sam & Dave by Gary Sperrazza in which he discusses the interplay and rapport of the duo:[1]

> All quick, very natural, and captured on vinyl. It's so hard to explain on paper, you'll just have to find the records and listen for yourself (because I truly believe—honest—that writing about music is, as Martin Mull put it, like dancing about architecture).

In December 1979 *Arts Magazine* published an article about the painter Michael Madore by the critic Thomas McGonigle. The saying here is attributed to Martin Mull; however, the domain of the quotation is knowingly transformed to painting. Even in 1979 McGonigle refers to the expression as a "famous dictum":[2]

> So with Madore we have the classic situation: no limits, thus all limits, or to slightly alter the famous Martin Mull dictum: Writing about painting is like dancing about architecture.

Based on current evidence, **QI** believes that Martin Mull is the most likely originator of this expression. It is not clear how Gary Sperrazza and Thomas McGonigle heard or read about the quotation. Mull did release several albums combining comedy and music in the 1970s. He also appeared in the television soap opera parody *Mary Hartman, Mary Hartman* and the talk show parody *Fernwood 2 Night* (later renamed *America 2-Night*). It is possible that he used the phrase in one of these venues, or perhaps he said it during a stage performance or interview.

Researchers have been attempting to trace this well-known saying for many years. It is a recurrent topic in discussion forums and on mailing lists. Alan P. Scott was the key pioneer in this endeavor, and he has created a wonderful webpage that records his gleanings and includes a comprehensive list of people that have been credited with the quotation.[3]

The clever maxim was probably not created ex nihilo. **QI** has found similar expressions that date back to 1918. There is a family of related sayings that comment about such difficult exertions as writing about music, talking about music, writing about art, and talking about art. This backstory helps to illuminate the aphorism, and it begins with a remark involving "singing about economics."

The earliest statement that **QI** has located that discusses the inherent difficulty of writing about music and compares it to singing about something is dated February 9, 1918, in the *New Republic*:[4]

> Strictly considered, writing about music is as illogical as singing about economics. All the other arts can be talked about in the terms of ordinary life and experience. A poem, a statue, a painting or a play is a representation of somebody or something, and can be measurably described (the purely aesthetic values aside) by describing what it represents.

In 1921 the remark reappears in the form of a sphinxlike simile, and over a period of decades, different words and phrases are substituted into the template "Writing about music is like [blanking] about [blank]." Also, sometimes "talking" is used instead of "writing" as is done here in 1921:[5]

> Like the musical critic who lamented impotently that "talking about music is like singing about economics," those musicians with a knack for literary expression may quite possibly be frightened

off from a task which is reputed to be as arduous as turning "Das Kapital" into a song.

There are a massive number of citations for this aphorism and for variants that fit the template; therefore, only a small sampling can be listed here. In 1930 the same author, Winthrop Parkhurst, repeated his observation in an influential scholarly musical journal called the *Musical Quarterly*. He also elevated the simile to the status of an apothegm:[6]

Some critic once observed that talking about music is like singing about economics; and it must be admitted that most conversation about music supports the apophthegm, for it is commonly as strange a perversion of the subject as would be the transformation of *Das Kapital* into a lullaby.

The next citation in chronological order is the 1979 one mentioned above where Gary Sperrazza attributes the maxim to Martin Mull. This version refers to writing about music as did the first 1918 quotation.

Also in 1979, an altered version of the saying is presented in *Arts Magazine* by the critic Thomas McGonigle crediting Mull, as noted previously.

In 1980 a revised version of Sperrazza's profile of Sam & Dave appeared in the publication *Black Music and Jazz Review*. The attribution to Mull is restated:[7]

I'm not going to attempt to describe the magic here, you'll have to check the record yourself, cos to write about this level of music is (as Martin Mull so aptly put it) like dancing about architecture.

Shortly before John Lennon's death in 1980, he granted an interview to *Playboy* magazine. When asked about the interpretation and misinterpretation of his song lyrics, Lennon responded with a simile that fits the template:[8]

Listen, writing about music is like talking about fucking. Who wants to talk about it? But you know, maybe some people do want to talk about it.

In 1982 the *Montreal Gazette* profiled musician Mike Oldfield, famous for the composition *Tubular Bells*. Oldfield explained his reluctance to grant interviews by using a simile that harks back to the early citations in 1918 and 1921 because it invokes singing:[9]

> It soon transpires that Oldfield doesn't generally do interviews in his native England. Not from any persecution complex or feelings of superiority, mind you, but simply because he feels that "talking about music is like singing about football."

In October 1983 *Musician* magazine interviewed artist Elvis Costello and asked about his treatment in the music press. Costello's response used the maxim as part of a general critique of written reviews of music. (Further below is an excerpt from a 2008 magazine interview in which Costello disclaimed credit for creating the maxim):[10]

> Framing all the great music out there only drags down its immediacy. The songs are lyrics, not speeches, and they're tunes, not paintings. Writing about music is like dancing about architecture—it's a really stupid thing to want to do.

For several years the quotation above was the earliest known citation for this famous saying. That is one reason the words are strongly associated with Costello. *The Quote Verifier* and *The Yale Book of Quotations* also cite Costello's words.[11]

On October 9, 1983, a Nebraska newspaper published an interview with flutist Eugenia Zukerman. The interviewer queried Zukerman, who is also a novelist, about her experiences writing:[12]

> When asked, she admits that writing about music, as humorist Martin Mull once quipped, is like dancing about architecture.
> "It's very hard," she said. "It's easy to write in such a silly way about music. It is its own language. You don't write about English in Italian . . ."

It is not completely clear to **QI** from the text if the crediting of Mull is directly based on Zukerman's remarks or if the interviewer Rick Ansorge is adding the attribution.

Other musicians were credited with the saying in the 1980s. For example, on June 18, 1985, a story in the *Los Angeles Times* used the adage as a subtitle for an article and attributed the words to Frank Zappa:[13]

INDIAN RAGA IS JOINED BY A LATIN BEAT
"Talking about music is like dancing about architecture."

—Frank Zappa

The article by Kenneth Herman began with the following:

La Jolla—Encountering music from non-Western cultures lends credibility to the barb Zappa hurled at his less-than-favorable critics. The more engaging a performance of exotic music, the more that description and metaphor tend to diminish its unique character.

The performance artist Laurie Anderson is another popular figure for attribution, and she did use the quotation in a high-profile work titled *Home of the Brave*. A 1986 review of the piece in the *Philadelphia Daily News* noted that the memorable saying was flashed on the screen during her concert. (Further below is an excerpt from a 2000 radio interview during which Anderson disclaimed credit for creating the adage):[14]

Anderson's direction is varied and competent on the whole. But some of the slogans flashed on the rear screen projections ("Talking about music is like dancing about architecture.") rush by so fast that the jokes are easily missed.

In 1990 a variant of the saying occurred in quotation marks and was assigned to the musician Jackson Browne. This variant with the word "singing" is identical to the one used by Mike Oldfield in 1982:[15]

Jackson Browne: "As they say in the studios of L.A., talking about music is like singing about football."

In 1991 an article in the *Times* of London discussed a group of paintings. The author depicted the difficulty of cogently writing about art by employing two similes that follow the template of the family of aphorisms under discussion:[16]

Writing about art is like dancing about architecture or knitting about music. It is a category mistake. But here goes.

In 1995 Martin Mull, who is also a painter, used a variant of the saying in one of his own books; however, he did not attribute the saying to himself. He stated that he heard it as part of a story about a teacher. This may mean that Mull did not originate the saying, or it may mean that he was simply using a rhetorical distancing device. This variant contains the phrase "talking about art":[17]

I once heard a story about a painting instructor who told his class that "talking about art is like dancing about architecture." Immediately upon hearing this, one of his students leapt to his feet, did an impromptu tap routine, and proudly proclaimed his fancy footwork to be the Flatiron Building.

And so, with little more than this snippet from academia to guide me, I will now undertake the fool's errand of attempting to describe the methods and madnesses that constitute the process by which I make pictures.

In 2000 the NPR radio program *Morning Edition* investigated the saying, and the host Susan Stamberg contacted the artist Laurie Anderson. Anderson attributed the adage to the comedian Steve Martin. During the discussion Stamberg mentions a website; she is referring to the website of Alan P. Scott:[18]

SUSAN STAMBERG: Laurie Anderson, are you the one who first said, 'Talking about music is like dancing about architecture'?

Ms. LAURIE ANDERSON: Oh, no, no. It's one of my absolute favorite quotes, and I always try to–that's so funny that you should ask that. I always try to preface it by Steve Martin. Now, Steve Martin, the comedian, is the one who said that.

STAMBERG: Well, good. Thank you for clarifying it for us, we think. Although, you know, there's now a Web site on this question. And he lists Steve Martin on there. He says that there are at least three places where it says it was Steve Martin who said it, but he doesn't believe it. And you're one of three who names him.

In a 2005 interview with a *Boston Globe* journalist, bassist Jesse Keeler of the Canadian musical group Death from Above 1979 used a variant of the expression containing the word "singing." Keeler's statement immediately reminded the interviewer of the most common variant, which he attributed to Elvis Costello:[19]

> "I'm using a quote I saw the other day—'Talking about music is like singing about football,'" Keller says in a recent telephone interview during a tour that will bring them to the Middle East Downstairs on Monday. Or, as Elvis Costello once said, "like dancing about architecture," although if one could do such an abstract thing, DFA '79 could provide as appropriate a soundtrack as anyone.

In 2008 *Q* magazine, a UK music periodical, ran an interview with Costello in its March special issue, titled "50 Years of Great British Music." Costello denied creating the saying, and he credited Martin Mull. Below is an excerpt that begins with a question directed to Costello and follows with his reply:[20]

> These days you dabble in music journalism for *Vanity Fair* magazine. But wasn't it you who said "writing about music is like dancing about architecture"?
>
> Oh, God! Can I please put in print that I didn't say that! I may have quoted it, but I think [1970s US actor/singer] Martin Mull

coined that. It still follows me around, that one. It's probably in some book of quotations credited to me.

Contacting a candidate such as Martin Mull or Steve Martin directly to ask questions on this topic would help to resolve the mystery. A post dated July 17, 2010, on a blog named *The Online Photographer* discussed an attempt to contact Martin Mull and ask him about the saying "Writing about music is like dancing about architecture." The blog author, Mike Johnston, was interested in the provenance of the quote, so he asked Mull's art dealer to make an inquiry:[21]

> So one of the lines I threw into the water was an email to Martin's art dealer, Carl P. Hammer of Carl Hammer Gallery in Chicago. Carl contacted Martin for me, and Martin confirmed that he is indeed the originator of the famous one-liner.

Note that this datum was sent along a chain: Mull talked to Hammer, who talked to Johnston, who wrote about it on his blog.

A more direct statement from Mull with fewer intermediaries would, of course, be desirable. Perhaps Mull could provide details about where or when the quote was spoken or written. Mike Johnston deserves kudos for initiating a query and sharing the results.

The artist Grant Snider created an entertaining comic on this theme and depicted the "Postmodernist Pogo" and the "Bauhaus Bounce." The work was posted on his website Incidental Comics in June 2012.[22]

In conclusion, Martin Mull is the leading candidate for crafter of this maxim at this time. Similar sayings conforming to a general template began to appear and evolve by 1918.

Notes:

1. Gary Sperrazza, "Looka Here! It's Sam and Dave!" *Time Barrier Express* 3, no. 6, iss. 26 (September–October 1979): 25. Verified in scanned digital images obtained from the Music Library and Sound Recordings Archive at Bowling Green State University. Great thanks to the librarian there.

2. Thomas McGonigle, "Michael Madore," *Arts Magazine* 54, no. 4 (December 1979): 5. Verified in hard copy. Great thanks to Mike Kuniavsky for pointing out this citation.

3. "Talking About Music Is Like Dancing About Architecture," Alan P. Scott, last updated December 31, 2010, http://www.paclink.com/~ascott/they/tamildaa.htm.

4. H. K. M., "The Unseen World," *New Republic* 14 (February 9, 1918): 63. Accessed in Google Books, https://goo.gl/aHGLPO, which provides an incorrect date of 1969. Quotation also verified in microfilm.

5. Winthrop Parkhurst, "Music, Mysticism, and Madness," *Freeman* 4, no. 82 (October 5, 1921): 93. Accessed in Google Books, https://goo.gl/8dVVvc.

6. Winthrop Parkhurst, "Music, the Invisible Art," *Musical Quarterly* 16, no. 3 (July 1930): 298–99. Verified in hard copy.

7. Gary Sperrazza, "Sam and Dave," *Black Music and Jazz Review* 3, no. 3 (July 1980): 24. Accessed in Google Books, https://goo.gl/tzzMhV, and verified in scanned images from the University of Virginia Music Library. Great thanks to their librarian.

8. David Sheff, *All We Are Saying: The Last Major Interview with John Lennon and Yoko Ono*, G. Barry Golson, ed. (New York: St. Martin's Press, 2000), 88. Accessed in Google Books, https://goo.gl/wOfWPQ. Many thanks to Victor Steinbok for pointing out this citation.

9. John Griffin, "Oldfield Tackles North America, and It Takes Him by Storm," *Montreal Gazette*, April 12, 1982, B6. Accessed in Google News Archive, http://goo.gl/6vTLT.

10. Timothy White, "Elvis Costello: A Man Out of Time Beats the Clock," *Musician*, October 1983, 52. Verified in hard copy. This valuable citation was located by Mark Turner and appeared on the webpage of Alan P. Scott, http://www.paclink.com/~ascott/apshome.htm.

11. Ralph Keyes, *The Quote Verifier: Who Said What, Where, and When* (New York: St. Martin's, 2006), 256–57. Verified in hard copy; Fred R. Shapiro, *The Yale Book of Quotations* (New Haven: Yale University Press, 2006), 175. Verified in hard copy.

12. Rick Ansorge, "Eugenia Zukerman: Renaissance Woman," *Omaha World-Herald* (Omaha, NE), October 9, 1983. Accessed in NewsBank. The *Globe and Mail* columnist Doug Saunders found this fine citation and placed it on the webpage of Alan P. Scott, http://www.paclink.com/~ascott/apshome.htm.

13. Kenneth Herman, "Indian Raga Is Joined by a Latin Beat," *Los Angeles Times*, June 18, 1985. Accessed in ProQuest.

14. Jonathan Takiff, "A Sense of Laurie Anderson," a review of *Home of the Brave*, by Laurie Anderson, *Philadelphia Daily News*, July 18, 1986, http://articles.philly.com/1986-07-18/entertainment/26095839_1_popular-music-artist-shadow-figures. Also accessed in NewsBank.

15. Loose Lips, *Buffalo News* (Buffalo, NY), August 5, 1990, M22. Accessed in NewsBank.

16. Philip Howard, "The Comfort of a Nude in the Bathroom," Enthusiasms, *Times* (London, UK), August 3, 1991. Accessed in Academic OneFile.

17. Martin Mull, *Martin Mull: Paintings, Drawings, and Words* (Boston: Journey Editions, 1995), 7. Accessed in Google Books, https://goo.gl/CreUp0, and verified in hard copy.

18. *Morning Edition*, "Profile: Letters from Listeners (10:00–11:00 AM)," broadcast transcript, NPR, January 14, 2000. Accessed in Academic OneFile.

19. Renée Graham, "Categorize This Duo's Sound as Loud," *Boston Globe*, April 29, 2005, http://archive.boston.com/news/globe/living/articles/2005/04/29/categorize_this_duos _sound_as_loud/.

20. "Elvis Costello: A Man Out of Time Beats the Clock," *Q*, March 2008, 67. Verified in photocopied pages from the article. Special thanks to the librarian in the periodical center at the Cleveland Public Library for locating this text in hard copy in the March 2008 issue when given an inaccurate citation to the February 2008 issue.

21. Mike Johnston, "OT: We Hear from Martin Mull," *The Online Photographer*, July 27, 2010, http://theonlinephotographer.typepad.com/the_online_photographer/2010/07 /ot-we-hear-from-martin-mull.html. The blog post on The Online Photographer website was mentioned on the excellent *Quotes Uncovered* blog of Fred R. Shapiro, based on an email sent from the mathematician William C. Waterhouse.

22. Grant Snider, "Dancing About Architecture," Incidental Comics, June 19, 2012, http:// www.incidentalcomics.com/2012/06/dancing-about-architecture.html.

9. "Those who dance are considered insane by those who can't hear the music."

—Friedrich Nietzsche

—George Carlin

QI has not yet located substantive evidence that Friedrich Nietzsche wrote or said the statement given above. But that is where the English tabloids pointed once the actress and supermodel Megan Fox was seen on a beach in 2011 with the unattributed phrase tattooed across her back.

The sole piece of evidence **QI** could locate that ties Nietzsche to this saying is highly suspect. A 2003 message in the alt.quotations newsgroup on Usenet attributes the quote to him.[1] But Nietzsche died in 1900, so 2003 is an absurdly late date.

A precursor to this quotation appeared in the early nineteenth century. In 1813 the influential writer Anne Louise Germaine de Staël published the work *De l'Allemagne* in French. The English title was *Germany*, and in 1814 *Universal Magazine* printed an excerpt. Madame de Staël envisioned herself watching a ballroom filled with dancers, and she imagined her reaction if she had been unable to hear the music:[2]

> [S]ometimes even in the habitual course of life, the reality of this world disappears all at once, and we feel ourselves in the middle of its interests as we should at a ball, where we did not hear the music; the dancing that we saw there would appear insane.

This figurative language was employed powerfully to illustrate an episode of dissociation. Madame de Staël was temporarily alienated from the normal rush of living, and the actions of those around her seemed purposeless and absurd.

In 1848 another precursor appeared in a letter written by an American journalist named William Cowper Prime. However, Prime described the dancers as "ludicrous" and not "insane":[3]

> Did you ever pass the windows of a room in which there was dancing, and watch the figures when you could not hear the music? Try it sometimes, and if the graceful movements of the dance do not become positively ludicrous, then I am no judge.

In 1860 the notable American writer Harriet Elizabeth Prescott Spofford published *Sir Rohan's Ghost: A Romance*. In a passage about love, Spofford discussed a metaphorical dance of love. She commented on the confusion experienced by some observers of this dance:[4]

> And those who stand without, who see the dance and do not hear the music—what more weird fantastic folly, the madness of the saturnalia, the sacred fury of eleusinian or evantian choir, ever dawns upon their dazzled darkness!

In an address found in the complete sermons of the preacher Thomas Manton, published in 1873, Manton invoked the following simile about watching dancers from a distance:[5]

> [I]f a man riding in an open country should see afar off men and women dancing together, and should not hear the music according to which they dance and tread out their measures, he would think them to be fools and madmen, because they appear in such various motions, and antic gestures and postures. But if he come nearer, so as to hear the musical notes, according to which they dance, and observe the regularity of the exercise, he will change his opinion of them . . .

In 1883 Nietzsche released *Also Sprach Zarathustra* in German. The English title was *Thus Spoke Zarathustra*. The work contained the following thematically relevant aphorisms. The translation from German to English given here was performed by Walter Kaufmann:[6]

I would believe only in a God who could dance.

One must still have chaos in oneself to be able to give birth to a dancing star.

These sayings are notably different from the quotation being examined. Nevertheless, the shared theme of dancing provides a connection, and it may have made the ascription plausible to some people.

In 1885 British-American writer Amelia Edith Huddleston Barr released *The Hallam Succession: A Tale of Methodist Life in Two Countries*, which contained the following passage:[7]

Did you ever watch a lot of men and women dancing, when you could not hear the music, but could only see them bobbing up and down the room? I assure you they look just like a party of lunatics.

The prominent French philosopher Henri Bergson published a series of three essays about laughter in the periodical *Revue de Paris*. The combined essays were published in 1900, and an English translation was released in 1911. In the following excerpt dancers are depicted as "ridiculous" without sound:[8]

Now step aside, look upon life as a disinterested spectator: many a drama will turn into a comedy. It is enough for us to stop our ears to the sound of music in a room, where dancing is going on, for the dancers at once to appear ridiculous. How many human actions would stand a similar test?

In 1927 the *Times* of London printed a version similar to the common modern examples of the saying and labeled it an "old proverb." This concise instance used the word "mad" instead of "insane":[9]

They who dance are thought mad by those who hear not the music.
The truth of the old proverb was never more surely borne out than
it is just now.

In 1929 the expression appeared in the reference work *English Proverbs and
Proverbial Phrases: A Historical Dictionary.* The citation given was to the 1927
newspaper instance that was presented immediately above. Hence, the editor
was unable to trace the phrase further back in time:[10]

They who dance are thought mad by those who hear not the music.

—Spoken of as an "old proverb." 1927: Times, 16 Feb., p. 15,
col. 4.

In 1936 the *Boston Globe* newspaper printed an instance using the word
"mad" in the title of an article and called it a "modern proverb":[11]

MODERN PROVERBS
"Those Who Dance Are Thought Mad by Those Who Hear Not
the Music"

In 1967 a column in a California newspaper ascribed the expression to a
person named John Stewart. Note that this is not the comedian Jon Stewart of
today:[12]

John Stewart says those who dance are thought mad by those who
don't hear the music.

In 1969 the popular magazine *Life* included a version of the saying without
attribution as the prefatory statement to an article:[13]

Those who dance are thought mad by those who don't hear the
music.

In 1972 an instance using the word "insane" instead of "mad" was ascribed to a radio program director working at the station KHYT in Arizona:[14]

> Those who dance are thought to be insane by those who can't hear the music.
>
> —Norman Flint, KHYT

In 1989 the Pennsylvania Folklore Society published an issue of the journal *Keystone Folklore* that focused on the science fiction community. An article about slogan buttons noted that the following statement was written on some buttons worn by sci-fi aficionados:[15]

> Those who dance are thought mad by those who hear not the music.

Also in 1989 the *San Francisco Chronicle* published a nostalgic article looking back at the famous Woodstock music festival. The article included an interview with musician Paul Kantner, a member of the rock group Jefferson Airplane, which had played at Woodstock. Kantner stated a version of the saying and connected it to the Sufis, a religious group:[16]

> I've got you a little quote I just pulled out: I think it goes back to the Sufis, but it says: "Those who danced were thought to be quite insane by those who couldn't hear the music." It has a lot to do with Woodstock and its observation by the media.

In 1997 the provocative comedian George Carlin published *Brain Droppings*, which included the following remark:[17]

> Those who dance are considered insane by those who can't hear the music.

Carlin's jokes are enjoyed by many who exchange information on the Internet. Indeed, the demand for Carlin one-liners has been so strong that many jokes have simply been reassigned to him. Hence, today many counterfeit Carlin quips are in circulation. Back in 2001 a *Los Angeles Times* article presented some fake Carlin jokes, including this one:[18]

If a pig loses its voice, is it disgruntled?

The same article presented some real Carlin jokes as well:

I never eat sushi. I have trouble eating things that are merely unconscious.

Those who dance are considered insane by those who can't hear the music.

Also in 2001 George Carlin published *Napalm and Silly Putty*, a sequel to his 1997 bestseller. The new book included the same quip about dancing, but this time Carlin explicitly disclaimed credit:[19]

Those who dance are considered insane by those who can't hear the music.

—Anon.

In 2002 the reference work *Thesaurus of Traditional English Metaphor* included a version of the adage and assigned it the remarkably early date of 1575. A precise citation to support this date was not given, and **QI** has so far been unable to locate a sixteenth-century work containing the saying:[20]

[T]hey who dance are thought mad by those who hear not the music [1575]. Said when someone's motivation is not appreciated; we should not judge others without knowing all the facts.

Also in 2002 a newspaper in Colorado attributed the adage to a woman named Angela Monet:[21]

Those who danced were thought to be quite insane by those who could not hear the music.

—Angela Monet

In 2003, as discussed at the beginning of this section, a message in the alt. quotations newsgroup ascribed a version of the sentiment to Nietzsche.

A 2004 updated translation of selected writings by the thirteenth-century poet and mystic Rūmī includes a thematically related passage about music and dancing:[22]

We rarely hear the inward music,
but we're all dancing to it nevertheless,
directed by the one who teaches us,
the pure joy of the sun,
our music master.

In 2005 a Florida newspaper printed a short piece with the title "They Said It" and ascribed the words to Nietzsche:[23]

"And those who were seen dancing were thought to be insane by those who could not hear the music."

—Friedrich Wilhelm Nietzsche philosopher (1844–1900)

In 2010, as mentioned in the opening of this chapter, a writer at the *Guardian* newspaper in the United Kingdom discussed the new tattoo adorning Megan Fox:[24]

Tabloid reports suggest that it's the work of a little-known poet called Angela Monet, and a quick Google search confirms as much. Thing is, though, Monet doesn't appear to exist. Staff at the Poetry Society have never heard of her, while Chris McCabe, head librarian at the Poetry Library, says, "There's no record of her in the library's database."

In 2012 the BBC website published a "Quiz of the Week's News" that included the following question:[25]

> A tattoo featuring musings by philosopher Nietzsche—"and those who were seen dancing were thought to be insane by those who could not hear the music"—was airbrushed out of a photo of . . .

The answer was Megan Fox. The cover image of the French magazine *Grazia* depicted Fox, but with the tattoo on her back photoshopped off her skin.

In conclusion, **QI** has not yet located any substantive evidence that Nietzsche used this expression. The general idea of the saying has a long history, as shown above. The 1927 instance in the *Times* of London is similar to the common modern version although it uses the word "mad" instead of "insane." Also, in 1927 the saying was called an "old proverb." Based on current evidence, the statement origin seems to be anonymous.

Notes:

Thanks to Gaby Clingman, whose query led to the construction of this question by **QI** and the initiation of this trace. Thanks to Barry Popik, who suggested that **QI** include a mention of Angela Monet.

1. Dougk, "IM Friedrich Nietzsche," alt.quotations Usenet newsgroup, August 28, 2003. Accessed in Google Groups, https://goo.gl/tYtcrR.
2. "On the Moravian Mode of Worship by Madame De Staël [From Her 'Germany']," *Universal Magazine* 22, no. 125 (April 1814): 296. Accessed in Google Books, https://goo.gl/KUbvJN. Thanks to commenter RobotWisdom, who shared this citation at the *Shortcuts* blog of the *Guardian*, https://www.theguardian.com/books/2010/jun/06/megan-fox-tattoo-angela-monet.
3. William Cowper Prime, *The Owl Creek Letters: And Other Correspondence* (New York: Baker and Scribner, 1848), 143–44. Accessed in Google Books, https://goo.gl/rh4Gv2. Hat tip to *Guardian* commenter RobotWisdom.
4. Harriet Elizabeth Prescott Spofford, *Sir Rohan's Ghost: A Romance* (London: Trübner, 1860), 279. Accessed in Google Books, https://goo.gl/nK7EIA. Hat tip to *Guardian* commenter RobotWisdom.

5. *The Complete Works of Thomas Manton, D. D.*, vol. 13 (London: James Nisbet, 1873), 113. Accessed in Google Books, https://goo.gl/zCScnC. Hat tip to *Guardian* commenter RobotWisdom.

6. Fred R. Shapiro, *The Yale Book of Quotations* (New Haven: Yale University Press, 2006), 552. Verified in hard copy.

7. Amelia [Edith Huddleston] Barr, *The Hallam Succession: A Tale of Methodist Life in Two Countries* (London: T. Woolmer, 1885), 95. Accessed in Google Books, https://goo.gl/wYKt8U. Hat tip to *Guardian* commenter RobotWisdom.

8. Henri Bergson, *Laughter: An Essay on the Meaning of the Comic*, trans. Cloudesley Brereton and Fred Rothwell (New York: Macmillan, 1911), 5. Accessed in HathiTrust, https://goo.gl/YDYqHF.

9. The Dance, *Times* (London, UK), February 16, 1927, 15. Accessed in *The Times* Digital Archive by Gale Cengage.

10. G. L. Apperson, ed., *English Proverbs and Proverbial Phrases: A Historical Dictionary* (London: J. M. Dent and Sons, 1929), 133–34. Accessed in Questia.

11. Vida Hurst, "Modern Proverbs: Those Who Dance Are Thought Mad by Those Who Hear Not the Music," *Boston Globe*, October 3, 1936, 10. Accessed in ProQuest.

12. "Nosegays from DeMuth," *Arcadia Tribune* (Arcadia, CA), November 19, 1967, 3. Accessed in NewspaperARCHIVE.com.

13. "Incredible '68—An Almanac," *Life* 66, no. 1 (January 10, 1969): 6. Accessed in Google Books, https://goo.gl/xZ4yH3.

14. R. Kent Burton, "The Music Called Rock: Fun Is All That Ever Was Intended," *Tucson Daily Citizen*, April 22, 1972, magazine supplement, 15. Accessed in NewspaperARCHIVE.com.

15. Stephanie A. Hall, "'Reality Is a Crutch for People Who Can't Deal with Science Fiction': Slogan-Buttons Among Science Fiction Fans," *Keystone Folklore* 4, no. 1 (1989): 25. Accessed in Google Books, https://goo.gl/qr4mzG.

16. Edward Guthmann, "Woodstock Remembered: A Sentimental Journey—Participants Recall the Music, the Mood, the Mud 20 Years after Legendary Concert," *San Francisco Chronicle*, August 13, 1989, Sunday Datebook section, 20. Accessed in NewsBank.

17. George Carlin, *Brain Droppings* (New York: Hyperion, 1997), 74. Verified in hard copy.

18. Ann O'Neill, "Hello, Mr. and Mrs. J. Lo," City of Angles, *Los Angeles Times*, October 2, 2001, E2. Byline note: "Ann O'Neill is on vacation. This column was written by staff writers Gina Piccalo and Louise Roug." Accessed in ProQuest.

19. George Carlin, *Napalm and Silly Putty* (New York: Hyperion, 2001), unnumbered page before introduction. Verified in hard copy.

20. P. R. [Peter Richard] Wilkinson, ed., *Thesaurus of Traditional English Metaphors*, 2nd ed. (New York: Routledge, 2002), 897.

21. Kevin Williams, "Deeper Meaning—Kabbalah Teaches Mystical Side of Judaism," *Daily Camera* (Boulder, CO), July 20, 2002, D1.

22. Jalāl ad-Dīn Rūmī, *The Essential Rumi*, trans. Coleman Barks and John Moyne, new expanded ed. (New York: HarperOne, 2004), 106.

23. "They Said It," *Ledger* (Lakeland, FL), February 8, 2005, East Polk section, F4. Accessed in NewsBank.

24. Patrick Kingsley, "Who Is the Mystery Poet Behind Megan Fox's New Tattoo?" *Guardian* (London, UK), June 1, 2010, https://www.theguardian.com/lifeandstyle/2010/jun/01/megan-fox-mystery-tattoo-poet.

25. Quiz of the Week, BBC News, April 12, 2012.

10. "If I had more time, I would have written a shorter letter."

—John Locke
—Benjamin Franklin
—Woodrow Wilson

The first known instance in the English language of the above quip was a translation of a text written by the French mathematician and philosopher Blaise Pascal. The statement appeared in a 1657 letter he wrote:[1]

> Je n'ai fait celle-ci plus longue que parce que je n'ai pas eu le loisir
> de la faire plus courte.

Here is one possible modern-day English translation of Pascal's statement. Note that the term "this" refers to the letter itself:

> I have made this longer than usual because I have not had time to
> make it shorter.

An English translation was created in 1658 and published in London. Here is an excerpt from that early rendition of the letter:[2]

> My Letters were not wont to come so close one in the neck of
> another, nor yet to be so large. The short time I have had hath been
> the cause of both. I had not made this longer than the rest, but that
> I had not the leisure to make it shorter then it is.

Pascal's notion was quite memorable, and it was discussed in a French book about language. That work was translated and published in London in 1676 as *The Art of Speaking*:[3]

These Inventions require much wit, and application; and therefore it was, that Mons. Pascal (an Author very famous for his felicity in comprising much in few words) excused himself wittily for the extravagant length of one of his Letters, by saying, he had not time to make it shorter.

In 1688 a religious controversialist named George Tullie included a version of the witticism in an essay he wrote about the celibacy of the clergy:[4]

The Reader will I doubt too soon discover that so large an interval of time was not spent in writing this discourse; the very length of it will convince him, that the writer had not time enough to make a shorter.

Below are several variations of the expression as used by well-known, lesser-known, and unknown individuals. The philosopher John Locke, the statesman Benjamin Franklin, the transcendentalist Henry David Thoreau, and the president Woodrow Wilson all presented statements matching this theme, and the details are provided. (Mark Twain is also often connected to this saying, but he did not use it, according to the best available research. However, one of his tangentially related quotations is given later for your entertainment.)

In 1688 Edmund Bohun published *A Geographical Dictionary*. This reference work presented an alphabetical list of cities, towns, rivers, mountains, and other locations together with descriptions. The author crafted the following variant of the remark:[5]

The Reader may pardon this long Discourse, because the Subject so well deserved it, and I wanted Art to make it shorter.

In 1690 the philosopher John Locke released his famous work *An Essay Concerning Human Understanding*. In a prefatory section called "The Epistle to the Reader," Locke commented on the length of his essay and indicated why he had decided not to shorten it:[6]

I will not deny, but possibly it might be reduced to a narrower Compass than it is; and that some Parts of it might be contracted: The way it has been writ in, by Catches, and many long Intervals of Interruption, being apt to cause some Repetitions. But to confess the Truth, I am now too lazy, or too busy to make it shorter.

In 1704 the *Philosophical Transactions of the Royal Society of London* printed a letter from William Cowper that contained the following:[7]

If in this I have been tedious, it may be some excuse, I had not time to make it shorter.

In 1750 Benjamin Franklin composed a letter describing his groundbreaking experiments involving electricity and sent it to a member of the Royal Society of London. Franklin excused the length of his report as follows:[8]

I have already made this paper too long, for which I must crave pardon, not having now time to make it shorter.

The quotation is sometimes attached to famous figures in antiquity. For example, in 1824 a version of the quote was assigned to the Roman orator Cicero:[9]

Cicero excuses himself for having written a long letter, by saying he had not time to make it shorter.

The German theologian Martin Luther died in 1546. A biographical work published in London in 1846 attributed the following words to him:[10]

If I had my time to go over again, I would make my sermons much shorter, for I am conscious they have been too wordy.

In 1857 Henry David Thoreau wrote a letter to a friend that offered commentary about story length:[11]

Not that the story need be long, but it will take a long while to make it short.

In 1871 Mark Twain wrote a letter to a friend that included a remark about the length of his note. Twain's comment does not really match the quotation under investigation, but it is related to the general theme:[12]

You'll have to excuse my lengthiness—the reason I dread writing letters is because I am so apt to get to slinging wisdom & forget to let up. Thus much precious time is lost.

According to an anecdote published in 1918, Woodrow Wilson was asked about the amount of time he spent preparing speeches, and his response was illuminating:[13]

"That depends on the length of the speech," answered the President. "If it is a ten-minute speech it takes me all of two weeks to prepare it; if it is a half-hour speech it takes me a week; if I can talk as long as I want to it requires no preparation at all. I am ready now."

Notes:

The investigation was motivated by an inquiry from a brilliant and entertaining writer, who is also a strong leader of a writing group in Florida.

1. Fred R. Shapiro, *The Yale Book of Quotations* (New Haven: Yale University Press, 2006), 583. Verified in hard copy; Ralph Keyes, *The Quote Verifier: Who Said What, Where, and When* (New York: St. Martin's, 2006), 119–20. Verified in hard copy; Elizabeth Knowles, ed., *Oxford Dictionary of Quotations* in Oxford Reference Online, s.v. "Blaise Pascal."
2. Blaise Pascal, *Les Provinciales, or, The Mystery of Jesuitisme*, trans., 2nd ed. (London: Printed by J. G. for Richard Royston, 1658), 292. Accessed in Google Books, https://goo.gl/bqADC8.
3. Bernard Lamy, Antoine Arnauld, and Pierre Nicole, *The Art of Speaking* (London: W. Godbid, 1676), 8. Accessed in Google Books, https://goo.gl/Uyn9hB.

4.   George Tullie, *An Answer to a Discourse Concerning the Celibacy of the Clergy* (Oxford: printed at the Theater for Richard Chiswell, 1688), preface. Accessed in Google Books, https://goo.gl/xHCPTC.

5.   Edmund Bohun, *A Geographical Dictionary, Representing the Present and Ancient Names of All the Countries, Provinces, Remarkable Cities* . . . (London: printed for Charles Brome at the Gun, at the west end of St. Paul's, 1688), page header AT, column 2. Accessed in Google Books, https://goo.gl/x2BOMq.

6.   John Locke, *The Works of John Locke Esq.: In Three Volumes* (London: John Churchill, 1714), vii. Accessed in Google Books, http://goo.gl/UHOUhU.

7.   William Cowper, "A Letter to Dr. Edward Tyson: Giving an Account of the Anatomy of Those Parts of Male Opossum that Differ from the Female," *Philosophical Transactions of the Royal Society of London* 290 (March–April 1704): 1586. Accessed in Google Books, https://goo.gl/ts1iOw.

8.   Benjamin Franklin, *New Experiments and Observations on Electricity Made at Philadelphia in America*, 2nd ed. (London: D. Henry and R. Cave, 1754), 82. Accessed in Google Books, https://goo.gl/fAzKrF.

9.   "Signor Rossini and Signor Carpani," *Harmonicon* 20 (August 1824): 156. Accessed in Google Books, https://goo.gl/8EJxBE.

10.   *The Life of Luther Written by Himself*, arr. M. Michelet, trans. William Hazlitt (London: David Bogue, 1846), 293. Accessed in Google Books, https://goo.gl/uaqQX1.

11.   Henry David Thoreau, *Letters to Various Persons* (Boston: Houghton, Osgood, 1879), 165. Accessed in Google Books, https://goo.gl/qNv497. Letter with quotation is dated November 16, 1857, to Mr. B. [Harrison Blake].

12.   "SLC to James Redpath, 15 June 1871," Mark Twain Project Online, http://goo.gl/Io1Ihy.

13.   [Untitled article], *Operative Miller* 23, no. 4 (April 1918): 130. Accessed in Google Books, https://goo.gl/fsU5tK.

11. "If you want to know what a man's like, look at how he treats his inferiors."

—J. K. Rowling

One theme in the Harry Potter series by J. K. Rowling is the mistreatment of a class of servants called house elves. The term "inferiors" is generally used to refer to individuals who have a lower rank or status within a society. This group includes the house elves in Rowling's fantasy universe.

In the book *Harry Potter and the Goblet of Fire*, the character Hermione Granger is unhappy with the treatment of a house elf by Bartemius Crouch Sr., a powerful official. The character Sirius Black concurs with Hermione that Crouch's actions reveal a character defect. Here is an excerpt in which Hermione speaks of the dismissal of a house elf, and Sirius then addresses Ron Weasley:[1]

> "Yes," said Hermione in a heated voice, "he sacked her, just because she hadn't stayed in her tent and let herself get trampled—"
>
> "Hermione, will you give it a rest with the elf!" said Ron.
>
> Sirius shook his head and said, "She's got the measure of Crouch better than you have, Ron. If you want to know what a man's like, take a good look at how he treats his inferiors, not his equals."

The popularity of Rowling's books provided wide dissemination for this guideline about assessing character. But this general expression has a long history, and **QI** has located an example in 1910 that communicates the same idea using comparable language:[2]

> It is the way one treats his inferiors more than the way he treats his equals which reveals one's real character.

—Rev. Charles Bayard Miliken, Methodist Episcopal,
Chicago

Below are additional selected citations on this theme in chronological order starting in the 1700s.

The Fourth Earl of Chesterfield's letters to his son were published multiple times with editions available by the 1770s. These letters have historically been used to provide a model regarding proper manners and etiquette in the United Kingdom. A letter dated May 17, 1748, discussed the topic of communicating with inferiors:[3]

> The characteristic of a well-bred man is, to converse with his infe-
> riors without insolence, and with his superiors with respect, and
> with ease.

In 1805 a book about unrest in Ireland discussed the general high regard achieved by the Dean of Kilfenora, a member of the upper class. The author presented an interesting definition for "gentleman" that hinged on the appropriate treatment of inferiors:[4]

> The Dean of Kilfenora is the only instance of complete success. The
> reason is this: that he is, in the best sense of the word, a gentleman;
> that is, he treats his inferiors, whatever their station, with civility
> and affability. This is the real secret of conciliating the Irish peas-
> antry; it is not your money or your protection that will win their
> hearts, but the respectful kindness which removes from their minds
> the painful sense of degradation.

In 1852 the *Farmer's Cabinet* newspaper of Amherst, New Hampshire, printed an article titled "Courtesy to Inferiors" that contained a passage the-matically similar to the quotation under investigation:[5]

> But apart from spiritual motives, a man's true claim to refinement
> of character and good sense, is better tested by scarcely any social
> incident, than by the way he treats his inferiors in life. Nothing

shows a greater abjectness of spirit than an overbearing temper. To insult or to abuse those who cannot resist, or dare not resent the injury, is a sure mark of cowardice, as it would be to draw a sword upon a woman.

In 1902 the periodical *Printers' Ink* published a statement describing the behavior of a gentleman:[6]

> A gentleman is one who treats his inferiors with the greatest courtesy, justice and consideration, and who exacts the same treatment from his superiors.

> —*New York Daily News*

As earlier mentioned, in January 1910 an Ohio newspaper article titled "Religious Thought: Gems Gleaned from the Teachings of All Denominations" included a statement similar to the one written by Rowling.

The words of Miliken were published in multiple newspapers in 1910. By 1911 a comparable statement delivered by another religious speaker named Dr. M. C. B. Mason was printed in newspapers:[7]

> The measure of a man is how he treats his inferiors and that will be the test of a man in the days to come.

In 1913 a book about San Francisco was published that included a profile of Leland Stanford, the prominent industrialist who founded Stanford University. The book mentions the connection between character and the treatment of inferiors:[8]

> All who knew him personally recognized his kindly disposition and he was held in great regard by his employes [*sic*]. The poorest man in his employ could go to him and be sure of considerate treatment. It has been said that the surest criterion of the character of an individual is the way in which he treats his inferiors. Mr. Stanford never let it be known that he considered an individual an inferior.

In 1930 an article in the *Augusta Chronicle* discussed the standards that should be used when judging a society or an individual:[9]

> One of these standards is the treatment that the weak and inferior receive from the strong and superior. It is a matter of no great importance as to what church a lady belongs but it is highly important as to how she treats the social inferior who enters at the back door and does the menial tasks about a home.
>
> As a matter of fact there is no other standard of measurement more accurate than the manner in which a man treats his inferiors and dependents.

In conclusion, the adage spoken by Sirius Black in the 2000 book *Harry Potter and the Goblet of Fire* has a long historical resonance. Charles Bayard Miliken employed a similar expression in 1910, and the general theme of the saying can be traced back to at least the 1700s.

Notes:

1. J. K. Rowling, *Harry Potter and the Goblet of Fire* (New York: Scholastic, 2000), 525. Verified in hard copy.
2. "Gems Gleaned from the Teachings of All Denominations," Religious Thought, *Mansfield News* (Mansfield, OH), January 29, 1910, 15. Accessed in NewspaperARCHIVE.com.
3. *Letters Written by the Late Right Honourable Philip Dormer Stanhope, Earl of Chesterfield, to His Son, Philip Stanhope, Esq., Late Envoy Extraordinary at the Court of Dresden*, vol. 1, 4th ed. rev. (London: J. Dodsley, 1774), 289. Accessed in Google Books, https://goo.gl /5Ts96N. Letter in question is dated May 17, 1748.
4. An Irish Country Gentleman [William Parnell], *An Enquiry into the Causes of Popular Discontents in Ireland* (London: J. Milliken, 1805), 78. Accessed in Google Books, https:// goo.gl/btWbCA.
5. "Courtesy to Inferiors," *Farmer's Cabinet* 51, no. 8 (September 30, 1852): 1. Accessed in GenealogyBank.
6. [Freestanding quotation], *Printers' Ink* 40, no. 10 (September 3, 1902): 26. Accessed in HathiTrust, https://goo.gl/CXobt5.

7. "Freedman's Address," *Daily Review* (Decatur, IL), September 15, 1911, 1. Accessed in NewspaperARCHIVE.com. Many thanks to Suzanne Watkins for pointing out this citation and her pioneering exploration of the saying more broadly. She also pointed out the adage in Rowling's book to **QI**, and she showed that the saying could be traced back to the early part of the twentieth century.

8. Leland Stanford, *San Francisco: Its Builders, Past and Present: Pictorial and Biographical*, vol. 2 (Chicago: S. J. Clarke, 1913), 26. Accessed in Google Books, https://goo.gl/cwZ585.

9. I. S. Caldwell, "Civilization's Yard Stick," Let's Think This Over, *Augusta Chronicle* (Augusta, GA), August 15, 1930, 6. Accessed in GenealogyBank.

12. "We are made of star-stuff."

—Carl Sagan

The chemical elements of life, such as carbon, magnesium, and calcium, were originally created in the interior furnaces of stars and then released by stellar explosions. This fact can be expressed with a beautiful poetic resonance. Here are three examples:

We are made of star-stuff.

Our bodies are made of star-stuff.

There are pieces of star within us all.

In 1973 Carl Sagan published *The Cosmic Connection: An Extra-terrestrial Perspective*, which included the following passage.[1]

> Our Sun is a second- or third-generation star. All of the rocky and metallic material we stand on, the iron in our blood, the calcium in our teeth, the carbon in our genes were produced billions of years ago in the interior of a red giant star. We are made of star-stuff.

Sagan was an important locus for the dissemination of this expression; however, it has a long history. An interesting precursor appeared in a North Carolina newspaper in 1913. A columnist pointed out that the sun and Earth were made of star-stuff. This implied that humans were also made of star-stuff, though this was not directly stated.[2]

> The spectroscope analizes [*sic*] the light if you please, and shows what it is made of. What was the surprise of the tireless searchers when they found common earth metals burning in the mighty sun!

There was once a little girl who cried out with joy when she realized for one little moment that the earth is truly a heavenly body, and that no matter what is happening to us we are really living right up among the stars. The sun is made of "star stuff, and the earth is made of the same material, put together with a difference."

In 1918 the president of the Royal Astronomical Society of Canada delivered a speech with the phrase "our bodies are made of star-stuff," and he seemed to be reaching for a quasi-spiritual interpretation for this fact.[3]

It is true that a first thoughtful glimpse of the immeasurable universe is liable rather to discourage us with a sense of our own insignificance. But astronomy is wholesome even in this, and helps to clear the way to a realization that as our bodies are an integral part of the great physical universe, so through them are manifested laws and forces that take rank with the highest manifestation of Cosmic Being.

Thus we come to see that if our bodies are made of star-stuff— and there is nothing else, says the spectroscope, to make them of— the loftier qualities of our being are just as necessarily constituents of that universal substance . . .

In 1921 a newspaper in Michigan introduced a new columnist with an advertisement that highlighted a version of the adage.[4]

We're All Made of Dust—
But It's Star Dust!

Some comfort in that, says Dr. William E. Barton, the new contributor to *The Evening News*.

Astronomers know how to tell what sort of stuff those stars are made of—and how one bright speck up there in the sky lacks something other stars have.

Odd, though, that human beings have in their makeup about ALL the different elements of ALL those stars.

You'll be interested in this, as Dr. Barton tells it—and in his comment, putting new zest in life for every human that's made of star-stuff.

In 1929 the *New York Times* printed an article titled "The Star Stuff That Is Man" on the first page of its magazine section. The astronomer Harlow Shapley, director of Harvard College Observatory, who was interviewed in the article, stated the following.[5]

> We are made of the same stuff as the stars, so when we study astronomy we are in a way only investigating our remote ancestry and our place in the universe of star stuff. Our very bodies consist of the same chemical elements found in the most distant nebulae, and our activities are guided by the same universal rules.

The last statement of the article was also used as a caption for the accompanying illustration depicting a human figure with a backdrop of planets and galaxies:

> We Are Made of Star Stuff and Are Part of a Magnificent Creation.

In 1971 Nobel laureate Doris Lessing touched on this theme in her novel *Briefing for a Descent into Hell.*[6]

> No one knows what has existed and has vanished beyond recovery, evidence for the number of times Man has understood and has forgotten again that his mind and flesh and life and movements are made of star stuff, sun stuff, planet stuff . . .

In 1973 Carl Sagan published a book with the following statement as noted previously in this article:

> We are made of star-stuff.

Guy Murchie's 1978 book *The Seven Mysteries of Life* stated that "most of the matter in the universe in fact is now known to pass at some time through the caldron of the stars." Murchie included an intriguing adage that he labeled an "ancient Serbian proverb." **QI** does not currently have adequate research tools for determining the age of this proverb.[7]

> When you can really grasp the universality of such relationships you have gained a new insight into the ancient Serbian proverb: "Be humble for you are made of dung. Be noble for you are made of stars."

In 1980 the landmark science series *Cosmos: A Personal Voyage* was televised, and Carl Sagan was the host and a cowriter. The first episode was titled "The Shores of the Cosmic Ocean," and it included the following words spoken by Sagan.[8]

> The surface of the Earth is the shore of the cosmic ocean. On this shore we've learned most of what we know. Recently, we've waded a little way out, maybe ankle-deep, and the water seems inviting. Some part of our being knows this is where we came from. We long to return, and we can because the cosmos is also within us. We're made of star stuff. We are a way for the cosmos to know itself.

In 1981 *The View from Planet Earth* by Vincent Cronin included a version of the adage.[9]

> Our bodies contain three grams of iron, three grams of bright, silver-white magnesium, and smaller amounts of manganese and copper. Proportionate to size, they are among the weightiest atoms in our bodies, and they come from the same source, a long-ago star. There are pieces of star within us all.

In 2006 the well-known science writer Michael Shermer credited Sagan with the saying.[10]

How can we connect to this vast cosmos? Sagan's answer is both spiritually scientific and scientifically spiritual; "The cosmos is within us. We are made of star stuff," he said, referring to the stellar origins of the chemical elements of life, which are cooked in the interiors of stars, then released in supernova explosions into interstellar space where they condense into a new solar system with planets, some of which have life that is composed of this star stuff.

In conclusion, Carl Sagan did employ a version of this saying by 1973. But the expression was in circulation decades before this. The astronomer Albert Durrant Watson used a version in a speech in 1918. In 1973 an interesting, thematically related proverb appeared in a book together with the claim that the words were ancient. But the proverb's accurate age is currently not known to **QI**.

Notes:

Special thanks to Joseph M. Moreno, who inquired about the quotation credited to Vincent Cronin. Also, special thanks to Lim Pin, who asked about the proverb being categorized as Serbian.

1. Carl Sagan, *The Cosmic Connection: An Extraterrestrial Perspective* (Garden City, NY: Anchor, 1973), 189–90. Verified in hard copy.
2. Ellen Frizell Wyckoff, "Star Land," *Greensboro Daily News* (Greensboro, NC), June 15, 1913, 8. Accessed in GenealogyBank.
3. Albert Durrant Watson, "Astronomy: A Cultural Avocation," Retiring President's Address at Annual Meeting, January 29, 1918, in *Journal of the Royal Astronomical Society of Canada* 12, no. 3 (March 1918): 89. Accessed in HathiTrust, https://goo.gl/3iyHML.
4. [Advertisement promoting a new contributor to the *Evening News*], *Evening News* (Sault Ste. Marie, MI], January 24, 1921, 2. Accessed in GenealogyBank.
5. H. Gordon Garbedian, "The Star Stuff That Is Man," *New York Times Magazine*, August 11, 1929, SM1. Accessed in ProQuest.
6. Doris Lessing, *Briefing for a Descent into Hell* (New York: Vintage International, 2009), 180. Verified in Amazon's "Look Inside" feature, https://goo.gl/I6aPLN.
7. Guy Murchie, *The Seven Mysteries of Life: An Exploration in Science & Philosophy* (Boston: Houghton Mifflin, 1981), 402. Verified in scans.

8. "Carl Sagan—Profound Words of Wisdom," YouTube video, 2:32, posted by "braincandy," January 22, 2011, https://www.youtube.com/watch?v=ECuarAmpKoo. Quotation starts at 1:58. This video excerpt is from the episode "The Shores of the Cosmic Ocean" from the 1980 television series *Cosmos: A Personal Voyage*. Sagan delivers the line in an introductory speech near the beginning of the episode.

9. Vincent Cronin, *The View from Planet Earth: Man Looks at the Cosmos* (New York: William Morrow, 1981), 282. Verified in scans.

10. Michael Shermer, *Why Darwin Matters: The Case Against Intelligent Design* (New York: Henry Holt, 2007), 158. Accessed in Google Books, https://goo.gl/QeQPTv.

13. "Comedy is tragedy plus time."

—Tig Notaro
—Woody Allen
—Jon Stewart

Some people are able to transform disastrous or mortifying episodes in their own lives into hilarious comedy routines. With enough time, a painful memory can be transmuted into something funny. The popular performer Carol Burnett once said the following:[1]

> I got my sense of humor from my mother. I'd tell her my tragedies. She'd make me laugh. She said comedy is tragedy plus time.

QI has observed this formula attributed to Woody Allen and Tig Notaro, as well as Burnett. Jon Stewart repeated the phrase with great distress and ire during the December 3, 2014, episode of *The Daily Show* on Comedy Central:

> If comedy is tragedy plus time, I need more fucking time. But I would really settle for less fucking tragedy to be honest with you.

The earliest evidence of this saying located by **QI** was published in *Cosmopolitan* magazine in February 1957. The television personality, actor, and polymath Steve Allen presented his viewpoint on the genesis of comedy.[2]

> When I explained to a friend recently that the subject matter of most comedy is tragic (drunkenness, overweight, financial problems, accidents, etc.) he said, "Do you mean to tell me that the dreadful events of the day are a fit subject for humorous comment?" The answer is "No, but they will be pretty soon."

Man jokes about the things that depress him, but he usually waits till a certain amount of time has passed. It must have been a tragedy when Judge Crater disappeared, but everybody jokes about it now. I guess you can make a mathematical formula out of it. Tragedy plus time equals comedy.

The "Judge Crater" that Allen mentions refers to a New York City judge named Joseph Crater who puzzlingly disappeared in 1930. Newspaper reports on the never-solved case mentioned a secret blonde mistress, missing money, corrupt politicians, and purloined papers.[3] Eventually the event became grist for comedy and even graffiti scrawls such as the following example:[4]

Judge Crater—Call Your Office

In June 1958 the *New Yorker* magazine reviewed a recent television program entitled *The Sound of Laughter*, which was part of a series called *Wide Wide World*. The show explored humor by presenting multiple samples together with general remarks on the theme. In the review, Steve Allen further disseminated the formula he gave in *Cosmopolitan*.[5]

Harry Hershfield said "Humor is the great common denominator;" Al Capp said "The comic strip is the world's most popular literary form;" Neil Schaffner, operator of a tent show, said "Ours is a folk theatre, one that springs from the soil, almost self-creative;" Steve Allen said "Tragedy plus time equals comedy;" and Bob Hope said "Laughter is our most precious commodity."

Here are additional selected citations about the saying in chronological order.

In July 1958 a correspondent with the news service United Press International interviewed Steve Allen, who spoke about writing for his NBC television program. Allen presented an amended version of his equation with a new additive term.[6]

Allen also has another formula for laughs: "Tragedy plus time plus
the will to be amused equals comedy. If you don't have the will to
laugh, you won't be amused—whether it's by a Chaplin or anyone
like him."

In November 1962 popular comic Bob Newhart employed a version of the
equation satirically, but he used the locution "they say" to indicate that he was
not the originator.[7]

I've already gotten a routine out of the interior decorating job on
our apartment in Westwood. They say that comedy is tragedy plus
time. After getting the bills I believe it.

In February 1963 the television star Carol Burnett stated a close variant of
the formula.[8]

Like most clowns who take their comedy seriously, Carol grasps
every opportunity to explain her artistic philosophy. To her,
"Comedy is tragedy mellowed by time."

Burnett illustrated the principle with a humiliating tale about hiding in a
closet to avoid being given a shot of penicillin by her doctor when she was
a child.

"I'd just as like have died than face him, but now it's a howl. Tragic
then, funny now, see?"

The Essential Lenny Bruce, published in 1967, contained material from multiple performances by the comedian and satirist who had died the year before.
Dates were not specified for the comedy routines discussed, but some of them
referenced trials for obscenity and narcotics possession that took place in the
1960s. Bruce used a version of the formula with the word "satire" instead of
"comedy." The following passage mentioned John Foster Dulles, a US secretary
of state who died of cancer in 1959.[9]

I definitely know that I could do a satire on the assassination of Abraham Lincoln and really get screams with it on television. Although Abraham Lincoln was a wonderful man.

But, here's the thing on comedy. If I were to do a satire on the assassination of John Foster Dulles, it would shock people. They'd say, "That is in heinous taste." Why? Because it's fresh. And that's what my contention is: that satire is tragedy plus time. You give it enough time, the public, the reviewers will allow you to satirize it. Which is rather ridiculous, when you think about it.

Note that Dulles was not assassinated, but died of cancer. So this passage is rather odd. It is conceivable that Bruce's routine actually referred to the assassination of John F. Kennedy, and the name was changed during transcription or editing because the tragic event was too recent.

In 1972 *TV Guide* printed an article about Carol Burnett that included the equation quoted at the start of this discussion.

Burnett's 1986 autobiography *One More Time: A Memoir* included a slightly different version of the adage that she attributed to her mother.[10]

I liked Mama's "sayings" better: "Most comedy is tragedy plus time . . ."

In 1987 Steve Allen released *How to Be Funny: Discovering the Comic You*, which included the following discussion.[11]

As I've said earlier, however, nearly all comedy could be classified under the heading "Tragedy." That is, the raw material of almost all jokes is serious subject matter. Being broke, hung over, fired from your job—whatever is bad news, that's what we kid about. Tragedy plus time equals comedy. Given a little time for the pain to subside, dreadful experiences often can be the basis of funny jokes or stories.

In the 1989 Woody Allen film *Crimes and Misdemeanors*, the somewhat unsympathetic character named Lester played by Alan Alda delivered a monologue elaborating on the formula. Lester states that during a visit to Harvard

University, some students asked him "What's comedy?" and he gave the following reply.[12]

> I said "Comedy is tragedy plus time . . . tragedy plus time." You see when—the night Lincoln was shot you couldn't joke about it. You couldn't make a joke about that. You just couldn't do it. Now time has gone by, and now it's fair game. See what I mean. It's tragedy plus time.

In 2012 an Associated Press news story reported on a stand-up performance by the comic Tig Notaro, who had very recently been diagnosed with cancer. Using stream-of-consciousness and dark humor, she spoke to the audience.[13]

> "It's weird because with humor, the equation is tragedy plus time equals comedy," Notaro told a stunned crowd. "I am just at tragedy right now."

In conclusion, based on current evidence, Steve Allen was the first person to represent the relationship between tragedy and comedy using this formula. Several other artists have employed the adage in the years since 1957. Carol Burnett credited her mother, who died in 1958. So it is possible that the adage was in circulation before Allen expressed it in *Cosmopolitan*.

Alternatively, Burnett's mother read it in *Cosmopolitan* near the end of her life and shared the saying with her daughter.

Notes:

Thanks to David Haglund, editor of *Slate*'s culture blog, whose query caused **QI** to formulate this question and initiate this exploration. Many thanks to the participants in a mailing-list discussion of this phrase in 2011, including Jon Lighter, Ben Zimmer, Victor Steinbok, Bill Mullins, Fred R. Shapiro, Laurence Horn, and others. Thanks to Barry Popik, who also examined this saying and wrote a blog post about it.[14]

1. Dwight Whitney, "Carol and Joe and Fred and Marge," *TV Guide*, July 1, 1972, 10. Verified in microfilm. The issue's table of contents states the article title as "Carol Burnett and Her Silent Partners."

2. Steve Allen, Steve Allen's Almanac, *Cosmopolitan* 142 (February 1957), 12. This column was part of a series published between 1956 and 1957. Verified in scans from the Browne Popular Culture Library at Bowling Green State University. Great thanks to the librarians there who provided a digital image of a document from the Steve Allen Collection.

3. Janet Cawley, "Judge Crater Case Slips into History—Police File Is Closed on 'Missingest' Person," *Chicago Tribune*, August 5, 1980, 1. Accessed in ProQuest.

4. Norton Mockridge, "A Rash of Graffiti," New York Scene, *Springfield Union* (Springfield, MA), September 12, 1966, 6. Accessed in GenealogyBank.

5. John Lardner, "What Humor Means, with Samples," The Air, *New Yorker* 34 (June 7, 1958): 78. Verified in hard copy.

6. Fred Danzig, "It's Simpler Writing Gags," *Bakersfield Californian* (Bakersfield, CA), July 21, 1958, 21. Accessed in NewspaperARCHIVE.com.

7. Bob Thomas, "Humorist Disproves Romanticists' Idea," *Corpus Christi Times* (Corpus Christi, TX), November 21, 1962. 8. Accessed in NewspaperARCHIVE.com.

8. "An Evening with Carol Burnett," Variety Show of the Month, *Show: The Magazine of the Arts* 3 (February 1963): 22. Verified in scans. Thanks to a librarian at the University of Florida Gainesville Library.

9. Lenny Bruce, *The Essential Lenny Bruce*, John Cohen, ed. (New York, Ballantine, 1974), 116.

10. Carol Burnett, *One More Time: A Memoir* (New York: Avon, 1987), 52. Verified in scans.

11. Steve Allen and Jane Wollman, *How to Be Funny: Discovering the Comic You* (New York: McGraw-Hill, 1987), 29. Verified in hard copy.

12. "If_it_breaks.avi," YouTube video, 1:00, posted by "Stephen Crane," December 5, 2008, https://www.youtube.com/watch?v=lYn3IPTnkQM. Quotation starts at 0:40. This video clip is from the 1989 film *Crimes and Misdemeanors* directed by Woody Allen.

13. Associated Press, "Comic's Unique Opening Leaves Impression," *Erie Times-News* (Erie, PA), October 14, 2012. Accessed in NewsBank.

14. Barry Popik, "Comedy Is Tragedy Plus Time," The Big Apple, June 22, 2011, http://www.barrypopik.com/index.php/new_york_city/entry/comedy_is_tragedy_plus_time/.

14. "Easy reading is hard writing."

—Nathaniel Hawthorne

The earliest match of the above quotation, located by **QI**, appeared in the London periodical the *Athenaeum* in 1837. The humorist, poet, and essayist Thomas Hood wrote a letter to the editor that was printed under the title "Copyright and Copywrong." Hood commented on the process of writing. In the original text, the word "damned" was partially censored to yield "d__d."[1]

> And firstly, as to how he writes, upon which head there is a wonderful diversity of opinions; one thinks that writing is "as easy as lying," and pictures the author sitting carefully at his desk "with his glove on," like Sir Roger de Coverley's poetical ancestor. A second holds that "the easiest reading is d__d hard writing," and imagines Time himself beating his brains over an extempore.

Hood placed the adage between quotation marks, suggesting that it was already in use. In fact, variant statements containing the phrases "easy reading" and "hard writing" were already being disseminated, and the expression probably evolved from those antecedents. Hence, apportioning credit for the formulation of this maxim is a difficult task.

An important precursor of the saying under investigation appeared in the poem "Clio's Protest or, the Picture Varnished" by the influential Irish poet and playwright Richard Brinsley Sheridan. This poem was in distribution by 1772.[2]

> You write with ease, to shew your breeding;
> But easy writing's vile hard reading.

The meaning of the maxim in the couplet above certainly differs from the expression employed by Hood. The pairing of the words "reading" and "writing" was swapped. Also, Hood used "easiest" instead of "easy." Nevertheless,

QI believes that the existence of Sheridan's couplet facilitated the emergence of the later saying from Hood. Indeed, some individuals have misremembered the words of Sheridan and credited him with the one used by Hood.

Another important precursor appeared in the 1818 poem "Beppo, A Venetian Story" by the famous Romantic poet Lord Byron. In the following excerpt, Byron lamented that he had not acquired "the art of easy writing":[3]

> Oh that I had the art of easy writing
> What should be easy reading!

Hood's statement was further disseminated in 1837 when his letter to the *Athenaeum* discussed above was excerpted in a weekly compilation called *Waldie's Select Circulating Library* based in Philadelphia, Pennsylvania.[4]

In 1845 *Douglas Jerrold's Shilling Magazine* printed a book review that included an instance of the saying without attribution.[5]

> It is a work that the most cultivated may read with advantage, who will be delighted with its skill and taste; and if easy reading is hard writing, we are exceedingly obliged to the author, for anything easier and more skilfully graceful on such knotty subjects it has seldom, if ever, been our lot to peruse.

In 1848 a text titled *The Satires and Epistles of Horace: With Notes and Excursus* by Thomas Keightley included an instance without ascription.[6]

> They objected to the light and careless flow of his verses as a fault, forgetting that easy reading is usually very hard writing.

In 1849 *Graham's American Monthly Magazine* favorably reviewed a history work by the famous philosopher David Hume. The reviewer complimented the text by using an oddly garbled version of the maxim, which he attributed to Sheridan, presumably the Irish playwright mentioned above.[7]

> "Easy writing," said Sheridan, "is cursed hard writing." The easy style of Hume is an illustration. The reader, at the end, feels that

he has been keeping company with a great man, gifted with an extraordinary grasp and subtlety of mind, but during the journey he thought he was but chatting with an agreeable and intelligent familiar companion.

In 1851 a book reviewer in the *Daily National Intelligencer* of Washington, DC, employed an instance when discussing a book by a journalist. The writer ascribed the maxim to an archetypal schoolboy.[8]

His readers have little appreciation of the labor expended on these articles, which seem to come off trippingly at the end of his flowing pen; but, should they attempt an imitation, they will have reason to say, with the schoolboy, "easy reading is darned hard writing."

The linkage of the adage to Thomas Hood was not lost, because his works continued to be reprinted. For example, an 1857 compilation titled *Prose and Verse* included the essay with the saying.[9]

In 1860 Charles Allston Collins, a painter and a regular contributor to the weekly London journal *All the Year Round*, included an instance of the saying in an article titled "Our Eye-Witness Among the Buildings." Collins elevated the saying to the status of a "rule," but he did not provide an attribution.[10]

The easy-looking, and the simple things in all art matters are more difficult than the complex and intricate. It is a rule that easy reading is hard writing, and to construct anything that the mind takes in without effort, and without being puzzled by it, is a triumph of art.

In 1867 a writer in the *Methodist Quarterly Review* incorrectly assigned the maxim to Sheridan.[11]

But the witty Sheridan once well remarked that "easy reading is terribly hard writing."

In 1882 the popular and prolific novelist Anthony Trollope placed the maxim into the thoughts of one of his characters.[12]

> She wrote such letters, letters so full of mingled wit and love and fun, that she was sure that he must take delight in reading them. "Easy reading requires hard writing," she said to herself as she copied for the third time one of her epistles . . .

In 1884 a book reviewer in the *Daily News* of London incorrectly assigned the adage to Lord Byron.[13]

> It seems an odd thing to say of a book dealing with the profoundest questions of human faith and destiny that it is easy reading; but as Byron used to say, easy reading means hard writing, and there is no mistaking the amount of laborious thought and investigation that has been spent upon these chapters.

In 1898 a book reviewer in the New York periodical the *Engineering Magazine* attributed the saying to the well-known novelist William Makepeace Thackeray.[14]

> "Easy reading means hard writing," said Thackeray, and if it is true, there can be no doubt that "De Pontibus" is the result of hard work and harder thought, for here is found the gist of matter which might easily have occupied double the space.

In 1979, at a press conference in Richmond, Virginia, Maya Angelou employed the saying and attributed the words to Nathaniel Hawthorne.[15]

> That preference, she said, recalls the comment of Nathaniel Hawthorne: "Easy reading is damned hard writing."

Years later, in a 1990 interview with the *Paris Review*, Angelou spoke the adage again with the same attribution.[16]

> Nathaniel Hawthorne says, "Easy reading is damn hard writing." I try to pull the language in to such a sharpness that it jumps off the page. It must look easy, but it takes me forever to get it to look so easy. Of course, there are those critics—New York critics as a

rule—who say, Well, Maya Angelou has a new book out and of course it's good but then she's a natural writer. Those are the ones I want to grab by the throat and wrestle to the floor because it takes me forever to get it to sing.

In conclusion, **QI** would provisionally credit Thomas Hood with coining the maxim, based on the version he used in 1837. Yet, it is certainly possible that future researchers will locate earlier instances.

Richard Brinsley Sheridan and Lord Byron can be credited with the words given in the 1772 and 1818 citations, respectively. There is no substantive evidence that Sheridan, Byron, or Hawthorne employed the maxim under investigation. Charles Allston Collins, Anthony Trollope, and Maya Angelou used the maxim after Thomas Hood. They helped to popularize the saying but did not coin it.

Notes:

Great thanks to Laurelyn Collins and Eric Feezell, whose inquiries led **QI** to initiate three explorations of interlinked sayings including this one. Special thanks to Bonnie Taylor-Blake, who accessed the 1772 citation.

1. Thomas Hood, letter to the editor, *Athenaeum*, April 22, 1837, 286–87. Accessed in Google Books, https://goo.gl/fbhFcs.

2. *The Rival Beauties; A Poetical Contest, Poem Information: Clio's Protest; Or, The Picture Varnished, Addressed to The Honourable Lady M-rg-r-t F-rd-ce* (London: Printed for W. Griffin, at Garrick's Head, in Catharine-Street, 1772), 16. Accessed in ECCO Eighteenth Century Collections Online.

3. Lord Byron, *Beppo: A Venetian Story* (London: John Murray, 1818), 25. Accessed in Google Books, https://goo.gl/sbjWu3.

4. The Journal of Belles Lettres, *[Waldie's] Select Circulating Library, Containing the Best Popular Literature* 25 (June 20, 1837), 3. Accessed in Google Books, https://goo.gl/6wgKf6.

5. Review of *Lectures, Addressed Chiefly to the Working Classes* by W. J. Fox, *Douglas Jerrold's Shilling Magazine* 2, no. 8 (1845): 192. Accessed in Google Books, https://goo.gl/F5EipW.

6. Thomas Keightly, *The Satires and Epistles of Horace with Notes and Excursus* (London: Whittaker, 1848), 94. Accessed in Google Books, https://goo.gl/EuvJN7.

7. Review of *History of England from the Invasion of Julius Caesar to the Abdication of James the Second*, by David Hume, *Graham's American Monthly Magazine* 35, no. 6 (December 1849): 379. Accessed in Google Books, https://goo.gl/uqyJup.

8. Review of *Hurry-graphs; or Sketches of Scenery, Celebrity, and Society, Taken from Life*, by N. Parker Willis, *Daily National Intelligencer* (Washington, DC), June 7, 1851, 2. Accessed in GenealogyBank.

9. Thomas Hood, *Prose and Verse*, new ed. (New York: Kiggins and Kellogg, 1857), 90. Accessed in Google Books, https://goo.gl/Sa2nRo.

10. Charles Allston Collins, "Our Eye-Witness Among the Buildings," *All the Year Round*, June 2, 1860, 189. Accessed in Google Books, https://goo.gl/dnDz3V.

11. Review of *Cyclopedia of Biblical, Theological and Ecclesiastical Literature*, by John Mclintock and James Strong, eds., *Methodist Quarterly Review* 27 (July 1867): 460. Accessed in Google Books, https://goo.gl/hjH2GP.

12. Anthony Trollope, *Kept in the Dark* (Leipzig: Bernhard Tauchnitz, 1882), 267. Accessed in Google Books, https://goo.gl/PNMrfJ.

13. Review of *Ancient Religion and Modern Thought*, by William Samuel Lilly, *Daily News* (London, UK), August 21, 1884, 3. Accessed in 19th Century British Newspapers by Gale Cengage.

14. Review of *De Pontibus: A Pocket Book for Bridge Engineers*, by J. A. L. Waddell, *Engineering Magazine* 15 (June 1898): 534. Accessed in Google Books, https://goo.gl/DYHp3J.

15. C. A. Bustard, "Richmond Compared to 'Living in Museum,'" *Richmond Times Dispatch* (Richmond, VA), April 20, 1979, A14. Accessed in GenealogyBank.

16. George Plimpton, "Maya Angelou: The Art of Fiction No. 119," Interviews, *Paris Review*, no. 116 (Fall 1990), http://www.theparisreview.org/interviews/2279/the-art-of-fiction-no -119-maya-angelou.

15. "In the future, everyone will be anonymous for fifteen minutes."

—Banksy

The graffiti provocateur Banksy fabricated a crudely painted pink television set with the message above stenciled on the screen. The saying is a twist on a famous pronouncement from the pop artist Andy Warhol concerning the velocity of modern fame:[1]

In the future everyone will be famous for fifteen minutes.

The earliest instance found by **QI** of a saying similar to the one in Banksy's artwork was printed in the music magazine *Spin* in 1989. It appeared in a hostile profile of the singer and songwriter Richard Marx by the journalist and critic John Leland. In the following text, the term "the 90s" referred to the near future:[2]

A success story for the 90s—when everyone will be anonymous for 15 minutes—Marx is rock's invisible man. No one has sold so many records and made so little impact on the culture. Even his press kit, the expensive, glossy cardboard portfolio of a major star, reads more like a corporate annual report than the story of a life.

The passage above concerns the transposable and indistinguishable elements of fame. By May 1996 an interesting variant quotation aimed at another topic was circulating: the computer-mediated invasion of privacy. This maxim had different implications because "cyberspace" was substituted for "the future." The periodical *PJ: Privacy Journal* reported on the saying and credited a legal scholar:[3]

In cyberspace, everyone will be anonymous for 15 minutes.

—Graham Greenleaf, associate professor of law at
University of New South Wales and member of the
New South Wales Privacy Committee in Australia

In August 1996 Greenleaf employed the saying again in an article in the
journal *Privacy Law and Policy Reporter*:[4]

> It has been said with appropriate irony that "in cyberspace, every-
> one will be anonymous for 15 minutes." [1] Cyberspace presents
> both an unexpected opportunity for private (and even anonymous)
> communications and transactions over distance, and the potential
> for a panopticon, surveillance more extensive than any previous
> form of social control.

In the footnote contained in the excerpt above, Greenleaf acknowledges two
individuals who inspired his remark:

> I stole this quip from John Hilvert, via Andy Warhol and who
> knows who else . . .

In 1998 the social critic Neal Gabler deployed a version of the adage in his
book *Life: The Movie; How Entertainment Conquered Reality* while discussing the
increase in the number of marginal demi-celebrities:[5]

> Indeed, the profusion of celebrity was so overwhelming that it also
> seemed to void another oft-quoted dictum. In the future everyone
> would not be famous for fifteen minutes, as Andy Warhol had
> prophesied. In the future, it seemed, everyone would be anony-
> mous for fifteen minutes.

The adage was further disseminated in a *New York Times* interview with
Gabler:[6]

> In the fame-driven future he envisions, everyone will be anony-
> mous for 15 minutes, but Mr. Gabler, looking every bit the cultural

critic (Armani black, stubbly salt-and-pepper whiskers), doesn't seem overly worried. "Anyone who writes seriously about American culture is not in danger of becoming a celebrity," he said.

A photo dated September 15, 2006, taken at a Los Angeles show captured Banksy's television art piece.[7] In 2008 an interview and profile of the actor Dennis Hopper at the website of the UK newspaper the *Telegraph* included a picture of Hopper adjacent to Banksy's modified television:[8]

> Upstairs, he poses for a final shot next to a sculpture by another friend, the elusive British graffiti artist Banksy: a TV set sprayed with the words, "IN THE FUTURE, EVERYONE WILL BE ANONYMOUS FOR 15 MINUTES."

In 2010 the book *Cracking Codes and Cryptograms for Dummies* gave the adage, credited to Greenleaf, as the solution to a puzzle:[9]

> Puzzle 247: In cyberspace everyone will be anonymous for fifteen minutes.
>
> —Graham Greenleaf

In 2011 a *New York Times* article about a fashion show in Milan, Italy, invoked Banksy:[10]

> Banksy said it best: "In the future, everybody will be anonymous for 15 minutes." The British graffiti artist and prankster's inversion of the weary Warhol dictum about fame comes as a tonic in an age of self-promotion and so-called social media.

In conclusion, the expression predates Banksy's television art piece with the saying. Indeed, more than one variant was in circulation before 2000. The phrasings and the meanings were fluid. The statement by Neal Gabler seems to be the closest precursor to the words painted on Banksy's television.

Notes:

1. Andy Warhol, *The Andy Warhol Diaries*, ed. Pat Hackett (New York: Warner Books, 1989), 156. Text is found in the diary entry dated July 27, 1978. Verified in hard copy.

2. John Leland, "The Invisible Man," *Spin* 5, no. 9 (December 1989): 13. Accessed in Google Books, https://goo.gl/QB8Tk4.

3. Quotable, *PJ: Privacy Journal*, May 1996, 2. Verified in hard copy.

4. Graham Greenleaf, "The Inevitability of Life in Cyberspace," *Privacy Law and Policy Reporter* 48, no. 5 (August 1996): http://goo.gl/KsAbyS.

5. Neal Gabler, *Life: The Movie; How Entertainment Conquered Reality* (New York: Vintage, 2000), 160. Verified in Amazon's "Look Inside" feature, https://goo.gl/qQKJBH.

6. Ralph Blumenthal, "Neal Gabler: Roll 'Em: Life as a Long Starring Role," At Lunch With, *New York Times*, December 8, 1998, E1. Accessed in ProQuest.

7. "Photos from Banksy's LA Show," Flickr photostream, 25 photos, Peggy Archer, September 15, 2006, https://goo.gl/SPPhaZ.

8. Sheryl Garratt, "Dennis Hopper: The Ride of His Life," *Telegraph* (London, UK), September 25, 2008, http://www.telegraph.co.uk/culture/film/3561177/Dennis-Hopper-the-ride-of-his-life.html.

9. Denise Sutherland and Mark E. Koltko-Rivera, *Cracking Codes and Cryptograms for Dummies* (Hoboken, NJ: Wiley, 2010), 316.

10. Guy Trebay, "Fashion Review: Designers Anonymous," *New York Times*, January 19, 2011, http://www.nytimes.com/2011/01/20/fashion/20MILAN.html.

HOST

16. "I fear the day that technology will surpass our human interaction."

—**Albert Einstein**

The statement above is usually displayed next to a portrait of Albert Einstein and accompanied by a set of pictures of young people staring intently at mobile phone screens. The oblivious individuals are shown engaging in miscellaneous activities, such as attending a sporting event, sitting at a bar, and visiting a museum. Perhaps the word "engaging" should be replaced by the more accurate word "disengaging."

There is no substantive evidence that Albert Einstein made this statement. It does not appear in the comprehensive collection of quotations *The Ultimate Quotable Einstein* from Princeton University Press.[1]

The saying and two variants were in circulation by 2012. For example, a now defunct website called answerbag.com presented a variant in a message with an attached date of October 21, 2012:[2]

Einstein: I fear the day when the technology overlaps with our humanity. The world will only have a generation of idiots. Was he right?

Dates on websites are sometimes inaccurate because the retroactive alteration of text and dates is easy to accomplish. Sometimes the content of a webpage is altered, and the date associated with the content is not updated to reflect the modification. Luckily, a snapshot of the webpage at answerbag.com with the saying was stored in the Internet Archive Wayback Machine database on October 25, 2012. Thus, the accuracy of that date is supported.

Another now defunct website called imfunny.net displayed an elaborate nine-panel composite image dated November 3, 2012, with the title "The Day That Albert Einstein Feared May Have Finally Arrived." Eight panels showed people preoccupied by phones. The ninth panel presented the following saying superimposed on a picture of Einstein. No name was given for the person posting the message:[3]

"I fear the day that technology will surpass our human interaction. The world will have a generation of idiots."

—Albert Einstein

The "Talk" webpage for Albert Einstein at the Wikiquote website lists a third version of the quotation in a section titled "Unsourced and Dubious/ Overly Modern Sources." The revision history of the webpage indicates that an unnamed person added the expression on November 3, 2012:[4]

I fear the day when technology overlaps our humanity. It will be then that the world will have permanent ensuing generations of idiots.

As previously discussed, in the 1995 movie *Powder* a quotation was credited to Einstein that has a thematic overlap with the sayings above. Note that there is no substantive support linking this quote to Einstein:

It's become appallingly clear that our technology has surpassed our humanity.

It is possible that the existence of this expression influenced the development of more recent sayings ascribed to the famous physicist.

In conclusion, **QI** believes that Albert Einstein did not write or say any of the three variant quotations. Individuals aggravated by the behavioral patterns of cell phone users probably facilitated the construction, evolution, and dissemination of this meme. The phrasing of the saying has changed over time, and different images have been attached to it. **QI** hypothesizes that the origination date is relatively recent, perhaps as late as 2012. The efforts of the creators have been successful for now—the basic saying has achieved viral status with its dubious ascription.

Notes:

Many thanks to the perceptive individuals—Guy MacPherson, Doug Wrotenbery, and M. Scott Gravlee—who contacted **QI** and implicitly or explicitly expressed skepticism about these quotations ascribed to Einstein. Thanks also to Douglas and Matze, who placed queries in the comment section of **QI**'s website. Their messages provided impetus for this investigation.

1. Alice Calaprice, ed., *The Ultimate Quotable Einstein* (Princeton: Princeton University Press, 2010). Verified in hard copy.

2. Susan_madari, "Life and Society: More Life and Society," Questions, answerbag.com, accessed March 19, 2013. The website answerbag.com is now defunct, but the webpage cited here can be found via the Internet Archive Wayback Machine, which captured a snapshot of the webpage on October 25, 2012. See https://web.archive.org/web/20121025152939/http://www.answerbag.com/q_view/2809436.

3. "The Day That Albert Einstein Feared May Have Finally Arrived," imfunny.net, November 3, 2012. The website imfunny.net is now defunct, but the webpage cited here can be found via the Internet Archive Wayback Machine, which captured a snapshot of the webpage on November 10, 2012, although, unfortunately, the picture with the quotation was not part of the snapshot. (The Internet Archive Wayback Machine does not

always store all images.) See https://web.archive.org/web/20121110025042/http://imfunny
.net/the-day-that-albert-einstein-feared-may-have-finally-arrived/.

4. "Talk:Albert Einstein," [discussion page], Wikiquote, https://en.wikiquote.org/wiki
    /Talk:Albert_Einstein.

17. "To be is to do" —Socrates / "To do is to be" —Jean-Paul Sartre / "Do be do be do" —Frank Sinatra.

—Kurt Vonnegut

The 1982 novel *Deadeye Dick* by the popular author Kurt Vonnegut presents the humorous tripartite message shown above.[1] But Vonnegut is not responsible for this eccentric philosophical wordplay. The earliest published description located by **QI** of a graffito that conforms to the template appeared in the *Dallas Morning News* in January 1968. According to columnist Paul Crume, the graffito was created in an incremental process by three different people. The initiator was a local businessman in Richardson, Texas:[2]

> Bud Crew says that a month ago he wrote this on the warehouse wall at Bud's Tool Cribs in Richardson: "'The way to do is to be.' —Leo-tzu [*sic*], Chinese philosopher."
>
> A few days later, a salesman wrote under that: "'The way to be is to do.'—Dale Carnegie."
>
> Recently, says Crew, an anonymous sage has added still another axiom: "'Do be, do be, do.' —Frank Sinatra."

The phrase ascribed to the famous vocalist Frank Sinatra derives from his version of the song "Strangers in the Night," a number-one hit in 1966. Near the end of the track, Sinatra sings a sequence of nonsense syllables that could be transcribed as "do de do be do" or "do be do be do."[3] Many listeners remembered this distinctive stylization.

In July 1968 this graffito tale was included in a syndicated series called "Weekend Chuckles" from General Features Corporation; hence, it achieved wide dissemination. Some details were omitted; for example, Bud Crew's name was not given. But the graffito was nearly identical. The spelling of "Leo-tzu" was changed to "Lao-tse":[4]

One fellow was inspired to write on a warehouse wall: "The way to do is to be. —Lao-tse, Chinese philosopher."

A few days later, a salesman wrote under that: "The way to be is to do. —Dale Carnegie."

Recently an anonymous sage has added still another message: "Do be, do be, do. —Frank Sinatra."

In January 1969 a real estate agent named Joe Griffith ran an advertisement in a South Carolina newspaper that included the tripartite message. The first two statements in this instance were shortened and simplified. In addition, one of the attributions was switched to Socrates:[5]

Joe Griffith Sez:
"TO BE IS TO DO" —Dale Carnegie
"TO DO IS TO BE" —Socrates
"DO BE DO BE DO" —Frank Sinatra

The message continued to evolve over the decades, and many philosophers and authors have been substituted into the template, including Dale Carnegie, Socrates, Plato, Aristotle, Jean-Paul Sartre, Albert Camus, John Stuart Mill, William James, William Shakespeare, and Bertrand Russell. The punch line ascribed to Sinatra, in some form, is usually preserved, though a variety of other lines have been added to the joke as shown in the 1990 citation further below.

In November 1971 a sports columnist for the *Dallas Morning News* published the following version of the message, which in this instance included two French philosophers:[6]

"To be is to do." —Sartre
"To do is to be." —Camus
"Do be do be do." —Sinatra

In 1972 *Aequanimitas*, the yearbook of the medical and nursing schools at the University of Michigan, printed a version with four parts instead of three. Also, Sinatra's line was distinct:[7]

To be or not to be —William Shakespeare
To be is to do —Jean Paul Sartre
To do is to be —Bertrand Russell
Scoo be doo be doo —Frank Sinatra

In August 1972 the *Boston Globe* published a report by a journalist who visited women's restrooms in the Boston area and examined the graffiti. She found the following instance:[8]

To be is to do . . . John Stuart Mill
To do is to be . . . William James
Do be do be do . . . Frank Sinatra

In January 1973 "The Times Diary" column of the *Times* of London described a graffito "in the gentlemen's lavatory at Cambridge University Library" that was spotted by a reader. Three different hands wrote the three parts:[9]

To do is to be —J. S. Mill.
To be is to do —Jean-Paul Sartre.
Do be do be do —Frank Sinatra.

A few days later the *Times* of London printed a follow-up describing a graffito in a prominent museum in New York:[10]

In the Guggenheim Museum, New York, "to do is to be" is attributed to Plato, not J. S. Mill and "to be is to do" to Aristotle, not J. P. Sartre. "Do be do be do" remains the work of Frank Sinatra.

The same article relayed assertions of precedence from Oxford University:

And Oxford, predictably, claims to have been there first. A man from St Catherine's says the text first appeared at the Bodleian several years ago and has since spread through many colleges.

A week later, on January 12, 1973, the *Times* of London described a six-part graffito found on the library wall at the University of Guelph:[11]

> To be is to do —Aristotle
> To do is to be —J. P. Sartre
> Do be do be do —F. Sinatra
> What is to be done? —Lenin
> Do It! —J. Rubin
> O.K.! O.K.! —T. Mann

The line concerning "J. Rubin" was probably a reference to the political activist Jerry Rubin, who published a book titled *Do It: Scenarios of the Revolution* in 1970.[12] **QI** has not attempted to provide rationales for each of the myriad lines inserted into this extended comical mélange over the years.

In January 1982 the personals section of *Reason* magazine printed the following instance:[13]

> TO DO IS TO BE —Kant
> To be is to do —Hegel
> Do be do be do —Sinatra

Vonnegut's aforementioned 1982 novel *Deadeye Dick* featured a fictional metropolis called Midland City and an imaginary airfield called the Will Fairchild Memorial Airport. The protagonist of the novel visited the bathroom at the airport:[14]

> For a few moments there, I was happier than happy, healthier than healthy, and I saw these words scrawled on the tiles over a wash basin:
>
> "To be is to do" —Socrates.
> "To do is to be" —Jean-Paul Sartre.
> "Do be do be do" —Frank Sinatra.

Longer and more elaborate lists have been constructed over time. Here is a subset of the lines that were posted in a message to the rec.humor newsgroup of Usenet in 1990:[15]

> To do is to be. —Socrates
> To be or not to be. —Shakespeare
> To be is to do. —Sartre
> Dooby dooby doo. —Sinatra
> Yabba dabba doo. —Fred Flintstone
> Dabba dabba doo. —Kate Bush
> Do be a do be. —Miss Louise, *Romper Room*
> Scooby-doobee-doo. —Scooby Doo
> Hey-boo-boo. —Yogi Bear

The long-running children's television show *Romper Room* featured a character in a bumblebee costume named Do-Bee, who displayed emulation-worthy behaviors. Thus, the line in the above instance should have said "Do be a Do-Bee."

In conclusion, based on current evidence, this family of multipart messages is traceable to a report from Texas in January 1968. The graffito evolved through replication and mutation. Individual lines were assigned to a wide variety of philosophers and thinkers. The attributions were primarily comical, and typically they did not correspond to actual quotations.

Notes:

Great thanks to Victor Steinbok, who suggested this topic and gave impetus to **QI** to formulate this question and perform this exploration. Special thanks to David A. Daniel and Barry Popik for pointing to the song "Strangers in the Night." Thanks to correspondent R. Gentile, who suggested mentioning "Strangers in the Night." Thanks to multiple members of the American Dialect Society discussion group for valuable comments. Thanks to A Very Defiant Duckling Named Ender, who asked about the line featuring "J. Rubin." Thanks to Hildegard Lindschinger, who told **QI** about the *Romper Room* character Do-Bee.

1. Kurt Vonnegut, *Deadeye Dick* (New York: Delacorte, 1982), 224. Verified in scans.

2. Paul Crume's Big D, *Dallas Morning News*, January 29, 1968, A1. Accessed in GenealogyBank.

3. "Strangers in the Night—Frank Sinatra," YouTube video, 5:10, posted by "kumpulanvideo," July 6, 2007, https://www.youtube.com/watch?v=hlSbSKNk9f0. Quotation starts at 2:23.

4. Weekend Chuckles, *Times-Picayune* (New Orleans, LA), July 28, 1968. Accessed in GenealogyBank.

5. [Advertisement for Joe Griffith Inc.] *News and Courier* (Charleston, SC), January 31, 1969, 15B. Accessed in GenealogyBank.

6. John Anders, "Wishbone for Pros?" *Dallas Morning News*, November 10, 1971, 4B. Accessed in GenealogyBank. The original text contained "Sarte" instead of "Sartre."

7. "Medical Education—A Review," *Aequanimitas* 1972: Yearbook of the Medical and Nursing Schools, University of Michigan Medical School, 120. Accessed in HathiTrust, https://goo.gl/5yS69p.

8. Diane White, "Graffiti by the Girls," *Boston Globe*, August 31, 1972, 42. Accessed in ProQuest.

9. P. H. S., The Times Diary, *Times* (London, UK), January 2, 1973, 10. Accessed in *The Times Digital Archive* by Gale Cengage.

10. P. H. S., The Times Diary, *Times* (London, UK), January 5, 1973, 12. Accessed in *The Times Digital Archive* by Gale Cengage.

11. P. H. S., The Times Diary, *Times* (London, UK), January 12, 1973, 12. Accessed in *The Times Digital Archive* by Gale Cengage.

12. Jerry Rubin, *Do It! Scenarios of the Revolution* (Simon and Schuster, 1970).

13. Personals, *Reason*, January 1982, 58, http://unz.org/Pub/Reason-1982jan-00055.

14. Vonnegut, *Deadeye Dick*, 224.

15. "Do," rec.humor Usenet newsgroup, March 21, 1990. Accessed in Google Groups, https://goo.gl/3RhS05.

18. "Well-behaved women seldom make history."

—Marilyn Monroe

The earliest evidence of a version of this phrase known to **QI** appeared in an academic paper in the journal *American Quarterly* in 1976 by Laurel Thatcher Ulrich. Ulrich's statement used the word "seldom" instead of "rarely" or "never":[1]

> Well-behaved women seldom make history . . .

In 1976 Ulrich was a graduate student at the University of New Hampshire, and she earned her PhD in history there in 1980. She is now an eminent Pulitzer Prize–winning professor of early American history at Harvard University. The article containing the phrase was titled "Vertuous Women Found: New England Ministerial Literature, 1668-1735." The goal of the paper and much of Ulrich's work was the recovery of the history of women who were not featured in history books of the past. She was interested in limning the lives of ordinary women who were considered "well-behaved" or "vertuous" (an alternative spelling of "virtuous").

The introductory sentences to Ulrich's 1976 paper provide further context for her quotation:[2]

> Cotton Mather called them "The Hidden Ones." They never preached or sat in a deacon's bench. Nor did they vote or attend Harvard. Neither, because they were virtuous women, did they question God or the magistrates. They prayed secretly, read the Bible through at least once a year, and went to hear the minister preach even when it snowed. Hoping for an eternal crown, they never asked to be remembered on earth. And they haven't been. Well-behaved women seldom make history; against Antinomians and witches, these pious matrons have had little chance at all.

Ulrich's article explored the experiences of these "pious matrons" by using sources such as the following, which are mentioned in her paper:[3]

> For the years between 1668 and 1735, *Evans' American Bibliography* lists 55 elegies, memorials, and funeral sermons for females plus 15 other works of practical piety addressed wholly or in part to women.

The maxim has been altered and reassigned to other individuals over time. For example, in 2002 a book credited a version of the saying to Marilyn Monroe:[4]

> Well-behaved women rarely make history.
>
> —Marilyn Monroe (June 1)

The popularity of the adage ultimately led Ulrich to write a 2007 book with the title *Well-Behaved Women Seldom Make History*. That same year the *Deseret News* of Salt Lake City, Utah, published an interview with Ulrich, and she discussed the phrase she made famous.[5]

> [T]he phrase has appeared on T-shirts, placards, placemats, mugs, bumper stickers and greeting cards throughout the country, sometimes with attribution and sometimes without.
>
> "It was a weird escape into popular culture," Ulrich said by phone from her home in Cambridge, MA. "I got constant e-mails about it, and I thought it was humorous. Then I started looking at where it was coming from. Once I turned up as a character in a novel—and a tennis star from India wore the T-shirt at Wimbledon. It seemed like a teaching moment—and so I wrote a book using the title."

Notes:

Thanks to Twitter user Love Goddess (@Aphrodite44), who pointed out this quotation to **QI** and identified Laurel Thatcher Ulrich as its likely creator. Thanks also to Twitter user Denise Lescano (@DeniseLescano), whose use of the saying initiated the cascade that led to this entry.

1. Laurel Thatcher Ulrich, "Vertuous Women Found: New England Ministerial Literature, 1668–1735," *American Quarterly* 28, no. 1 (Spring 1976): 20. Accessed in preview page in JSTOR, http://goo.gl/YwJe8z.
2. Ibid.
3. Ibid.
4. Hazel Dixon-Cooper, *Born on a Rotten Day: Illuminating and Coping with the Dark Side of the Zodiac* (New York: Fireside, 2003), 42.
5. Dennis Lythgoe, "Ulrich Touts Women in History," *Deseret News* (Salt Lake City, UT), October 21, 2007, E10. Accessed in NewsBank.

19. "Nobody goes there anymore; it's too crowded."

—Yogi Berra

Yogi Berra was a brilliant baseball player who became a successful coach and manager. He appeared in the World Series many times, and his teams often won. Outside of the sports realm, he is best known for a fascinating collection of humorous quotations that have become known as "Yogi-isms."

A shallow analysis of a Yogi-ism might highlight its self-contradictory, nonsensical, or comical aspects. But a deeper analysis often reveals a practical insight or a koanlike wisdom.

Determining the number of Yogi-isms that Berra actually said is a daunting task. The man himself extemporaneously delivered perfect commentary on this enigma in 1986 in the form of a self-referential Yogi-ism:[1]

I really didn't say everything I said.

In 1987 the well-known language columnist William Safire inquired about the popular funny saying "It's déja vu all over again," and Berra told him that the words were not his.[2] But a decade later, Berra stopped disavowing the saying and accepted the credit, delighting his fans.[3] Nevertheless, current evidence points to a movie reviewer named Clifford Terry, who used the phrase in 1966, several years before it was linked to Berra.[4]

And what about the classic listed at the beginning of this section? Is this saying an authentic Yogi-ism? Berra stated on multiple occasions that he made this remark, and detailed citations for this claim are given further below. But this joke has a long history, and it was already circulating before Berra was born. A thematic precursor about parties appeared in 1882 in a London periodical called the *Nonconformist and Independent*. The comedy hinged on the impossibility of all the guests delaying attendance until all the other guests had already arrived:[5]

"I'm afraid you'll be late at the party," said an old lady to her stylish granddaughter, who replied, "Oh, you dear grandma, don't you know that in our fashionable set nobody ever goes to a party till everybody gets there?"

In December 1907 another variant appeared in a New York newspaper humor column called Sparklets. The creator of the joke was unidentified, and the person delivering the punch line was also not named:[6]

Ambiguous, Yet Clear—Oh, don't go there on Saturday; it's so frightfully crowded! Nobody goes there then!

In the ensuing days, months, and years, other newspapers, such as the *Philadelphia Inquirer*, reprinted the jest with minor alterations.[7] The saying was still circulating in 1914 when its same text appeared in the *Middletown Daily Times-Press* of Middletown, New York.[8]

In 1941 Hollywood gossip columnist Paul Harrison spoke with a comedian named Rags Ragland. Ragland claimed that his girlfriend Suzanne Ridgeway had used a version of the quip. However, it was possible that Ragland was simply providing entertaining fodder for Harrison's newspaper readers by recycling an old joke.[9]

For laughs off the set, Rags goes around with a flutter-brained cutie named Suzanne Ridgeway. He says he took her to a concert at the Hollywood Bowl the other night, and as they inched their way up the ramp with the throng she remarked: "Now I know why nobody ever comes here; it's too crowded."

In 1943 the *New Yorker* published a short tale titled "Some Nights When Nothing Happens Are the Best Nights in This Place" by the journalist John McNulty, whose lauded literary style was distinctive. McNulty included an instance of the expression.[10]

Johnny, one of the hackmen outside, put the whole thing in a nutshell one night when they were talking about a certain hangout and Johnny said, "Nobody goes there any more. It's too crowded."

Also in 1943 a sportswriter in a Pennsylvania newspaper assigned the joke to an archetypal Irishman.[11]

"Speaking of places did you see that one about the Irishman who says 'No one goes to Murphy's saloon anymore because it's too crowded.'

"If you don't get that one on the first hop it's not the fault of the gag."

In January 1961 the columnist Earl Wilson indicated that the jest was still being used by comedians such as Ukie Sherin.[12]

Appearing at the Losers Club in Hollywood, Ukie said, "No wonder nobody ever comes in here—it's too crowded."

In April 1962 the *Cleveland Plain Dealer* assigned the joke to Yogi Berra.[13]

A Yogi Berraism: At Ft. Lauderdale Yogi was listening to his teammates talk about a restaurant in the area. Said Yogi, "Aw, nobody ever goes there. It's too crowded."

In 1963 the gag was ascribed to Berra again, but a detail of the story was changed—the restaurant was in New York instead of Fort Lauderdale.[14]

New York Yankee coach Jim Hegan attributes this story to Yogi Berra, the new resident genius of the Bombers.

Berra was asked if a certain restaurant in New York was as popular as ever. "Naw," quoth Yogi. "Nobody ever goes there anymore—it's too crowded."

In 1984 the writer Roy Blount Jr. published a profile of Berra in *Sports Illustrated*, and he inquired about the history of the well-known quip.[15]

> "How about the one about the restaurant being so crowded nobody ever goes there?" I asked. "You didn't really say that, did you?"
>
> Yogi smiled. "Yeah! I said that one," he assured me.
>
> "You did?" I said. "About Charlie's in Minneapolis?"
>
> "Nahhh, it was about Ruggeri's in St. Louis. When I was head-waiter there." That would have been in 1948.
>
> "No," said Carmen, "you said that in New York."
>
> "St. Louis," Yogi said firmly.
>
> So there you are.

In 1996 a journalist named Joe Sharkey spoke to Berra and printed his comments about the saying in the *New York Times*.[16]

> We were stalled in crosstown traffic. Mr. Berra glanced at a restaurant awning on 50th Street and recalled something he once said about a nightclub. "That place, it's so crowded nobody goes there anymore."
>
> Mrs. Berra shook him off. "No, you said, 'It's so popular nobody goes there,'" she said.
>
> "Right, popular," he agreed, and tossed out another one: "Thank you for making this day necessary."

Berra's 1998 *The Yogi Book: I Really Didn't Say Everything I Said!* discussed many of his celebrated remarks. The volume included a date and setting for the joke under investigation:[17]

> Nobody goes there anymore. It's too crowded.
>
> I was talking to Stan Musial and Joe Garagiola in 1959 about Ruggeri's restaurant in my old neighborhood in St. Louis. It was true!

In conclusion, the earliest instances of this remark were anonymous. The comedians Rags Ragland and Ukie Sherin employed the quip, as did the writer John McNulty. In addition, there is some evidence that Yogi Berra employed the joke; however, in all documented cases, the jest was already in circulation.

Notes:

In memoriam: thanks to my brother Stephen, who greatly enjoyed Yogi-isms.

1. Steve Marcus, "Color Yogi a Happy Guy; Now Wearing Astros' Rainbow Uniform, Berra's Relaxed, Popular," *Newsday* (Long Island, NY), February 24, 1986, sports section, 92. Accessed in ProQuest.
2. William Safire, "Mr. Bonaprop," On Language, *New York Times*, February 15, 1987, A8. Accessed in ProQuest.
3. Yogi Berra, *The Yogi Book: I Really Didn't Say Everything I Said!* (New York: Workman, 1998), 30. Verified in hard copy.
4. Clifford Terry, "Gimmicks Jam 'The Silencers,'" *Chicago Tribune*, February 22, 1966, B5. Accessed in ProQuest.
5. Gleanings, *Nonconformist and Independent* (London, UK), February 23, 1882, 178. Accessed in NewspaperARCHIVE.com.
6. Sparklets, *Daily People* (New York, NY), December 7, 1907, 2. Accessed in GenealogyBank.
7. "Here and There: Clear but Confusing," *Philadelphia Inquirer*, December 19, 1907, 8. Accessed in GenealogyBank; "Clear but Confusing," *Titusville Herald* (Titusville, PA), March 9, 1908, 5. Accessed in NewspaperARCHIVE.com.
8. "Clear, but Confusing," *Middletown Daily Times-Press* (Middletown, NY), March 4, 1914, 7. Accessed in NewspaperARCHIVE.com. Thanks to top researcher Barry Popik who identified this primal version and located other valuable citations. See his post about this quote on his website: "'Nobody Goes There Anymore. It's Too Crowded' (Restaurant Joke)," The Big Apple, July 22, 2004, http://goo.gl/VPMVtC.
9. Paul Harrison, Harrison in Hollywood, *Racine Journal Times* (Racine, WI), September 8, 1941, 14. Accessed in NewspaperARCHIVE.com; Paul Harrison, In Hollywood, *Trenton Evening Times* (Trenton, NJ), September 30, 1941, 14. Accessed in NewspaperARCHIVE.com.
10. John McNulty, "Some Nights When Nothing Happens Are the Best Nights in This Place," *New Yorker*, February 20, 1943, 13. Verified in hard copy.

11. Havey J. Boyle, "Mirrors of Sport," *Pittsburgh Post-Gazette*, April 12, 1943, 22. Accessed in Google News Archive, https://goo.gl/t39Ysy.

12. Earl Wilson, "Emotional Bit Better Now That Phil Can't See Critics Leaving," Best of New York, *St. Petersburg Times* (St. Petersburg, FL), January 6, 1961, 10D. Accessed in Google News Archive, https://goo.gl/ku1EQp.

13. Hal Lebovitz, "Flap Your Arms, Hitters Tell Perry," *Cleveland Plain Dealer* (Cleveland, OH), April 1, 1962, 2C. Accessed in GenealogyBank.

14. Fred Tharp, Fred Tharp on Sports, *Mansfield News Journal* (Mansfield, OH), December 29, 1963, 20. Accessed in NewspaperARCHIVE.com.

15. Roy Blount Jr., "Yogi: As a Reincarnated Yankee Skipper, Yogi Berra Is Working for George Steinbrenner," *Sports Illustrated*, April 2, 1984. Accessed in Sports Illustrated Archive.

16. Joe Sharkey, "Commencement Ain't Over Till It's Started," *New York Times*, May 19, 1996, NJ1. Accessed in ProQuest.

17. Berra, *The Yogi Book*, 16. Verified in hard copy.

20. "If your only tool is a hammer, then every problem looks like a nail."

X

—Mark Twain

Expert Ralph Keyes examined this saying in his reference work *The Quote Verifier*, and he noted that the linkage to Mark Twain was unsupported:[1]

Credit for this familiar quotation has been given to everyone from Buddha to Bernard Baruch. Mark Twain is the most common recipient, based on no evidence whatsoever.

In 1868, a London periodical called *Once a Week* published a thematic precursor involving an overeager boy indiscriminately wielding destructive implements:[2]

Give a boy a hammer and chisel; show him how to use them; at once he begins to hack the doorposts, to take off the corners of shutter and window frames, until you teach him a better use for them, and how to keep his activity within bounds.

At a conference of the American Educational Research Association held in February 1962, Abraham Kaplan, a UCLA professor of philosophy, gave a banquet speech. Several months later, in June 1962, the *Journal of Medical Education* published a report on the gathering. The following excerpt about the speech includes the earliest strong match for the adage known to **QI**.[3]

The highlight of the 3-day meeting, however, was to be found in Kaplan's comment on the choice of methods for research. He urged that scientists exercise good judgment in the selection of appropriate methods for their research. Because certain methods happen to be handy, or a given individual has been trained to use a specific method, is no assurance that the method is appropriate for all problems. He cited Kaplan's Law of the Instrument: "Give a boy a hammer and everything he meets has to be pounded."

Interestingly, this instance did not contain the word "nail." Instead, "nail" was referenced implicitly via the word "hammer" and the verb "to pound."

In the pioneering 1963 book *Computer Simulation of Personality: Frontier of Psychological Theory*, a passage in the first chapter, written by psychologist Silvan S. Tomkins, used a hammer and nails as part of an analogy that paralleled the adage under study.[4]

This was the tendency of jobs to be adapted to tools, rather than adapting tools to jobs. If one has a hammer one tends to look for nails, and if one has a computer with a storage capacity, but no feelings, one is more likely to concern oneself with remembering and with problem solving than with loving and hating.

Computer Simulation of Personality also contained a chapter by the psychiatrist Kenneth Mark Colby titled "Computer Simulation of a Neurotic Process." Colby presented a version of the "Law of the Instrument." A *Science* magazine review of the work published in November 1963 reprinted the following passage from the book.[5]

The First Law of the Instrument states that if you give a boy a hammer, he suddenly finds that everything needs pounding. The computer program may be our current hammer, but it must be tried. One cannot decide from purely armchair considerations whether or not it will be of any value.

In 1964 Kaplan's *The Conduct of Inquiry: Methodology for Behavioral Science* included a passage about the "Law of the Instrument."[6]

I call it the law of the instrument, and it may be formulated as follows: Give a small boy a hammer, and he will find that everything he encounters needs pounding. It comes as no particular surprise to discover that a scientist formulates problems in a way which requires for their solution just those techniques in which he himself is especially skilled.

In October 1964 Kaplan published an article in *Library Quarterly* that also contained pertinent sentences.[7]

We tend to formulate our problems in such a way as to make it seem that the solutions to those problems demand precisely what we already happen to have at hand. With respect to the conduct of inquiry, and especially in behavioral science, I label this effect "the law of the instrument." The simplest formulation I know of the law of the instrument runs this way: give a small boy a hammer and it will turn out that everything he encounters needs pounding.

In 1966 the prominent psychologist Abraham Maslow published *The Psychology of Science: A Reconnaissance*. He presented an instance of the adage that is closer to the common modern versions. The word "nail" was part of this instance.[8]

I remember seeing an elaborate and complicated automatic washing machine for automobiles that did a beautiful job of washing them. But it could do only that, and everything else that got into its clutches was treated as if it were an automobile to be washed. I suppose it is tempting, if the only tool you have is a hammer, to treat everything as if it were a nail.

In 1967 the *Washington Post* reported on remarks made by a powerful US government regulator named Lee Loevinger of the Federal Communications Commission. Loevinger attached his own name to an instance of the saying.[9]

"There is one principle of behavioral science," Commissioner Loevinger has said, "that has been well established over the years. This is 'Loevinger's law of irresistible use' which says that if a boy has a hammer, this proves something needs pounding. The political science analogue is that if there is a government agency, this proves something needs regulating."

In September 1974 a columnist for the *Times-Picayune* newspaper of New Orleans, Louisiana, printed an instance of the expression sent by an inquirer who was eager to know the identity of the maxim's creator:[10]

Who said "If all you have is a hammer, you treat everything as a nail?" inquired "Puzzled."

In November 1974 the same New Orleans columnist relayed an answer to his readers. The saying was traced back to Abraham Maslow and not to Abraham Kaplan. Also, the wording was slightly altered.[11]

MAGICIAN Ernie Heldman turned himself into The Times-Picayune with the source of the quotation: "If the only tool you have is a hammer, you tend to treat everything as if it were a nail." Abraham Maslow said it in "The Psychology of Science," published in 1966.

In 1981 the financial adviser Howard J. Ruff published *Survive and Win in the Inflationary Eighties*. The title of the book's fourth chapter was an instance of the saying:[12]

CHAPTER 4
When You Have a Hammer in Your Hand, Everything Looks Like a Nail

In 1982 an MIT professor attributed an instance of the saying to Maslow, as reported in the *New York Times*.[13]

"Abraham Maslow once said that to him who has only a hammer, the whole world looks like a nail," said Joseph Weizenbaum, a professor of computer science at M.I.T.

In 1984 the famous investor Warren Buffett used the adage when criticizing academic studies of financial markets that emphasized inappropriate mathematical techniques.[14]

> It isn't necessarily because such studies have any utility; it's simply that the data are there and academicians have worked hard to learn the mathematical skills needed to manipulate them. Once these skills are acquired, it seems sinful not to use them, even if the usage has no utility or negative utility. As a friend said, to a man with a hammer, everything looks like a nail.

By August 1984 the saying had been reassigned to the brilliant humorist Mark Twain. The computer periodical *InfoWorld* printed a received missive with the title "Twain Said It." The letter writer presented an instance with the words "only" and "everything" italicized and credited Twain:[15]

> For the record, the accurate quote is: "If the *only* tool you have is a hammer, *everything* looks like a nail." I have added emphasis that Mark Twain left to his rhetoric.

In 1985 the award-winning author William Gaddis cleverly permuted the maxim to yield a fresh and emotionally insightful remark for a character in his novel *Carpenter's Gothic*:[16]

> [W]hen you feel like a nail everything looks like a hammer . . .

In 1995 a Florida newspaper printed an instance without attribution and labeled it "an old adage":[17]

> "If your only tool is a hammer," goes an old adage, "then every problem looks like a nail."

The important 2012 reference work *The Dictionary of Modern Proverbs* from Yale University Press includes an entry for this saying that lists the key citations in the 1960s that were earlier discussed.[18]

In conclusion, by 1962 Abraham Kaplan had formulated a version of the saying featuring a boy that expressed the central idea. However, Kaplan did not use the important word "nail." In 1963 Silvan S. Tomkins wrote a version with the word "nail," but it differed from popular modern instances. In 1966 Abraham Maslow wrote a version that is similar to popular expressions circulating today.

Notes:

Great thanks to Mark Halpern, Benjamin Howard, and Snarxist Agent, whose inquiries led **QI** to formulate this question and perform this exploration. Thanks also to John Cowan and Susan Holmberg for their comments.

1. Ralph Keyes, *The Quote Verifier: Who Said What, Where, and When* (New York: St. Martin's, 2006), 87. Verified in hard copy.

2. "Toys," *Once a Week* (London, UK), April 18, 1868, 344. Accessed in Google Books, https://goo.gl/5VCWKn.

3. Milton J. Horowitz, "Trends in Education," *Journal of Medical Education* 37, no. 3 (June 1962), 637. Verified in hard copy.

4. Silvan S. Tompkins, *Exploring Affect: The Selected Writings of Silvan S. Tomkins*, E. Virginia Demos, ed., Studies in Emotion & Social Interaction series (New York: Cambridge University Press, 1995), 445. Accessed in Google Books, https://goo.gl/Z12rlg. Article originally appeared in Silvan S. Tompkins and Samuel Messick, eds. *Computer Simulation of Personality: Frontier of Psychological Theory* (New York: Wiley, 1963).

5. Harold Borko, review of *Computer Simulation of Personality: Frontier of Psychological Theory*, by Silvan S. Tomkins and Samuel Messick, *Science* 142, no. 3593 (November 8, 1963): 656. Accessed in JSTOR.

6. Abraham Kaplan, *The Conduct of Inquiry: Methodology for Behavioral Science* (San Francisco: Chandler, 1964), 28. Verified in hard copy.

7. Abraham Kaplan, "The Age of the Symbol—A Philosophy of Library Education," *Library Quarterly* 34, no. 4 (October 1964): 303. Accessed in JSTOR.

8. Abraham H. Maslow, *The Psychology of Science: A Reconnaissance* (New York: Harper and Row, 1966), 15–16. Verified in hard copy.

9. Richard Harwood, "FCC Is Divided on Regulating 'Quality,'" *Washington Post*, October 23, 1967, A22. Accessed in ProQuest.

10. Howard Jacobs, "Checks May Soon Be Thing of the Past," Remoulade, *Times-Picayune* (New Orleans, LA), September 10, 1974, 15. Accessed in GenealogyBank.

11. Howard Jacobs, "Today Is Dedicated to Local Versifiers," Remoulade, *Times-Picayune* (New Orleans, LA), November 21, 1974, 19.

12. Howard J. Ruff, *Survive and Win in the Inflationary Eighties* (San Ramon, CA: Target, 1981), 44. Verified in scans.

13. Edward B. Fiske, "Computers Alter Lives of Pupils and Teachers," *New York Times*, April 4, 1982, A1. Accessed in ProQuest.

14. Warren E. Buffett, "The Superinvestors of Graham-and-Doddsville" *Hermes: A Magazine for Alumni of Columbia Business School*, Fall 1984, 8. Verified in scans.

15. David Lenfest, letter to the editor, *InfoWorld* 6, no. 34 (August 20, 1984): 6. Accessed in Google Books, https://goo.gl/pZ4WIY.

16. William Gaddis, *Carpenter's Gothic* (New York: Viking, 1985), 223. Verified in scans.

17. "Race Relations in U.S.: A Dilemma Which No Commission Can Solve," Viewpoint, *News Herald* (Panama City, FL), October 21, 1995, 8A. Accessed in NewspaperARCHIVE.com.

18. Charles Clay Doyle, Wolfgang Mieder, and Fred R. Shapiro, eds., *The Dictionary of Modern Proverbs* (New Haven, CT: Yale University Press, 2012), 114. Verified in hard copy. Special thanks to Charles Clay Doyle and his colleagues for their research.

21. "Better to remain silent and be thought a fool than to speak and remove all doubt."

—Abraham Lincoln
—Mark Twain
—Proverbs 17:28

There is a biblical proverb that expresses a similar idea to the adage above, namely Proverbs 17:28. Here is the New International version, followed by the King James version of the verse:[1]

> Even a fool is thought wise if he keeps silent, and discerning if he holds his tongue.
> Even a fool, when he holdeth his peace, is counted wise: and he that shutteth his lips is esteemed a man of understanding.

The adage is certainly more humorous. In the biblical version, one is thought wise if one remains silent, but in the adage, the word "wise" is not used. Remaining silent simply allows one to avoid the fate of being thought a fool. This maxim has many different forms, and it is often ascribed to Abraham Lincoln or Mark Twain. However, there is no substantive evidence that either of these famous individuals employed the maxim.

The wonderful *Yale Book of Quotations* investigated the saying and presented the earliest known attribution to Lincoln in *Golden Book* magazine in November 1931:[2]

> Better to remain silent and be thought a fool than to speak and to remove all doubt.
>
> —Abraham Lincoln

Since Lincoln died in 1865, this is a suspiciously late instance, and the *Golden Book* mention provides very weak evidence. Further, *The Yale Book of Quotations* indicates that the phrase was in use years before 1931 with no attachment to Lincoln.

The ascription of the saying to Mark Twain is also dubious. The companion book to the 2001 Mark Twain documentary by Ken Burns lists the following variant of the adage in a section titled "What Twain Didn't Say." The statement uses "keep your mouth shut" instead of "remain silent":[3]

> Better to keep your mouth shut and appear stupid than to open it
> and remove all doubt.

There are many proverbs extolling silence. Several examples from an 1887 collection called *Proverbs, Maxims, and Phrases of All Ages* are reminiscent of the biblical proverb:[4]

> Silence is the virtue of those who are not wise
> Silence is wisdom and gets a man friends
> Silence is wisdom when speaking is folly

In 1893 a New York newspaper column titled Jewels of Thought included an alternative maxim presenting a different rationale for silence:[5]

> It is better to remain silent than to speak the truth ill-humoredly,
> and spoil an excellent dish by covering it with bad sauce.
>
> —St. Francis de Sales

The earliest appearance of a close match to the adage discovered by **QI** occurs in a book titled *Mrs. Goose, Her Book* by Maurice Switzer, published in 1907 with a copyright notice of 1906. The book consists primarily of clever nonsense verse, and the phrasing in this early version of the saying is slightly different:[6]

It is better to remain silent at the risk of being thought a fool, than to talk and remove all doubt of it.

Most of the humorous content of *Mrs. Goose, Her Book* has the imprint of originality, and based on currently available data, **QI** believes that Maurice Switzer is the leading candidate for originator of the expression. This 1906 citation was also given in *The Dictionary of Modern Proverbs*, an indispensable reference work from Yale University Press.[7]

The choice of Switzer's book title is illuminated by the fact that another book, *Father Goose, His Book*, was a popular sensation in 1899. The author of that book, L. Frank Baum, went on to write an even bigger hit, *The Wonderful Wizard of Oz*.

In 1922 the saying appeared as a banner on the front page of the society section of a Minnesota newspaper. The words were credited to a person or entity named Empeco. The phrase "keep quiet" was used instead of "remain silent":[8]

It Is Better to Keep Quiet and Be Thought a Fool Than to Speak and Remove All Doubt.

—Empeco

In 1923 the newspaper of Evansville College (now the University of Evansville) in Indiana published the adage. The word "thought" was spelled "thot":[9]

'Tis better to keep quiet and be thot a fool than to speak and remove all doubt.

In 1924 an instance of the saying was credited to a person named Arthur Burns:[10]

"It is better to keep silent and be thought a fool." says Dr. Arthur Burns, "than to speak and remove all doubts."

In March 1931 a humorist with the moniker Doc Rockwell presented a version of the maxim with the phrase "keep your mouth shut" instead of "remain silent," "keep silent," or "keep quiet":[11]

> Some great man once made a famous remark about something or other that I will never forget. I can't recall it at this moment, but it was to the effect that it is better to keep your mouth shut and let people think you're a fool than to keep it open and leave no doubt about the matter.

In May 1931 a columnist printed a version with "dumb" instead of "fool." No attribution was given:[12]

> Listen to this: "It is better to be silent and be thought dumb, than to speak and remove all doubt!"

In October 1931 the student newspaper of Northwestern University published a letter to the editor that defended gangster Al Capone. The letter contained another instance of the adage with "keep your mouth shut":[13]

> But when you try to dictate what to do to others, remember this—
> It is better to keep your mouth shut and be thought a fool than to
> open it and remove all doubt!

In November 1931 *Golden Book* magazine assigned the saying to Abraham Lincoln, as noted previously. In 1936 a Nebraska newspaper printed the maxim rephrased as a question, and an Asian origin was suggested:[14]

> YOU ANSWER IT.
> (Old Chinese Proverb.)
>
> Is it better to keep your mouth shut and seem a fool, or to open
> your mouth and remove all doubt?

In 1938 a Florida newspaper ascribed the words of the aphorism to Confucius, but the intent was jocular:[15]

> The following wise-crack was written by Confucius—unless I'm
> confusing him with somebody else:
> "It is better to keep one's mouth shut and be thought a fool
> than to open it and remove all doubt."

In 1953 a newspaper columnist in Saskatoon, Saskatchewan, assigned the expression to Mark Twain. Currently, this is the earliest connection to Twain known to **QI**:[16]

> Maybe Mark Twain had something when he said, "It is better to
> keep your mouth shut and be thought a fool than to open your
> mouth and prove it," and often, in these cases, it's the informant
> who feels the fool.

In 1958 the *New York Times* published a profile of the famous economist John Maynard Keynes, and the article noted that a version of the dictum had been attributed to Keynes:[17]

> "It is better to keep quiet and seem ignorant," he reportedly advised
> an American dignitary, "than to speak up and remove all doubt."

The aphorism appeared in the 1961 collection *Mark Twain: Wit and Wisecracks* edited by Doris Benardete. No citation to Twain's oeuvre was provided:[18]

> It's better to keep your mouth shut and appear stupid than to open
> it and remove all doubt.

The ascription to Abraham Lincoln has been common for decades. In 1962 a South Carolina newspaper printed:[19]

> Abe Lincoln said:

Better to remain silent and be thought a fool than to speak out and remove all doubt.

Sometimes Mark Twain has been assigned the version of the maxim using the phrase "remain silent." For example, in 1980 a newspaper in Ottawa, Ontario, printed the following:[20]

Mark Twain put it well. . . . "[I]t is better to remain silent and be thought a fool than to talk and remove all doubt."

In conclusion, there is no substantive evidence that this popular adage was coined or employed by either Abraham Lincoln or Mark Twain. The earliest ascriptions to these famous figures appeared many years following their deaths. **QI** thinks that Maurice Switzer is currently the top choice for coiner of the expression, though future data may reveal alternative claimants.

Notes:

Thanks to John Baker for pointing out the connection between *Mrs. Goose, Her Book* and *Father Goose, His Book.*

1. Proverbs 17:28, Bible Hub, accessed October 24, 2012, http://biblehub.com/proverbs /17-28.htm. The website Bible Hub contains several translations from the Online Parallel Bible Project of Biblos.com.

2. Fred R. Shapiro, *The Yale Book of Quotations* (New Haven: Yale University Press, 2006), 446. Verified in hard copy; "Advice," *Golden Book* 14 (November 1931): 306. Verified in hard copy.

3. Geoffrey C. Ward, Dayton Duncan, and Ken Burns, *Mark Twain: An Illustrated Biography* (New York: Alfred A. Knopf, 2001), 189. Verified in hard copy.

4. Robert Christy, *Proverbs, Maxims, and Phrases of All Ages* (New York: G. P. Putnam's Sons, 1887), 268. Accessed in Google Books, https://goo.gl/uO3OOH.

5. Jewels of Thought, *Stamford Mirror* (Stamford, NY), August 8, 1893, 1. Accessed in Old Fulton NY Post Cards, fultonhistory.com.

6. Maurice Switzer, *Mrs. Goose, Her Book* (New York: Moffat, Yard, 1907), 29. Accessed in Google Books, https://goo.gl/waA7Kh.

7. Charles Clay Doyle, Wolfgang Mieder, and Fred R. Shapiro, eds., *The Dictionary of Modern Proverbs* (New Haven, CT: Yale University Press, 2012), 83. Verified in hard copy.

8. [Front-page banner text], *Duluth Sunday News-Tribune* (Duluth, MN), December 17, 1922, society section, 1. Accessed in GenealogyBank.

9. [Freestanding quote], *Crescent* (Evansville, IN), June 19, 1923, 3. Accessed in NewspaperARCHIVE.com.

10. Bob's Sportitorials, *Seattle Daily Times* (Seattle, WA), June 10, 1924, sports section, 1. Accessed in GenealogyBank.

11. Doc Rockwell, "Rockwell Tells How to Behave Like a Human Being," *Omaha World Herald* (Omaha, NE), March 22, 1931, 8. Accessed in GenealogyBank.

12. Tony Wons, As I Think It, *Albany Evening News* (Albany, NY), May 25, 1931, 9. Accessed in Old Fulton NY Post Cards, fultonhistory.com.

13. Not So Swell, letter to the editor, *Daily Northwestern* (Evanston, IL), October 16, 1931, 2. Accessed in GenealogyBank.

14. You Answer It, *Omaha World Herald* (Omaha, NE), July 13, 1936, 4. Accessed in GenealogyBank.

15. Lee Morris, Free Speeches, *Evening Independent* (St. Petersburg, FL), June 1, 1938, 4. Accessed in Google News Archive, https://goo.gl/QKoh4p.

16. Jane Gale, It's Always Same Answer, *Saskatoon Star-Phoenix* (Saskatoon, SK), May 29, 1953, 13. Accessed in Google News Archive, https://goo.gl/rnCyq3.

17. Henry C. Wallich, "Keynes Re-examined: The Man, the Theory," *New York Times*, April 20, 1958, SM13. Accessed in ProQuest.

18. Mark Twain, *Mark Twain: Wit and Wisecracks*, Doris Benardete, ed. (Mount Vernon, NY: Peter Pauper, 1961), 18. Verified in scans.

19. Phraseologies, *Aiken Standard and Review* (Aiken, SC), March 21, 1962, 2. Accessed in NewspaperARCHIVE.com.

20. Roger Appleton, "Calm, Reasonable Approach Best," Action Line, *Ottawa Citizen* (Ottawa, ON), December 26, 1980, 49. Accessed in Google News Archive.

22. "History does not repeat itself, but it rhymes."

—Mark Twain

On a tip, **QI** discovered in the *New York Times* a Twain-ism presented by a business columnist, who coupled it with a strong warning about authenticity:[1]

> "History doesn't repeat itself but it often rhymes," as Mark Twain
> is often reputed to have said. (I've found no compelling evidence
> that he ever uttered that nifty aphorism. No matter—the line is
> too good to resist.)

QI can confirm that there is no substantive evidence that Mark Twain, who died in 1910, made this remark. In 1970 the two earliest known matches appeared in print. Both instances were attributed to Twain.

QI located the saying in a poem by the Canadian artist John Robert Colombo in a collection called *Neo Poems*. The experimental work containing the saying is titled "A Said Poem," and the innovative format consists of a series of quotations. The first four lines are the following:[2]

> A SAID POEM
> for Ronald and Beatrice Gross
>
> "I have seen the future and it doesn't work," said Robert Fulford.
> "If there weren't any Poland, there wouldn't be any Poles," said
> Alfred Jarry.
> "We aren't making the film they contracted for," said Robert
> Flaherty.
> "History never repeats itself but it rhymes," said Mark Twain.

In April 2011 **QI** contacted John Robert Colombo to inquire about the source of the expression.[3] Colombo believed that he had encountered the saying in print sometime in the 1960s, perhaps in the columns of the *Times Literary Supplement.* He considered the saying to be part of "proverbial lore," and he had never seen a precise source.

The maxim also appeared in the pages of the *New York Times* in January 1970. An individual with the initials W.D.M. sent a query letter to the newspaper asking about the origin of the saying. The question was printed in a Q&A section of the newspaper, though unfortunately readers subsequently brought forth no satisfactory answer:[4]

> W.D.M. is seeking to locate the source of the following line, attributed to Mark Twain: "History never repeats itself but it rhymes."

These two citations are listed in the important recent reference work *The Dictionary of Modern Proverbs* from Yale University Press.[5]

In 1845 an interesting thematic precursor using the descriptive phrase "mystic rhyme" was printed in the publication the *Christian Remembrancer:*[6]

> The vision recurs; the eastern sun has a second rise; history repeats her tale unconsciously, and goes off into a mystic rhyme; ages are prototypes of other ages, and the winding course of time brings us round to the same spot again.

Twain did use the prefatory phrase "History never repeats itself" in a novel he cowrote with his neighbor Charles Dudley Warner. The 1874 edition of *The Gilded Age: A Tale of To-Day* employed wonderfully vivid figurative language based on a kaleidoscope:[7]

> History never repeats itself, but the Kaleidoscopic combinations of the pictured present often seem to be constructed out of the broken fragments of antique legends.

In 1896 the humorist Max Beerbohm employed a witticism about historians in his essay titled "1880":[8]

"History," it has been said, "does not repeat itself. The historians repeat one another."

Mark Twain also spoke about the repetition of history in a commentary to his famous story, "The Celebrated Jumping Frog of Calaveras County." An elaborate dual-language, extended edition of the 1865 short story was published in 1903. Twain had discovered a version of the frog tale set in classical Greece, and he initially thought the comical anecdote was ancient. Later Twain realized that a British professor had created the Greek version of the tale based on Twain's text:[9]

> NOTE. November, 1903. When I became convinced that the "Jumping Frog" was a Greek story two or three thousand years old, I was sincerely happy, for apparently here was a most striking and satisfactory justification of a favorite theory of mine—to wit, that no occurrence is sole and solitary, but is merely a repetition of a thing which has happened before, and perhaps often.

In 1941 the *Chicago Tribune* printed an article with the following thematically related headline:[10]

> History May Not Repeat, But It Looks Alike

In 1962 the California-based literary journal *Contact* published a work that depicted history as a rhyming poem. The fifth verse of "Suite of Mirrors" included the following:[11]

> You might think history teaches; it repeats;
> page after page, a poem in perfect rhyme
> tolls echoing bells from both sides of the sheets
> for births and funerals, tells the time
> of ageless Alice, Hamlet's fallacies—
> the latest light from vanished galaxies.

In 1970 John Robert Colombo published "A Said Poem," and as noted previously the following line was included:[12]

"History never repeats itself but it rhymes," said Mark Twain.

In January 1970 the *New York Times* printed a query seeking a source for the line ascribed to Twain, as mentioned earlier.

In 1971 the volume *Diplomacy and Its Discontents* by James Eayrs printed an instance of the saying attributed to Twain. This version differed slightly by using "does not" instead of "never":[13]

> The trouble with history is that while historians repeat each other, history never repeats itself. Not, at any rate, exactly. (When Mark Twain declared 'History does not repeat itself, but it rhymes,' he went about as far as he could go.)

The summer 1971 issue of the *University of Toronto Quarterly* contained a piece that evaluated the collection *Neo Poems* by Colombo. The reviewer considered the line ascribed to Twain worthwhile, and he reprinted it:[14]

> Meanwhile, I'm grateful for random gems that I might otherwise have missed, like Mark Twain's 'History never repeats itself but it rhymes.'

In May 1972 Professor James Eayrs wrote an opinion essay in the *Windsor Star* of Windsor, Ontario. He employed another variant of the adage, but he presented no ascription:[15]

History may not repeat itself. But it rhymes.

In December 1972 a columnist in the *Vancouver Sun* of Vancouver, British Columbia, credited the maxim to Eayrs. Perhaps the columnist saw the unattributed citation given immediately above:[16]

James Eayrs. "History may not repeat itself. But it rhymes."

In 1974 the journal *History Teacher* printed another version of the maxim ascribed to Twain. This instance used the word "past" instead of "history":[17]

> The relationship between the continuities and the discontinuities of history have rarely been better expressed than in Mark Twain's epigram, "The past does not repeat itself, but it rhymes."

In conclusion, the earliest known evidence of this popular quotation appeared in 1970, but that date is many decades after the death of Twain. Hence there is no substantive support for the Twain ascription. Precursors mentioning history and rhyme were published before 1970, but the statements were not compact and witty.

Notes:

Great thanks to Barry Popik for his research on this saying.[18] Thanks to Daniel Gackle and Ben Yagoda, who inquired about the Twain attribution. Special thanks to Dan Goncharoff, who located the 1845 citation. Thanks to Charlie Doyle, Wolfgang Mieder, and Fred R. Shapiro for their work on *The Dictionary of Modern Proverbs*. Thanks also to Victor Steinbok, Ken Hirsch, and Bill Mullins, whose comments were helpful. Lastly, in memoriam: for my brother Stephen, who also asked about this saying in 2011.

1. Jeff Sommer, "Funny, but I've Heard This Market Song Before," *New York Times*, June 19, 2011, BU5. Accessed in ProQuest.
2. John Robert Colombo, *Neo Poems* (Vancouver, BC: Sono Nis, 1970), 46. Verified in hard copy.
3. John Robert Colombo, email message to author, April 18, 2011.
4. [Untitled Q&A appeal to readers], *New York Times Book Review*, January 25, 1970, 47. Accessed in ProQuest.
5. Charles Clay Doyle, Wolfgang Mieder, and Fred R. Shapiro, eds., *The Dictionary of Modern Proverbs* (New Haven, CT: Yale University Press, 2012), 121. Verified in hard copy.
6. Review of *A History of the Church in Russia*, by A. N. Mouravieff, *Christian Remembrancer* 10 (October 1845): 265. Accessed in Google Books, https://goo.gl/83aKE2.

7. Mark Twain and Charles Dudley Warner, *The Gilded Age: A Tale of To-Day* (Hartford, CT: American Publishing, 1874), 430. Accessed in Google Books, https://goo.gl/T5DuiE.

8. Max Beerbohm, *The Works of Max Beerbohm* (New York: Charles Scribner's Sons, 1896), 41. Accessed in Google Books, https://goo.gl/tzt21x.

9. Mark Twain, *The Jumping Frog: In English, Then in French, Then Clawed Back into a Civilized Language Once More by Patient, Unremunerated Toil* (New York: Harper and Brothers, 1903), 64. Accessed in Google Books, https://goo.gl/rmFih5.

10. "History May Not Repeat, but It Looks Alike," Chicago Tribune, May 11, 1941, 16. Accessed in ProQuest.

11. Harold Witt, "Suite of Mirrors," *Contact: The San Francisco Collection of New Writing, Art, and Ideas* 3, no. 3 (August 1962): 21. Verified in hard copy.

12. Colombo, *Neo Poems*, 46.

13. James Eayrs, *Diplomacy and Its Discontents* (Toronto, ON: University of Toronto Press, 1971), 121. Verified in hard copy.

14. Michael Hornyansky, review of *Neo Poems*, by John Robert Colombo, *University of Toronto Quarterly* 40, no. 4 (Summer 1971): 375. Verified in hard copy.

15. James Eayrs, "Policy Toward Greek Colonels Found Wanting," *Windsor Star* (Windsor, ON), May 3, 1972, 11. Accessed in Google News Archive, https://goo.gl/PgIWCt.

16. Trevor Lautens, column, *Vancouver Sun* (Vancouver, BC), December 19, 1972, 33.

17. David Pratt, "The Functions of Teaching History," *History Teacher* 7, no. 3 (May 1974): 419. Accessed in JSTOR.

18. Barry Popik, "History Doesn't Repeat Itself, but It Does Rhyme," The Big Apple, June 5, 2010, http://www.barrypopik.com/index.php/new_york_city/entry/history_doesnt_repeat _itself_but_it_does_rhyme.

INDEX (BY NAME)

SELECTION OF PERSONS OF INTEREST

FROM QUOTEINVESTIGATOR.COM

INDEX (BY QUOTATION)

SELECTION OF KNOWN FALSEHOODS FROM QUOTEINVESTIGATOR.COM

"Choose a job you love and you will never have to work a day in your life." 103–6

"Comedy is tragedy plus time." 308–13

"Do good anyway" and the Paradoxical Commandments. 158–62

"Don't bend; don't water it down; don't try to make it logical; don't edit your own soul according to the fashion." 55–58

"Easy reading is hard writing." 314–19

"For sale: baby shoes, never worn." 183–91

"Genius is 1% inspiration and 99% perspiration." 46–50

"Give a man a fish, and you feed him for a day. Teach a man to fish, and you feed him for a lifetime." 97–102

"Good artists copy; great artists steal." 17–23

"Great invention, but who would ever want to use one?" 192–96

"Half of the town councilors are not fools." 208–13

"Heaven for the climate, and hell for the company." 258–61

"History does not repeat itself, but it rhymes." 358–63

"Hollywood is a place where they'll pay a thousand dollars for a kiss and fifty cents for your soul." 221–23

"I fear the day that technology will surpass our human interaction." 325–28

"If I had more time, I would have written a shorter letter." 292–296

"If you love someone, set them free. If they come back they're yours." 92–96

"If you want to know what a man's like, look at how he treats his inferiors." 297–301

"If your only tool is a hammer, then every problem looks like a nail." 344–50

"I'm so fast, I hit the light switch in my bedroom and jump into bed before it gets dark." 262–65

"In the future, everyone will be anonymous for fifteen minutes." 320–23

"In the struggle for survival, the fittest win out at the expense of their rivals." 59–62

"It has become appallingly obvious that our technology has exceeded our humanity." 214–15

"Life is what happens to you while you're busy making other plans." 252–57

"Life is a journey, not a destination." 63–67

"Money can't buy love, but it improves your bargaining position." 126–29

"No one can make you feel inferior without your consent." 29–32

"Nobody goes there anymore; it's too crowded." 338–43

"Not everything that counts can be counted." 266–71

"People who like this sort of thing will find this the sort of thing they like." 202–7

"Sometimes, I'm terrified of my heart, of its constant hunger for whatever it is it wants." 169–71

"Today a reader, tomorrow a leader." 142–45

"We are made of star-stuff." 302–7

"We do not inherit the Earth from our ancestors; we borrow it from our children." 82–91

"Well-behaved women seldom make history." 335–37

"What lies behind us and what lies before us are tiny matters compared to what lies within us." 163–68

"With great power comes great responsibility." 241–47

"Writing about music is like dancing about architecture." 272–81

"You can get much further with a kind word and a gun than with a kind word alone." 216–20

"You'll worry less about what people think of you when you realize how seldom they do." 235–40

ABOUT THE AUTHOR

Garson O'Toole has researched the origins of familiar quotations for years at www.quoteinvestigator.com. His work has been featured in the *New York Times, Slate, USA Today,* and many other publications.